A PASSION FOR

TANGO

by

DAVID TURNER

DINGLEY
PRESS

A DINGLEY PRESS
PAPERBACK

© Copyright 2006

DAVID TURNER

Second Edition 2006
First published in 2004
Reprinted in 2008

A CIP catalogue record for this title is
available from the British Library

ISBN 978-0-9547083-1-3

DINGLEY PRESS
16, Church Lane,
Dingley LE16 8PG
UK

For Alice and Bea

Acknowledgements

I am grateful for the generous help
and encouragement given to me during
the writing of this book by several people:

Rodolfo Aguerrodi
Joaquin Amenábar
Tony Arihanto
Christine Denniston
Stephanie Gögelein
John Hounam
Alex Krebs
Tony Lucas
Diana Mansfield
Chan Park
Wendy Rainbow

also

numerous fellow pupils on the Cambridge tango scene
and in particular
in memory of
Isabelle Bouhon.

My special thanks go to Mike Rose, who has spent many, many hours
vetting the contents, and making suggestions and technical corrections.
His support, wisdom, extensive knowledge of the subject and
enthusiastic comradeship have been invaluable to me.

Contents

The Illustrations

Chapter heading photographs, along with many others throughout the book are the work of Diana Mansfield, a tanguera and freelance photographer.

The text illustrations were taken by David Turner with the invaluable help of Tony Arihanto. Most of them were shot at an idyllic weekend tango workshop at Bylaugh Hall, Norfolk.

Prologo

En un prologo, se puede hablar de muchas cosas diferentes, y se pueden escribir muchas palabras, sentencias y parrafos, con o sin sentido. Como en nuestras vidas, ya que normalmente hacemos o experimentamos cosas con o sin sentido; cosas como una pasión, una addicción, conocer gente, relaciones, y algun ticket para viajar, quien sabe a donde.

El tango, como la vida, es es un viaje e incluye muchas cosas. Como la vida, el tango es un viaje de ida, sin regreso, pero tiene algo bueno, uno puede parar y bajarse en cualquier momento, aunque una vez que lo prueban, la mayoria de la gente sigue en el todo la vida.

La vida esta llena de cosas maravillosas, y nos permite elegir diferentes cosas en cada momento. Como un viaje, durante nuestras vidas en este mundo nosotros hacemos muchas y diferentes elecciones para continuar nuestro viaje en diferentes direcciones o para alcanzar diferentes objectivos exactamente . Lo mismo ocurre con el tango.

Este libro habla acerca un viaje; el viaje de un tango adicto. Este libro esta escrito con la pasión de vivir, antes y despues de descubrir el tango. Este libro nace en la necesidad de una persona de contarle al mundo lo que ha encontrado. Este libro habla acerca de tango, de mi mismo y habla mucho más de acerca de el (David)

Realmente, me siento muy honrado por ser parte del viaje David en el tango.

Rodolfo 'el Chino' Aguerrodi
Buenos Aires July 2003

Prologue

In any prologue to a book we can talk about a lot of different things. Similarly, we can write lots of words, sentences and paragraphs, some with and some without apparent sense. This mirrors real life, where many things we do and experience either have, or do not have, much sense; things such as passion, addictions, people, relationships. Some of us seem to have tickets to ride; but who knows where?

Tango is like life itself. It is a journey that encompasses many aspects. Life, like tango, is a one-way trip; there's no return ticket. But you can get off at any station you like, although many people stay on their single tango journey until the entire voyage of their lives is complete

Like any journey, life is full of many choices at every moment. During our lives on this earth we make many choices; we travel in different directions to achieve different goals. The same is true of tango.

This book describes a journey by one tango addict who has lived his life with passion, both before and since discovering tango. This book was born from the necessity a person has to tell others about what he has found. This book is about tango, to some extent about me, Rodolfo, and a lot about David.

I feel honoured to have been a part of David's tango journey.

Rodolfo 'el Chino' Aguerrodi
Buenos Aires July 2003

Foreword to the second edition

I can barely believe that I would be writing this foreword, less than two years after the launch of 'A Passion for Tango' and that I have learned enough to merit writing another three chapters. What pleases me most is that almost all the original material in the first edition still seems valid. What I have learned is to trust the logic of Rodolfo Aguerrodi's teaching since it applies to absolutely everything. I still believe his understanding of the reason why tango works is unique amongst teachers of tango. For two years now, I have now been teaching others what he taught me, using his methods and I have watched over the growth of a close, social group of dancers. All of them appear to have benefited hugely from the idea that this entire phenomenon of tango argentino is about relationships and not steps. Connection, connection, connection.

In the beginning, I wanted to create a tango environment near to my home with people who would be fun to dance with and who shared my - and Rodolfo's - view of tango. Therefore, Judith and I started up a group of our own, Market Harborough Tango. We had immense support from friends, including dear Mike Rose, and I am proud to report that there is now a live and thriving tango scene in the East Midlands.

Because it was my dream, I became, by default, the teacher. We had little idea if anyone would come or if we could cope with the teaching. Mike helped in that respect by organising a tango teachers' exposition, which was excellent. It is a great tribute to his skill, energy and dedication that so many of his pupils in Cambridge now also teach tango, and teach it well. To begin with, I borrowed from my own book and shamelessly from classes I attended in Cambridge. I would attend a class on a Tuesday night and run it, slightly adapted, for my group on the following Sunday evening. I kept faith with the Aguerrodi school of thought, avoiding the 'basic eight' and sequences, and it worked!

I am amazed but also delighted to find myself in this situation. I am even more amazed and delighted how many people have bought a copy of the book and the generous feedback that has been offered me. Writing a book about tango was, in itself, a journey of discovery and, although I did think it might have been of interest to a few people, I hardly expected it would have the appeal it has had. More surprising to me is that tango has gripped me so firmly that I am still excited by it. I want to learn more and more. Sure, I go through the doldrums from time to time, as we all do, but then the music speaks to something vital deep down inside me and I must dance.

A trip to Buenos Aires only served to reinforce all that I have come to believe about tango. I saw wonderful dancing and atrocious dancing. I watched people dancing in a social environment with more than half an eye on their audience. Sadly, those self-same dancers showed scant concern for the dancers around them. The more they tried to impress, the more they caused me to despise that attitude towards tango.

The best dancing I saw was from the older generation. By that I mean people even older than me! As they danced, they did very little in terms of variety and figures but with such style and elegance and with such evident commitment to each other and those around them. You don't haver to travel halfway round the world to see these things. They are present in Milongas all over the world.

I came to see that there is nothing wrong with developing my own style, suitable for somebody of my size and age. I just hope that I can encourage others who, like me, will never be like those young athletic tango dancers, never mind the tango stars of stage and screen. I want them to concentrate and practice what is well within the grasp of any dancer; simple, elegant togetherness.

I am still learning and loving every minute of it

Introduction to the first edition

Argentine tango is an absorbing, addictive and unique way of dancing. I love it! It is an entire body language in which two people communicate a wide variety of emotions to one another. These feelings are usually driven by the music, though tango is perhaps the only dance that is enjoyable even when danced in total silence. Indeed, I have been most moved when watching a couple dancing in a silent room, completely engrossed in each other and the dance

Please, please do not confuse Argentine tango with ballroom tango with its image of exotic dress, unnatural arm posture and bizarre, sharp head and neck movements. These elements, I believe, stand in the way of the newcomer to tango who may think of tango as 'showing off' and become overly concerned about performance. Tango, for me, is not a performance as such though it can be wonderful to watch. Tango is a conversation in body language between two people. How it looks to an observer is not half as important as how it feels. It may be the case that when it feels good, it looks good too.

Some have likened tango to a seduction; for some couples it will be. For some it may be a harmless flirtation with gentle teasing and for others it is a complex game of 'body chess'. It does take two to tango but each few minutes of dance are what you choose to make them.

Each dance is totally improvised by the leader (not necessarily a man) who takes the follower (not necessarily a woman) for a trip. The trip lasts for the duration of a song and will never be identical. The same leader will dance an entirely different dance any other time, even on an empty dance floor to the same tune; he invents the dance as he is moved by the moment and the music.

This may be the reason for the addictive properties of tango. However many times you attempt to reproduce the same conditions, it will always be a fresh experience because your mood, or that of your partner, will differ. Of course, on a crowded dance floor, the problems of navigation will throw yet another spanner in the works. As you become more skilled, your repertoire of possible choices of moves increases. In short, tango offers a huge and ever-changing kaleidoscope of dance possibilities and is always challenging and rewarding. It can never be boring

This book has several aims. I am most eager to show beginners how fulfilling such a dance can be and encourage them to try it this way. I hope that, at the same time, experienced tangueros will be able to use some of the ideas and exercises to enjoy their dancing all the more. Between these two extremes, I like the image of such a book taking the place of a 'rough guide' but with a smiley face. Perhaps the closest I can hope for is that, in passing on what I have learned, I can be like the useful older brother, a couple of years up the school ladder. You know, someone who is approachable for help but not so far advanced that he can't remember how it felt to struggle? I hope my book is helpful at all levels.

One more thing. Someone once said to me that tangueros could be divided into two broad groups: 'techies' and 'feelies'. The techies love all the history and the names of the moves. Sadly, they also like to teach them, even whilst dancing socially, to any partner that does not seem to know the particular move they just failed to lead. The feelies just love the dance and to hold a partner in their arms; they aren't interested in the technique or the history or the names. To a feely, there is no wrong move. They make it up as they go along, much to the confusion of their partners. In my more honest moments, I have to admit to being a bit of both. I hope that this book might make the techies more feely, and the feelies a little more techy.

David Turner
July 2004

CHAPTER 1

The history of tango

Tango! I wonder what that word conjures up in your mind? I would be surprised if it failed to induce images of passion. I dare go further. I wonder if there is a soul who has never actually heard of tango? I suppose I must concede that, somewhere on this planet, there may well be somebody so disconnected from the world of popular culture that the word means nothing to them; but I would be surprised. Certainly, in my experience, when I tell people of my passion for this dance and its music I always seem to receive a strong reaction. This usually takes the form of something between a 'wow!' of surprise and a chuckle. Why is this? I suspect that it

Fabiana and Cesar   *Photo DM*

has to do with one fairly common and conventional image that tango has acquired. The word 'tango', for some people, is synonymous with 'sex'. "It takes two to tango," they say, usually with a suggestive look. The Marlon Brando film Last Tango in Paris may have done wonders for the dairy industry but I am sad to say it has done tango few favours, except perhaps to provide one other reason why the name 'tango' lives in a corner of everyone's mind in some form or another. How remarkable is that?

How did this come about? How could it be that a dance, the tango, could grow from tiny origins over a hundred years ago in a far distant land, Argentina, to be almost a household name, and – what is more – to be so significant in so many people's lives today? Why is it that, after all these years, you can find couples dancing tango in every major city in the world, and why is its popularity rising so rapidly?

Perhaps it is the music, which is inextricably bound to the dance. Well, maybe so, since its unique rhythm, set at about the rate of the resting human heart, seems to move the human spirit wherever and whenever we hear it. The insistent beat, particularly of the earlier recordings, simply cries out to be danced to. It has an effect on me that continues to surprise me, even after years of familiarity. I feel sure that it speaks to me at an, unconscious level that I am at a loss to explain; it is so deep. I am sure that I am not alone in this.

It seems that mankind has always loved to dance, and we know that the courtship rituals of many animals and birds incorporate dance and display, so it is no stretch of my imagination to consider that dance as a form of expression probably preceded speech. I have always been moved by the words of the famous dancer Isadora Duncan, who said: "If I could explain myself, I wouldn't need to dance." Most people dance spontaneously in childhood almost as soon as they have conquered walking but, somehow, as they acquire self-consciousness, 'learn' not to as an adult. Those of us who do love to dance have usually learned to do so in many different ways. Speaking for myself, long before I learned to tango I had enjoyed country dances, such as 'Strip the Willow', at junior school, and later my mother taught me the Gay Gordons on the deck of a troopship that was carrying an entire regiment to the Far East. Weekly sessions in the sixth form with the local girls' school had us waltzing and quickstepping, and many of my contemporaries learned to jive, twist and do the Madison simply by copying what we saw on the television and at the movies. All these dances were formulaic and so had to be learned and practised, and – for me – that was a big element of the fun of them. You struggled to learn, but when you got it right you felt wonderful.

In the era following the 1960s dancing continued to be popular, of course, but increasingly the style of dance broke loose from the restrictions of lessons and form. I suppose that in that way it mirrored what was going on in popular music, where bands of three-chord, amateur guitarists could hit the big time. Many of these were unable to read a note of music but still felt free to express themselves. Dancers went out to enjoy themselves as before but now, although they were in company, effectively they danced alone. The huge advantage of this was that each dancer was free to develop his or her own style and be inventive. Sadly, however, these virtues were gained at the expense of the intimate experience of physical closeness that was the hallmark of the earlier dances. I still grieve at the sight of a ring of women dancing at a Christmas ball, only last year, merely moving from one foot to another in one corner of a heaving ballroom to music loud enough to shatter eyeballs. No touch, no skill, no finesse, no soul and

– which saddens me most of all – no men.

Tango offers something different. In a sense, it allows us to 'have our cake and eat it'. We have all the closeness with a partner we could ever want but we can combine it with the freedom of an improvised dance. This is its enduring character and its strength. Let us look at its origins, but, before we do, I feel the need to make some things clear to you.

First I want to say that, although the history of tango is fascinating in its own way, it contributes only a little, in a practical sense, to the we are taught. You could leave this whole chapter out completely and still tango satisfactorily. That would be a great shame, however, because it is fun to incorporate some of the flavour of tango's earlier days in our dancing today. I believe that tango is as much a language as speech. In the same way as many of us love the poetry of Shakespeare even though we don't communicate with each other in Tudor English, we are perfectly able to grasp the subtleties of tango without necessarily copying those who danced it in the past.

I dare to go one step further. I am eager to dispel the myth that there is some sort of 'authentic' tango that can and must be copied and is set in concrete for all time. I know a number of people who choose to believe this, and that's fine for them, though I wonder what they get out of that feeling. I just worry that, if we focus too much on the past, we may lose the joy of the present and – worse still – discover that there is no one to tango with in the future.

No one actually owns tango or can forbid anyone from connecting with it for any reason. It is a genuine, basically earthy dance of the proletariat; a dance created by the people, for the people. Tango did not evolve because people wanted to do only that which had been done before. It was new and fresh and dangerous. It pushed at the boundaries of human contact and was not subservient to form. I read somewhere that one lover of tango thought that, when Osvaldo Pugliese, a great bandleader, died in 1995, so did tango. That is exactly the attitude I feel we must fight against. While, at the moment of writing, there is no doubt a strong rise in the popularity of tango – both the music and the dance – it still needs all the friends it can get.

On the other hand, I recognise in myself as I dance more and become more familiar with those older recordings of tango from the Golden Era, how my tastes have changed. I hear more subtlety and nuances in those tunes which I fail to find in the newer music. Could it be that in a world of constant change and ephemera, we could learn something about the qualities of music, dances and even behaviours that manage to survive from the past?

The Internet, normally a wonderful way to trawl for information, contains a widely conflicting set of opinions. They vary from the useful and informative, posted by people with the highest ideals and the desire to spread the word about this wonderful dance, to nit-picking discussions of semantics. Some of the motivation of the writers seems to be to further engorge a few egos in Buenos Aires. The greatest sadness for me is that they may put people off from trying to develop their own tango language skills.

From other books you can read on the subject, and interviews with some of tango's current senior citizens, it would appear that even in the so-called 'golden era' there were many schools of thought about tango. This was true not only in different places in Argentina but even from one side of Buenos Aires to another. This is hardly surprising with a dance that evolved from such a melting pot of talents, different cultures, hardships and often violent rivalry.

Tango at Corrientes, London   *Photo DM*

In life it is good to be pure, but not to be a purist. I want to prevent newcomers to tango forming the impression that I gained in my early days: that tango could be taught or danced properly only by Argentinians. In particular, the film *The Tango Lesson*, lovely as it is, appears to support this view. Sadly, all that does is risk putting people off. I have been taught by many Argentinians. Some were very good at teaching while others were good to watch but, I am sad to report, very poor teachers. When I think about this seriously, I realise that some of the best teachers I have experienced were English, American or German. I know that this analogy is not watertight but think about this for a moment: football, cricket and rugby were invented in England, but I really can't believe that only the English can play these games well. No Argentine would accept that.

In learning to tango we should realise from the outset that we are who we are, and need to develop our own styles to suit our bodies and aptitudes, always remembering the goal: connecting with a partner and enjoying the experience. In this respect I must pay tribute to Rodolfo 'el Chino' Aguerrodi, an Argentine, whose method of teaching I recommend in this book because it offers you the key to open the door to tango for yourself.

There is a very special feeling about dancing in Buenos Aires but since, with tango, the deal is moving to the music with a partner you can enjoy tango anywhere. Besides, we can't all go to Argentina whenever we like. You can dance tango in very little space, too, which is just as well if you are on a crowded dance floor. Best of all, you can tango to any tune the band plays with a little thought. In that sense, once you have learned to tango, all other dances become unnecessary, even trivial in comparison.

What I am saying is that, irrespective of the history of it all, tango is alive and modern and growing every day, all over the world. Though I do not subscribe to the view of Henry Ford, the car man, that "History is bunk", we should use it for our own enjoyment, not be enslaved by it.

As I understand it, from 1875 to 1900 Argentina opened its doors to floods of immigrants, mostly from Europe. By the turn of the 20th century those immigrants outnumbered the original population by 40 to 1, and it is interesting to realise that in Buenos Aires in 1900 there were daily newspapers in English, German, Yiddish and Italian but only a weekly one in Spanish, the local language. Remember too that the local culture was also Spanish, with stiff rules of courtship. Often, at a social gathering, men outnumbered women by as much as 100 to 1. The gross discrepancy between the desire for women's company and the supply thereof must have led to a great deal of rivalry, tension and violence, and it is little surprise that the culture of 'machismo' was then at its peak. Isn't it interesting to consider that we have no equivalent single word in the English language?

Some of the women that accompanied the immigrants were – shall we say – not the most ladylike, and many worked in bordellos near to the docklands. As the male population rose so the need for brothels grew, but the supply of suitable woman to service them remained extremely limited. At this time only half the male population could have a wife and there was no chance of casual relationships with normal women. Men, being what they are, looked to prostitutes for female company. A man could buy various services from these women, including a chat. It was possible to buy a dance with a woman, who would make sure you wanted to keep on buying by flirting and teasing and seeking to arouse you. She would pay more attention to the more affluent customer and to the one who gave her a good time. She might even see herself able to marry such a man and become respectable before old age and/or disease put a stop to her trade. Incidentally, this brothel culture was not just found in Buenos Aires by any means, as anyone who remembers the song 'Hey, Big Spender!' from the show and film *Sweet Charity*, set in New York, will realise.

Many of the movements we still use in tango today have echoes of those days of sexual frustration, teasing and flirtation. I have friends who find close embrace slightly too arousing to attempt. The leads for sacadas in close embrace involve quite close pelvic contact, and all leg intrusions between the legs of our partners are suggestive, to say the least.

In those early days, if the man practised hard and became a good dancer he had more chance of a free dance – and maybe more. Men who wanted to be good dancers practised their skills with each other. They had to, because you would have to pay a prostitute and there was no way that any other woman would dance with you. So men – rip-roaringly, heterosexual, macho men – danced with men, and this is still a part of the tango culture today. It was common for the younger boys to be used as followers to assist the older men to practise new moves. I have danced with men on many occasions in lessons both as a leader and as a follower. This has helped me immensely, and this should not surprise us since, if we accept that the best leaders are those who are most acutely aware of their follower's needs, the more you understand the follower's problems the better a leader you become. It is interesting to realise that, despite all the evidence available, some dispute still exists as to whether, in those early days, men danced with men or not. Some seem to feel that even to suggest that men danced with each other is an affront to the macho image of the early Argentinian, or even implies that the men were gay. I find this difficult to accept, since it is a fact that the population of Buenos Aires rose from some 210,000 in 1880 to 1,200,000 by 1910; most were immigrants from Europe, where there is a long and honourable tradition of men dancing with each other.

So, to begin with (the story goes), tango arose within the bordellos of Buenos Aires, particularly in those dockland areas by the River Plate, such as San Telmo. Well, not really, some would say. They point to sources that say that no musicians worked in brothels. Others make the logical suggestion that musicians kept men happy to wait their turn before they went upstairs. That sounds entirely logical to me. We know for sure that establishments referred to as 'academies' became popular places where a man might drink, listen to music, flirt with the waitresses and dance as well. It would seem very likely that some of these places – dance halls – developed an unsavoury reputation for all sorts of criminal activities indulged in by their clientele. Perhaps the confusion lies in wanting to label these 'academies' as dance halls or brothels when their function was not so narrow. Furthermore, it seems very likely that the sort of venue providing music, dance, alcohol and whatever else you might seek would more likely to be found in the provinces than in Buenos Aires, where demand for prostitutes was high and so were rents. Whatever the truth is, tango has not exactly suffered from the slightly raffish image that surrounds it.

What certainly is the case is that, with male-female ratios being so adverse to a man's chances of female contact of any kind, brothels were – for some men – the only place they might meet women on an intimate level. Just to be able to touch a woman was better than nothing at all.

A whole new slang language, called lunfardo, also evolved in the docklands, and found itself intertwined into the music and the dance. It is reasonable to suppose that, like cockney rhyming slang, lunfardo represented, on the one hand, a form of social glue, bonding folk together and, on the other, a way of being able to exclude strangers from precious inside information and to intimidate them.

There is some confusion about the true musical origins of what we now see as tango, partly because of the period of time between 1955 and about 1983 when tango was at its lowest ebb. Orchestras that had flourished disbanded and dance halls fell into disuse, and so the chain of mostly verbal history about tango's very earliest days was largely broken. For this reason, opinions differ, but it seems most likely that tango evolved from several different music and dance sources. Primarily, there was the habanera, a slow dance, sharing the same background rhythm as tango, which originated – as the name suggests – from Havana, Cuba, but became very popular in Spain. Other sources quote the influence of tango Español and also the fandango. It is generally agreed that the milonga, with its dash-dot-dot-dash rhythm (used to such great effect by Astor Piazzolla in much of his work), preceded and contributed towards tango. Finally, most people acknowledge the influence of candombe, an African dance. When

The author with his lovingly restored Louis XV style bandoneon.. If only he could actually play the darned thing as well as he can restore them!

you listen to classic tango recordings, it is no stretch of the imagination to hear both European and African influences, and certainly some reminiscent of the Andes.

The flavour of older tango music also reflects the instruments those immigrants brought with them. Perhaps the most important of these is the bandoneon, a unique button-box version of the accordion, which was brought from Germany. It is the bandoneon that lends to the tango song some of the plaintive quality we expect. Add to this a violin for both crispness and fluidity, a piano for the small element of percussion needed and a double bass, and you have the basic authentic tango sound, with or without a vocalist. Carlos Gardel, probably the greatest tango singer of all time, made many recordings just with two guitars as backing, and it seems likely that the guitar would have played a very important role at the birth of tango even before the arrival of the bandoneon. What is certain is that the bandoneon replaced the flute in many ensembles and that some of the earliest street music was from barrel organs.

The lyrics of the songs frequently speak of unrequited love, homesickness and loss. I have always been drawn to the idea that, when the lyrics are in the voice of females, they can be feisty or confidently seductive, like 'A Media Luz', or defiant, like 'Nostalgias'. Many of those clearly referring to the male condition are a bit whiny, it seems to me. I mean to say, what do we make of 'La Cumparsita', probably the most famous tango tune in the world. I've heard it referred to as Argentina's unofficial national anthem. After three verses of pathetic whingeing about rejection, the last line wraps it up: "Even the puppy left me!" Is there any wonder, we all think? Perhaps these lyrics really do offer us a snapshot of what life must have been like in the Buenos Aires of the early 20th century. How must it have felt to be thousands of miles from your roots, working like a dog with no wife at home to offer solace, support and affection?

Several tango lyrics refer to another Argentinean obsession; that of gambling. 'Por una cabeza' links the image of a green young colt being pipped at the post 'by a head' with the chagrin of a young lover, at the last moment, losing the woman he has set his heart on. 'Suerte Loca', or 'Crazy Luck' is a wonderful lyric. It refers to the popular card game, 'Truco'. In it, an older man counsels a youngster to never believe in luck or that anything really happens by chance. That 'crazy luck' people think he has was hard earned experience, gained by watching himself fail. How true.

From these small beginnings tango grew. At first it was the property of street barrel organs and working-class dance halls, but as the middle classes explored these colourful dives they became attracted to the music and the dance, took it back to more respectable areas and refined it. It must certainly have been the affluent middle classes that bought the sheet music and the recordings that became so prolific in the first two decades of the 20th century. Soon tango was all the rage and huge orchestras with banks of fiddlers and bandoneonists were formed. The scene was similar to that which you might have seen once jazz had been discovered and emerged from the back streets of New Orleans into the commercial world. One bandoneonist, playing at that time in Anibal Troilo's orchestra, was Astor Piazzolla, who was to become very important to tango later on.

At the time of Eva Perón, around 1945 to 1950, tango was at its absolute peak. Performance shows went to New York, where they were smash hits. Famously, Rudolf Valentino, a decade earlier still, was filmed in gaucho costume performing a stylised tango routine, and – thanks to him – many people who hear the word 'tango' think immediately of a rose, clenched between the teeth. Thank you, Rudi, so much!

The American audiences did not just copy the styles they saw but changed the dance to suit their mood. Tango Americano then developed and, from this, the current style of – to my eyes at least – the somewhat uncomfortable-looking ballroom tango descended.

Similar spectacles were taken to Paris in the 1920s. Once Parisians thought that it was chic to tango it became even more fashionable for the upper classes, which gave tango another big boost back in Argentina. In Paris at this time, however, there appeared the 'tango apache'. This is the entertaining, but – dare I suggest? – laughable, dance-ballet with the pimp, in his striped T-shirt, flinging his hooker around the bar. I suspect that this version may have done much to spoil the image of tango for the public, and although, for certain, pimps and prostitutes must have tangoed in the early days, the dance – for me at least – is not about violence and humiliation but, rather, seduction.

I much prefer the image of the lonely, homesick dock worker dressing up in his only decent suit on a Saturday night and going out to the dance hall, hoping to meet the woman of his dreams. He knows he has very small chance of success of connecting with a woman except for brief moments, perhaps just two and a half minutes of a tango, and that watched, no doubt, by her brother or some other chaperone. He will have practised his floor skills with a friend all through the week.

At the dance hall he sees a girl who attracts him. She briefly returns his gaze but holds it for enough time to give him hope. He nervously awaits the moment he will be able to ask her to dance, and as he walks towards her she appears for a while to look in his direction but as he gets nearer she quickly and positively looks away. He gets the signal; he has been rejected and he veers away and goes to chat to some friends. No one else has seen the rejection but he feels it keenly. At least he has not lost face. He lifts his chin, sticks out his chest, flicks some imaginary fluff from his sleeve and, once again, looks about him for another partner.

This was the formula that worked so well in the dance halls of those days. As soon as the man came near enough to come properly into focus, if the girl did not like him she merely averted her gaze. If she maintained eye contact, no words needed to be said; she would rise from her seat to join him on the floor. They would assume the tango embrace and he would gain a further message from her by the way she came into his arms. She might play cool and hold him a little away from her with her left hand placed on his right biceps. So far so good. He still has the dance to convince her of his worth. On the other hand, she might slide her hand up his arm and as far round as his neck, no doubt making his back hairs stand up in a shiver of excitement. Even better, but the signal here is of more forwardness or familiarity and certainly of more expectation. Besides, dancing closer needs different skills from both dancers.

Whilst dancing further apart offers more room for manoeuvre it causes problems in two ways. Firstly, because we can do more things we may come to feel we ought to; then we are obliged to learn all those things in classes to make them possible and enjoyable. Secondly, and more vitally, the further apart our bodies are the greater the likelihood that we will lose the connection between each other. In an 'open' embrace we are forced to pay attention to the embrace, the 'frame' (explained in chapter 3) and our ability to dissociate at the waist. When we dance in close embrace, connection is almost inevitable and instinctual. The leader is obliged to understand what is and is not possible for his follower to do but he is never in any doubt as to where she is or whether she is with him when he moves. When the man moves, the couple moves; it just happens.

The message to me from this aspect of the history of tango is that connecting with a partner using body language was the very essence of tango, even before the dance began. That it is non-verbal must be a reflection of the variety of languages spoken in Buenos Aires at the time. I expect most immigrants could get by on a daily basis with limited skills in foreign tongues, but courtship demands more eloquence. Tango and its related dances – the tango vals and the cheeky milonga – could, and still can, speak volumes between a man and a woman.

In the dance halls there were other useful conventions that helped the dancers to use the environment as a place to meet and find a mate. The tango numbers were grouped in fours, usually linked by tempo, and this group was referred to as a 'tanda'. After each tanda a totally different tune would be played to signal the end of the section. This was referred to as 'la cortina' ('the curtain'), and the convention was that, during this tune, all couples left the floor. The lady was always escorted to her chair. This meant that no dancer could be monopolised for the whole evening. The tanda system had further advantages. For example, if you were accepted at the beginning of the tanda you expected to dance all four dances with the same lady. If she left the floor after the first dance you would feel disgraced. If you were in some doubt as to whether you really wanted to dance with a particular lady, you would wait to the fourth tune of the tanda to ask her to dance and, that way, if you didn't connect you had to dance with her only for three minutes. After all, you could always ask her for another tanda later if you found her appealing.

Very often you would notice a couple standing in an embrace for half a minute after the tune had started, perhaps gently swaying to the beat. Part of the reason for this was to allow the man to feel the 'resonance' of the woman and make a simple connection before entering into steps that might produce the wrong impression for both parties. Sometimes, however, it was the only opportunity the couple would have to talk without being overheard. Apart from these moments, all the communication was done by the different elements of the dance, some of which, as you will discover, represent questions and answers, proposals and responses, whether 'yes' or 'no'.

These formulas were valuable in the courtship rituals of early 20th century Argentina, but some of us still enjoy using them to this day, and if you are a visitor to a dance hall in – say – Barcelona they would work just as well now. They certainly still use the tanda system, with some very unusual cortinas from time to time.

The tango hall was always considered to be an arena for a man to ask a woman to dance and the woman was obliged to wait until he did. In recent years, however, not only has equality arrived in tango but also my personal experience is that women are more than confident in asking men to dance, and I can think of some who are positively rapacious! This new culture has yet to reach Buenos Aires.

In 1930 a military coup in Argentina produced an environment in which gatherings to dance tango fell away, and when there was a return to more political freedom at the end of that decade tango revived. The flavour of it changed with the feeling of the time. Out went some of the earlier vulgarity and in came a lyrical, sentimental and nostalgic quality. Elegance was the essential style, and because of the fact that dance halls were packed 'bouncers' would ask couples to leave if they performed antics that might lead to a fight. This refinement went as far as meaning that it was considered poor taste to let anyone see the sole of your shoe when dancing, and as good as ruled out ganchos and high boleos in social dancing, and rightly so.

Tango received a strong boost during the rule of Juan Perón from the mid-1940s to the mid-1950s, probably because working-class people found that they had more money. Life had become good for many families, even at the poorer end of the scale. Food was relatively cheap in comparison to other commodities and as a result a very extensive nightlife developed. It was very common that on Wednesday nights the whole family went out for dinner, then to the cinema, then maybe to dance after that to round off the evening. Monday, Thursday and Sunday were for other activities with mistresses. Saturday was for the official partner. This all required a lot of money, which was rather freely distributed by Perón. As we all know so well, a period of boom and money printing is conventionally followed by a period of bust, and this era was no exception. The great outcome of all this feel-good factor was that tango grew to be a massive industry and was developed so that it would never be forgotten.

At about the time of Eva Perón's death in 1952, however, the political stability of Argentina became fragile again. A military coup in 1955 worsened the situation. Curfews were imposed, making nightlife impossible. Very many of the dance halls fell into disuse, the young fell under the influence of American pop music and tango went underground. Astor Piazzolla, returning from Paris (where he had been studying composition), continued to compose more modern variants of tango and these were performed in concerts. The whole new genre of 'tango nuevo' began to flourish. Many find the varying of tempo and frequent elements of passion and violence in this new type of tango music impossible to dance to, preferring the more sedate, fixed-tempo recordings from the past. Actually, as I hope to show in this book, the very nature of tango as an improvised language means that, once you have learned to dance competently to the old style, tango nuevo adds a new spice to the recipe.

I hope I can convince you that, while all this background to tango is fascinating, we would do well to keep our eyes firmly on the reason that we do this dance at all. We are not attempting to keep alive a flagging old tradition, nor is tango just for a tiny fringe of the 'in' crowd. This is not the Argentine equivalent of morris dancing. Tango works today because it is the most liberating way to dance in the arms of someone else.

The level of enjoyment for beginners appears to be very high even in the first lessons and seems to rise as their experience and confidence mounts. Since the dance is about communication, it does not need the skills of a mountain goat, nor great stamina, nor flamboyance. What is needed is the ability to feel the body position of the partner and to connect.

One final point needs to be made here. Tango can be wonderful to watch and there are some terrific tango shows constantly touring the world. I used to love them and went to see them as often as I could. Many of the stars of these shows teach tango and are a fantastic inspiration to us all. I feel sure that, had you been alive in the 1930s in Buenos Aires, you would have seen a few of the amazing moves the show dancers do. The vast majority of the dancers then, however, did no such thing. The dance floors were just as packed as now. On those dance floors were men and women attempting to make connections with each other. There would have been little room for kicks and passion directed towards the rest of the dancers but lots for control and intensity of feeling within each couple. Let us not forget that when we see a tango show it is choreographed to the hilt. It is entirely sequenced to give the maximum pleasure to the audience by fitting in the biggest number of spectacular moves in the shortest time, in the space available. I dare say the dancers enjoy themselves a little too, from time to time, but they also suffer the pain of all professional dance performers. This is a different tango world from the one we inhabit in our social dancing. The shows usually attempt to show the tango era but they are a garish pastiche of that time, the fantasy of a show producer. They do not portray the history of tango any more than a performance of *Les Misérables* gives us real insight into the Paris Commune. We would not pay money to sit in a theatre and watch a film of real social dancing in the Sunderland Club in 1930, I think, so the shows are here to stay. I just make a plea that we all remember that it is ballet, rather than 'authentic' tango.

Let us now leave the history of tango behind and move forward. In my view, tango has a great future. Dwelling too lovingly on the past can be positively unhelpful.

CHAPTER 2

The different schools of tango teaching

It may not be apparent to those beginning to learn to tango, but there are quite a wide variety of teaching styles and philosophies used. This should not surprise us when we consider the origins of tango and the influences of the dancing on the teachers, the teachers on the dancing and the music on the entire thing. We think of tango as a single entity but, even now, it is not. The perceptions of what tango is vary from place to place and from time to time.

Costas and Susanna   *Photo DM*

In the beginning, Buenos Aires was small and quite distant in real terms from all those areas we now merely consider to be its suburbs. In each of these locations tango had its own style. The dancers moved little from place to place but the bands certainly travelled to make a living and brought back different things from their gigs. Those bands were like bees, pollinating as they collect nectar. As those smaller satellite townships were subsumed into the sprawling city over the first 30 years of the 20th century, what resulted was a cocktail of styles, all perfectly 'legitimate' within the remit of tango. The differences were immense.

Just think about it. Different dance floors – both floor surface and dimensions – led to different needs. Different dance floor traffic led to different embraces, as did individuals' desires for closeness and intimacy of embrace or, on the other hand, for more genteel distancing. None of these styles was weak and easily subservient to any other and they all survived because they were legitimate and valuable. Who could criticise the 'orillero' style of the docklands areas of San Telmo or La Boca because it differed from the styles of those dancers from Mataderos or Villa Urquiza? The same must be true for the teaching that both led the styles and, at the same time, was formed by them. I think it is reasonable, however, for us all to judge for ourselves which style of dancing we like and which style of teaching is most likely to allow us to dance as we want. I propose to nail my colours to the mast here and now on this issue in the hope that it will help some fellow dancers.

The 'basic eight'

There are many stories about the creation of the 'basic eight' and none is very complimentary. I refer to the 'paso basico', or basic step. Rather confusingly, you may also find this sequence of steps referred to as the 'salida' by some teachers. All dances have their basic characteristic step patterns, and tango is no exception. The problem with it for tango is that it tends to stifle the feelings that power the dance. If we lose the feelings, the dance becomes just another dance form. I know some people who prefer to see it that way but to my mind, they miss the entire point of tango as a dance form with a distinct, unique and wonderful quality.

In a nutshell, the 'basic' in tango, from the beginning, is: we walk; the woman adopts the cross position, or 'la cruzada', walk; then we walk to the closed side of the embrace ('resolution').

There is a story that, once upon a time, there was a very successful tango school in Buenos Aires. The principal of the school thought to himself: "How can I improve my business?" so he sat down and pondered. He constructed an eight-step sequence, involving the basic tango elements (walk, woman cross, walk, walk to the closed side of the embrace), and then linked in lots of steps – which had already been found and named – to these eight steps.

Teachers I have spoken to who have prepared for classes in both systems confirm that for them the basic eight is by far the easiest way to teach tango. As one who spends a great deal of time preparing classes for pupils, I can see how I could reduce my own preparation time considerably if I taught this way myself. Less effort for the teacher may not be better for the pupil, however. There are benefits for pupils in learning by this system, of course. It is easy to grasp the curriculum and pupils soon acquire a sense of achievement at having mastered something concrete. Many people find learning steps by numbers easy, and it is well known that there is a long tradition in the military of teaching by numbered sequences.

The reason this method of teaching people things is still used is that it works, but I would like you to pick up on the word 'concrete' and remember that it conjures up other meanings: grey, cold, heavy and – I suspect most of us would agree – unattractive.

The basic eight is based on a set pattern of eight steps and is taught as a sequence to be honed until grooved to perfection. The problem with it is that, although this may well teach poise and probably gets you up on the dance floor with confidence quite quickly, it does teach you to think in sequences. "What is the problem with that?" you ask. The problem with sequences for me is that they stifle improvisation and interpretation and, worst of all, they inhibit innovation. Only the teacher holds the 'secret' of the next new step and these are dribbled out from lesson to lesson. It must be attractive for the teacher to be able to prepare for a lesson with a 'concrete' item to get across. This works particularly well where a sequence taught in the previous week runs sweetly forward into the sequence for this week. This is how ballroom dancing is usually taught, so it appeals to those who learn and teach from that background.

I have discovered, however, that to learn a dance this way has its drawbacks. It is a little like learning a language by learning to speak a number of useful phrases extremely well. As long as you stick to those phrases, you will sound as if you really do understand the language well, because, within those few phrases, your accent will be perfect. The problem will arise when, fooled by the perfection of your accent, a native speaker throws at you, at speed, a sentence not including the words you have learned.

So, to my mind, the paso basico system of learning is quick and easy to grasp to begin with but after a while it needs to be, as it were, 'unlearned'. I shall describe it, however, for completeness and to further demonstrate how restricting it is in its nature. It is useful to know it because it is so widely taught but in my view it is more of a help to the teacher than to the pupil.

All the steps are numbered from one to eight and, considering the man's sequence first, step 1 is a back step on the right foot. Two problems become immediately apparent. Firstly, there is the potential for the man to step backwards onto someone else's foot, but, more importantly, the novice leader often finds it so convenient to initiate the dance by pulling on the follower's back. We should not be surprised. It works. The leader steps back and the follower steps forward and it feels like a result. The leader should be learning the proper way to indicate to the follower his intention, however, using his torso and never using his arms. Ballroom dancers are actually encouraged to use their arms for leading and, when they come to tango, they may have a problem learning not to do so. Step 1 of the paso basico allows them to dance tango just as another ballroom dance, but it really isn't.

Step 2 is a sidestep to the leader's left and at least those who teach the paso basico insist that, before this step happens, the leader must close left ankle to right. This is a very big and worthwhile lesson to learn. The collection of knees and ankles at each beat is very important and I have to admit that the teaching of the basic eight does achieve this quickly. If, however, leaders are allowed to lead the sidestep with a push from their right hand or a pull with the left, much has been lost. The sidestep must be led by a preparation for the step that ensures that the follower is on her left foot and able to move her right foot to her right. This follows easily from step 1, but it can be achieved from a starting position with feet together by shifting body weight from foot to foot. Often, therefore, teachers leave out step 1 to reduce toe crushing potential.

Step 2 is often referred to as the 'salida', and this sometimes produces confusion in the minds of beginners who also hear other teaches refer to the whole sequence of eight steps as the salida. Some even refer to salidas by numbers (e.g. 'salida no. 1', 'salida no. 2', etc.), referring to subtle differences in foot placing during the eight steps that allow the couple to turn a corner. Worse still, from a confusion point of view, some people refer to the last three steps of the eight, steps 6, 7 and 8, as la salida, because of the meaning in Spanish: 'the exit'. I do not wish to sound overly critical of such teachers, who have their reasons for these methods. I simply wish to show how differently tango may be taught.

Usually, when the leader takes step 2, he angles his upper body to the right, restricting somewhat the sidestep of the follower, while maintaining the embrace frame. The reason for this is that he will take step 3 forward on his right foot with the thigh outside the follower's right leg. Usually, right thigh touches right thigh as the follower steps back on her left foot. Some teachers teach that this thigh-to-thigh contact is the signal that the follower will "go to the cross", which I will describe in a moment. It is fine to learn the cross, but I hear that, lately, it may have fallen out of favour in some circles in Buenos Aires.

Step 4 is taken in the same direction, with the leader's left leg and the follower's right, maintaining the same upper body configuration.

Step 5 for the leader is simply to bring the right foot to join the left. Before he does this he must return his torso to the front by rotating it slightly anticlockwise. The effect for the follower is to simultaneously produce a deceleration and a need for the left foot to travel towards the right foot, and even further right, to maintain balance and stay in front of the leader. The outcome is, therefore, that the follower ends up standing on the right foot with the left ankle crossed in front of the right and ready to take the weight to enable the right foot to leave on the next beat. This position is referred to as 'the cross' ('la cruzada'), but very soon it comes to be thought of as '5' by those who sequence, particularly if they use some instructional videos. I believe this is another area where the constraints of a sequenced learning system may cause problems because it 'hard-wires' the pattern into our brains and prevents us from seeing it for what it truly is. We might ask ourselves: "What is the cross all about?" Call me fanciful if you will, but I suspect that the position is one that is designed to show the woman's legs to their best advantage. Why is it that every line-up of Miss World contestants shows them standing with one foot crossed in front of the other? Surely this pose accentuates the hips and gives the illusion of longer legs? Still in doubt? Contrast this artificial pose, then, with an image of the same woman standing with her legs like those of a table, and tell me you find that just as attractive!

A nice result of the woman's cross is that it places her in a 'pre-sprung' position with a slight coiled tension across her body that is useful for dynamic progression when she releases it. It is a useful preliminary position before that dramatic movement. As a prelude to a

La cruzada - the cross. Strictly speaking, illustrated here is the moment just before the completion of the cross because Frederique has yet to fully transfer her weight onto her left leg and come to arrive fully in front of James

19

forward ocho, the 'coiled spring' feeling of the cross allows for a bigger, more swoopy and altogether more satisfying feeling than when effected from a more neutral start. From a leader's point of view, any forward step led from the cross seems to be a little bigger, leaving a good gap into which we can intrude our legs; but I'll say more about that much later

I always think that the cross fulfils two vital functions. One is to act as a sort of punctuation; not so much as a full stop as a semi-colon. When we arrive at the cross, to a certain extent, we both know where we are. The other function is that the cross-legged position actively blocks some movements of the follower and allows a leader to settle her axis on that point and, for example, move round her central axis before she can move it.

So, it is quite a useful thing to know about the cross and how to arrive at it, but you don't necessarily have to go through the whole sequence of five steps to get to it. Theoretically, allowing the follower to step back on her right foot, then indicating a stop with first a right torso rotation to make her face her right and then a leftward movement, should indicate the cross to those who do it. Sadly, in my short experience, I have rarely found it possible to induce a cross with a partner who has been taught the basic eight exclusively except as part of the sequence, so, most of the time, I don't lead it. Quite contrary to the notion that the cross is an inevitable pose at step 5 of the paso basico, some believe that the cross is actually an advanced movement in fully improvised tango that has numerous permutations of positions. For them, it is not just the follower bearing weight on her right foot with the left held across the front of it. They see no reason why the cross could not be led from either side and with either leg held in front of the other. I am sure they are right. When we think of the cross, we ought to be more questioning about its purpose in our dance and not just throw it in because it comes at the fifth beat of the bar in the paso basico. In any case, so many women I dance with now have not been taught to cross at all and won't go to the cross for you even if you want them to.

Step 6 is taken with the leader's left foot, straight forward but with a range of variations. Possibilities range from straight ahead, torso facing straight ahead, to a preliminary left angulation of the torso and left angulation at the left ankle to prepare for step 7. This is where some teachers use different 'salidas' to teach turning. If the leader precedes step

6 with a positive torso turn to the left, the follower will copy this and be able to take a step backwards and slightly to her right with her right foot, the left crossed foot now having assumed the weight-bearing role. Remember that tango is left-right-left, so that, as the cross pose is momentarily held, there is a weight shift from one foot to the other, as usual. The left foot does not come across the right ankle into the cross and just hover.

Step 6 can be rotated as much as the leader wants. He indicates the amount during the early part of the step. Here, again, lies one of the key lessons of tango and, if nothing else, step 6 of the basic eight teaches a leader to use his chest and not his arms to indicate a requirement of his follower. What a palaver for teaching such a simple trick, though!

In step 7 both dancers collect their knees and ankles together and then step to the leader's right. They should now be squarely in front of one another so that step 8 is merely the final collection of leader's left and follower's right feet together.

Tango music tends to be eight beats to a phrase, so you can see how seductive it is to teach this pattern of eight movements to a class of beginners. They repeat it over and over, moving in the line of dance without fouling each other, and with the variation of rotation at step 6 to allow them to turn the corners. Lovely! At the end of the class they have all felt they have danced the tango, they can do the simple homework even in their own kitchens, and they enjoy the movement and music from day one. Do you remember my analogy with learning a language? After a few more lessons of the same regimentation they will be able to recite in a perfect accent "My postilion has been struck by lightning", and now they can be taught "My postilion's aunt has been struck by lightning" with minimal effort, and they will be well pleased. The problem will be when someone asks them for directions to the station!

I realise that my views on this subject will not find favour in many quarters. Teachers who approve of the basic eight system and have a vested interest in its survival may ask: "Who does he think he is to criticise?" I am no expert, nor do I dance particularly well. Whilst the passage of years forbids me to label myself any more as 'just a beginner', I still go to classes. I have taken instruction under both schools of thought and have arrived at a realisation that one has been more helpful to me than the other. More significantly, perhaps, after each lesson I still come home and write notes, and I am happy to share these with you. After all, information is like manure; best if widely spread.

Different teachers

I have always found it interesting to analyse the classes I have attended, and writing notes afterwards affords me a chance to consider what common features make a great lesson and why some lessons fail to impress. Why do some workshops seem to allow a great leap forward in our dancing? I think it may be a function of the depth of any given teacher's own understanding of tango. Some teachers seem very self-confident while others come with so much expectation and hype because they are great dancers themselves. Some of these teachers, however, instruct by the 'do it this way because I say so' method and appear to have little understanding of the underlying logic of the moves. I am more attracted to the teacher who shows us a move in order to demonstrate a basic principle that may be applied to the entire dance. I'm sure I am not alone in being interested in the reasons why things work. I always want to know what is going on inside. In addition to that, I want all new ideas that are presented to me as factual to be cross-referenced to other things I already know to be true. I always want to know why, if I do a certain thing in a particular way, it should work naturally or why it has failed to be successful. Sometimes, understanding the reason for failure teaches us much more than when things go well. I

El Chino and Miho

really cannot approve of a teacher who says "Copy me" but can't explain why that way works.

This is why I so respect the teaching method of Rodolfo Aguerrodi, nicknamed 'el Chino' ('the Chinaman'). His deep grasp of the mechanics of tango has allowed him to design classes that will convey the understanding to us. When I fail to achieve a set goal in a Chino class, I am able to say so. When I do, he relishes the task of solving my problem. He never interprets a question as an attack on his authority. In any case, he is forever asking us: "Any questions? Any doubts?" and is quite disappointed when we have none for him. When you present him with a problem he watches you move and grasps, in an instant, the reason something has felt uncomfortable.

22

It may be that, for example, I have failed to dissociate adequately and that, as a result, my pelvis is wrongly aligned to my partner. He spots it immediately because, over the years, he has boiled down the factors that make the dance successful to a handful of important issues. These usually relate to our individual posture, self-control and body alignment. Sure, dancing is an art, but underpinning that is a vast body of knowledge of mechanics, anatomy, physiology and logic. I admire a teacher who is capable of delving into those areas to help me expand my understanding and therefore my technique. But then how many tango teachers do you know that is also fully trained locksmith *and* physiotherapist like Chino?

An alternative approach to the basic eight: the Aguerrodi system.

There is another way of learning tango, which may sound simplistic to begin with but is actually harder to persevere with in the early stages because it does not appear to resemble the dance you see the good dancers perform. I can tell you from experience that it is harder to teach this way, too. When this system of tango is taught, it has the potential to frustrate the dancer who imagines he can learn a lot more quickly. Those who have mastered other dance disciplines may find it very hard to learn to walk properly when all they want to do is run as soon as they can. It's like the cherry cake: the novice wants the cherries, but the basic cake structure is of flour, water and eggs, and you need both. Actually, a good cook can make much of the basic ingredients and use the cherries sparingly to good effect. This is true of the good dancer, who always walks elegantly and is balanced, so that the partner is free to dance without being pulled about. There are few things sadder than those who try to run before they can really walk well. None of us has perfect balance all the time; even the best dancers have off days. The difference is that the good dancer chooses carefully the moment to introduce something flashy; when, and only when, he is in complete control. He may plan a move, but be able to abort it if something unexpected happens. The same is true of language. We chat away freely but occasionally we begin a sentence and someone else starts to speak at the same time. We don't just carry on. In purely practical terms we won't be heard over the other voice anyway.

So, in my pretty limited experience, it is best to begin as you mean to end up. To learn how to walk naturally and elegantly in the arms of any person who will dance with you would seem to be the basic ingredient of this cake. Long before showy figures enter our minds, leaders have to develop a good, balanced walking style. They must also become very sensitive to the body position of the follower and, in particular, on which foot her weight rests at any time. For her part, the follower needs to learn the rather different way of stretching her leg backwards, as she generally walks backwards along the line of dance. The follower also has to learn both to disengage her brain from the steps and anxieties about what she is expected to do next, and walk into those areas the leader has made available. She must learn to read the signals that come from the leader's whole body, but particularly his chest, and at the same time, once she has understood the indication of what is expected, listen to the music and interpret it in her own way.

I want to dispel any idea that you might have gained that, in this conversation of body language called tango, the leader talks and the follower listens – and that's it. As with speech, someone has to start talking, and this the leader does. He then needs to know that he has been understood. He picks up signals from the follower about how she feels and where she is and whether she is receptive to suggestions about the different movements the couple may make as a unit. The leader proposes a movement but then listens to the way the follower responds and learns to amend future propositions accordingly. The music is the driving force that makes it all happen.

It is a similar situation to that which musicians find when they play together. When a violinist performs a sonata with a pianist, for example, each has a part to play that is different from the other's but entirely complementary. The actual performance is not just a sum of those two parts but more than that; an amalgam with the ebb and flow of communication between the two performers, both listening to their own sound but each other's also. The audience feels something living is present as a third element and the players feel it too. The better the spark that exists between two musicians the more moving the experience is for all. So it is with tango.

Once both dancers have learned to walk together freely in someone's arms, the basic 'cake' is fit to have some 'cherries' added to it, and they will enhance it.

What follows, therefore, is my experience and understanding of a system of teaching and learning tango that is gaining acceptance, even in

Argentina. I call this the 'Aguerrodi system' after my friend and mentor, Rodolfo Aguerrodi, who for many years has studied tango extensively from both a physical and intellectual standpoint. His training as a chiropractor has allowed him a unique insight into the way our bodies may interact effectively and with pleasure. His teaching has had a profound effect on me.

Rodolfo believes that the basic elements of tango are very simple and limited in number but that they must be perfected by the use of exercises. He is very keen to insist that we, his pupils, learn to balance on our own axes and move crisply from on point to another with commitment. He teaches us to be able to dissociate the top halves of our bodies from the bottom. Leaders must learn how to lead with their chests irrespective of the actions of their feet. Leaders lead by displacement of their mass and not by setting up tensions in their arms. Leaders and followers learn very early on under his tutelage to pivot cleanly a full 180 degrees from a stationary position using their abdominal muscles by torso rotation followed by collection.

Chino and Miho on stage   *Photo RA*

The system Rodolfo uses reminds me very much of the well-known language courses by Michel Thomas, who starts by linking the new information with knowledge you already possess and then almost imperceptibly allows your skill to grow almost organically. As with Michel Thomas, classes with Rodolfo lead steadily deeper into greater complexity, step by step. It is almost like a continuous game of 'consequences'. You move in a particular way and then deal with the resultant position. Many leads have numerous possibilities for further improvisation. Rodolfo teaches us to complete each step fully before exploring all the available options our new state offers us. At all times the emphasis is on freedom to express our own feelings engendered by the music, the partner in our arms and the space available. Any manoeuvre that can be done to the right can be done to the left too. Any intrusion we make with one free foot can be done with the other once we have learned to balance properly and change weight.

The result may be different but all outcomes are legitimate tango moves so long as the balance is secure and we have not made our partner feel uncomfortable. Because the tango embrace is asymmetrical, movements are usually easier to one side than another, but Rodolfo ensures that we do not learn by any series of sequences that favour our most comfortable side and thus lead us into restrictive habits. In short, he frees us to choose any move we like, in any sequence we devise 'on the wing'.

I believe that, unlike the sequence-based system of teaching and the basic eight, the Aguerrodi philosophy of learning tango allows each dancer to think for themselves and evolve their own individual style, so that they may enjoy dancing tango with any partner, anywhere in the world. They will, in essence have learned to speak the language we call tango fluently and with confidence.

Sequencing

I want to make something quite clear about the business of dancing in sequences. I can see the attraction of it; a couple can hone a few skills together and become very comfortable on a dance floor and even look very competent fairly quickly. It is possible to use a video of set pieces and learn to tack them together neatly and even manage some variations to take account of the floor space available. So, what is the problem with that? Isn't that exactly how ballroom dancing is taught? Well, there is no actual problem as such and quite a number of couples dance just like this. It's just that it is not real tango. It is a pastiche of tango. It is very much like when you see an English actor in a foreign language movie speaking his lines with an impeccable accent; you come to believe he or she can actually speak that language. Maybe they can, but it is much more likely that they have been coached for hours to perfect a few lines, parrot-fashion.

The beauty of the real thing and what makes it worth bothering with and why so many of us keep trying to master it is that connecting deeply with a partner needs more risk taking than you get when you dance in sequences. It is the difference between flying a light aircraft with your instructor beside you and your first solo flight. In a sense, when we dance tango as it is possible to dance it – from the soul – we are flying by the seat of our pants.

Most of us will have seen elderly couples sequence dancing. Each couple performs the same steps as all the others in synchrony and progress round the room without collision. The sequence is small and you have all the others to copy if you forget. They even do a 'square tango', and on occasions when I have told such people that I dance tango they have said: "Oh, we can tango too!" They seriously believe they do. I accept that I am going to the extreme for an example, but I wish to suggest that those who dance a set of sequences are merely using an extension of the same mindset. It is very safe, lots of fun for a few minutes, but – to my mind – totally lacking in soul.

And yet, in all tango classes you attend, you will be taught a sequence. This is more than reasonable. How else can a teacher lead you to understand and remember a particular movement? For example, if you want to teach a class to lead a backward ocho to the leader's left, it makes sense to first teach them to lead a left sidestep to ensure that the follower's weight has been placed on her right foot ready for the pivot. The problem this creates in some minds is that they begin to feel that the *only* way that ocho can be danced is from a leader sidestep left, and now a two-element sequence has been hard-wired into the brain. It is much more useful to learn how to lead, and follow, more complex movements from where you are now, rather than feel obliged to 'take a run-up' to the movement you planned. Teachers such as 'el Chino' Aguerrodi realise this and deliberately

Mike in Cambridge   *Photo DM*

27

teach so many different entries within the same lesson that no pupil gets into that tempting groove. As soon as he sees that you have grasped one set of movements to one side, he makes you try it to the other. Then he turns it upside down, back to front, adds a twist, a change of direction. All the time, the accent is on balance, poise and – above all – connection. In a Chino lesson the brain has no time to set grooves. The exercises are indeed sequences but they are designed with a purpose, which is usually to enable you to pivot well or to be able to better dissociate upper body from lower. When el Chino teaches an exercise his aim may simply be to allow a lead to be conveyed without compromising the embrace, or it may be to encourage the follower to concentrate on the fine-tuning of the lead being offered. He does not expect us to rehash the exercise as a sequence when we dance socially, and he makes this quite clear. The sequences he uses are merely vehicles to demonstrate a point or reveal a deficiency in our technique.

This is a radically different concept from that which leads to sequencing in social dancing. El Chino's approach frees us from our teacher. We become fully adult and we actually speak the language of tango because we are thinking in that language, not trying to do rapid translations. We arrange our own choreography from moment to moment as the music drives us. We have no fear that we will find ourselves bereft of ideas and not be able to lead, or follow, because we have forgotten something we were taught. Nor do we come to the end of a dance thinking things such as "We didn't do a gancho". If you watch a couple dancing who have been recently taught from a sequence system you occasionally see that something they attempt fails to come off. What do they do then? They stop dancing. When I learned ballroom dancing, when things went wrong it was so tempting to try to start again by breaking away from each other and walking back to the start point in one corner of the room! If you watch a couple who have been taught by the Aguerrodi philosophy, when something intended fails to happen it simply does not matter. So, you have found yourself in some configuration that you had not planned? Never mind. The next movement begins right here where we find ourselves. Indeed, 'failure' in this philosophy of tango is actually 'serendipity', the joyous stumbling onto an unexpected pleasure by accident. What a happy philosophy that is? The perfect antidote to neurotic dancing.

When you join in with a group of people doing a sequence dance, your preoccupation is on remembering the sequence and watching the other dancers so that you stay uniform with them. It's a bit like marching in a squad: not much room for individuality but not too taxing on the brain. When we tango we keep an eye out for other dancers, of course, but the areas to concentrate on most are our partner, first and foremost, and the music. It is quite possible to chat while you dance sequence. It is the sure recipe for disaster if you chat in tango. There is just not enough brain to communicate properly on two separate levels at a time. The reason why those of us who love tango so much work so hard on the technique is not to be able to perform more difficult and flashier steps. That's a different dance altogether. What the tango dancer wants is sufficient technique to

be able to dance without thinking about technique at all, freeing up the brain for the music and the connection with the person in their arms. The inspirational Olga Besio puts it beautifully. She says: "The technique is something we learn to forget." Carrying a shopping list of sequences in your mind is as useful as a ball and chain round one ankle if you want to experience the rewards real tango can bring.

I have to admit that, to begin with, to learn to string together a series of set pieces is very tempting and, to the casual eye, the results will seem very impressive. I watched a couple that I had never seen

Tango Nuevo   *Photo DM*

before dancing recently and they looked wonderful. As the usual flow of dancers swept round the room, they stood out as being particularly stylish. At one point, right in front of me, the strikingly glamorous follower gave the most exotic, high, backward boleo. It looked superb. Unusually for me, I was sitting out for a while, so I was able to watch a few dancers more closely. What I came to realise was that there were some who hardly appeared to perform any set piece moves at all, yet moved as one with each other and in total sympathy with the music.

My glamorous couple continued to attract my eye and I decided that they were worth watching for longer than I would normally see them, so I took up a vantage point and watched them as they progressed all round the room. After a while I saw that the dance they did was heavily choreographed and sequenced and that the same, wonderful, high boleo could be seen, absolutely identical in every respect, every now and again. Sadly, there were times when it didn't quite suit the music, but I think that they were enjoying themselves. The whole evening they danced exclusively with each other, and that's fine too. I just wondered, however, how either of them would have coped with dancing with any of the rest of us. I would guess that many who normally dance with several partners through the evening as a rule might have been put off by the exotic display and feared to ask for a dance. I know I was. I suspect too that, denied their usual partner and their choreography, in the arms of one of us devoted to improvisation and the conversational style of tango, they might not have enjoyed themselves so much. Sequencing has that effect. It makes you look more skilled than you truly are but actually restricts you to dancing in one way only. We free spirits, on the other hand, are able to dance with anyone who simply understands the principle of leading and following and of full connection. Thankfully, such partners are to be found all over the world.

Dissociation

There are a handful of teachers who learned their tango in the 1980s, at the very time it was being reborn. That has given them credibility, with some justification. The human brain is a rare and wonderful thing and its facility for memory unique. Sadly, we all know what the passage of time does to that. One such teacher is prepared to declare categorically that dissociation was not a feature of the tango learned by people prior to 1955. I find that almost impossible to accept and, because it comes with no logical explanation why such a belief would be reasonable,

I prefer to see dissociation as a valuable tool. I know that being unable to dissociate makes dancing quite difficult for friends who are less flexible because of age or back surgery. That would make believing that dissociation was irrelevant a wonderful advantage for them. I watch them struggle and I know, in my guts, it is untrue. I am quite prepared to accept that extreme levels of dissociation are not needed other than in gymnastic moves better suited to the stage. I only know that, once I had grown comfortable with more flexibility about my own waistline, tango enjoyment rose to greater heights. The message here is this. Value everything you are taught but weigh it against your own good sense.

CHAPTER 3

Leading and following

Though it is usual for a tango couple to be a man and a woman, this is not Holy Writ and frequently men dance with men and women with women. However... I am prepared to dispense with political correctness – and point out that men and women are different!

Jay in 'tango heaven'   *Photo DT*

When a man dances with a man it is simply not the same as dancing with a woman, although I am prepared to consider that if both men are gay then maybe it is very similar. Given that when tango began it was about male-female contact, not to mention the sublimation of sexual desires, then we should not be too surprised that many of the modern-day needs for tango demand the same sort of body shapes and 'chemistry' to work fully. I realise that there are people who think of tango as 'just another dance' and even some who consider it to be a form of exercise but, for me, it is a means of relationship between two people, preferably of different sex.

To this end, then, in tango, generally speaking, there is a man's role and a woman's role. Those who dispute this might try following without wearing high heels or lifting their heels up. It feels very odd. Similarly, try to lead with high heels. It is very difficult. I have seen female tango professionals dance the woman's role with low heels, and it either looks strange or they raise their heels off the floor. Interestingly, put a man in high heels and he is able to follow quite elegantly because the high heel changes the body posture, most significantly by encouraging a 'weight forward' posture even when you walk backwards.

Commonly in tango, in Europe and the United States at least, the two roles are referred to as 'leader' and 'follower'. These two terms more accurately describe the roles of the individual members of the couple than the gender, but I think this convention has yet to find much favour in Argentina. More recently, a concept has arisen that is referred to as 'shaping', to attempt to refine even more accurately what the man does in the dance. It is an attractive notion and attempts to get away from the image of a man 'leading' an animal on a halter or a small child by the hand. As far as I know, this has not caught on as a term yet, and I cannot guess what a 'shaper's' partner might be called that would be suitable. I dread to think of the reaction from some quarters if it became 'shaper' and 'plasticine'! To be serious, the notion of shaping is that it is the shape of the dance each couple does that the leader is responsible for; he is not responsible for the shape his partner is in! And I promised to be serious, too. For the moment, then, I propose to use the terms 'leader' and 'follower' because they have become well established.

The ship of tango has one captain, the leader. This is a huge responsibility, particularly with an unfamiliar partner on a crowded dance floor. The leader therefore needs to learn how to make decisions, make them with confidence and convey a clear and unambiguous message of intent to the follower. The timing of this message is vital. It is interesting to note from teachers in the United Kingdom that one problem we all have with male newcomers to tango is their reluctance to become macho enough to drive the dance. Does this tell us something about the culture of the time, or Anglo-Saxon attitudes to women? We are, after all, not talking about aggression here; just decision making with style and thoughtfulness. Perhaps the word 'shaping' does fit in with this concept rather well? The leader 'shapes' the dance. That has a nice feel about it for me.

For her part, the follower must accept the role and try not to second-guess the wish of the leader. The follower should learn to be able to read, by feeling the signals of intention coming from the body of the leader. When I was first taught to follow, I was encouraged to focus intensely on the upper chest of my leader. I now realise that this was one of those helpful simplifications that made it possible for me to cope with following. The reality is that signals flow between leader and follower from the whole body. To start with, though, I do think it is helpful to keep it as simple as we can. I rather like the image offered by the expression 'tango eye'. This is the imaginary, non-swivelling eye in the middle of a tango dancer's breastbone that looks at the partner all the time. If we look each other in the 'tango eye' all the time, we stand a chance of learning to tango well.

Having grasped the meaning of the leader, the follower has to be skilled enough to execute the manoeuvre requested without interfering with the balance of the leader or the couple as a unit, or (for that matter) with the leader's continuing decision-making process.

I suppose we could use words to convey our intention. I am reminded of "Left hand down a bit, Number One", and "Aye, aye, Skipper". However...words would never convey enough information quickly enough to work in the context of a dance. Reading body language, moment to moment, is quite hard to begin with, but once you have grasped it the fun can really start between you. This is the essence of tango, and if you think about its history it should be no surprise to imagine how a non-verbal courtship might suit the rare mix of languages and cultures that was Argentina when tango was born.

To make life easier for me, the writer, I shall from here on maintain the assumption that the leader is male and the follower female. In this way I hope to avoid confusion. I must hasten to say at this point, however, that many women are great leaders and many men, including me, have learned to be followers and enjoy it immensely.

Daniel Trenner and Rebecca Shulman have produced a really entertaining instructional video on 'Exchange of Lead and Follow', in which they show how to switch the lead back and forth. They achieve this either by stealing the lead or by giving it up. As a spectacle it is great to watch and I can tell you, having done it a good bit, it is great fun to do on a dance floor. My regular partner, my wife Judith, is a pretty good

Sam and Annette, here demonstrating a boleo. Both women are excellent followers and also happen to be competent leaders. I have led them both and I have been led by them both, with immense pleasure. Exchange of lead and follow within the dance adds another fun dimension which must surely be unique to tango.

leader but finds the mental effort of it rather exhausting and usually gives the lead back after a short while. Similarly, it takes some agility of mind for me to stop leading and relax in the arms of another leader and trust them to take care of me. Interestingly, several of my friends have discovered that role reversal is quite easy when both people are averagely competent in both roles. It makes us suspect that it does not have to be taught.

One lovely tradition you can see in Cambridge is the 'teacher's birthday, anything goes, all comers, excuse me tango'! After singing 'Happy Birthday to You' and the presentation of a card signed by all the pupils, a tango track is played and the teacher dances with whomsoever butts in, be they leader or follower, cheerfully dropping into the required role quite seamlessly. Fun to watch and fun to join in.

One big problem about reversing roles is the very important difference between the way a leader initiates a movement and the way the follower responds. There is absolutely no problem for either dancer to learn the 'vocabulary' of the other. Indeed, the more experienced you become at tango the more you realise that both dancers can use all the possible movement options (giro, sacada, gancho and so on) perfectly compatibly within the dance. There are really no exclusively 'leader steps' or 'follower steps' at all. For the convenience of learning it is wise to have some structure to begin with but pretty soon you realise that you are both free within the connection relationship to do anything you find pleases you. No, what I am referring to is something much more significant, and it relates to timing and the initiation of motion. The leader begins the couple's movement by transmitting to his follower his intention to move with his upper body; he begins to shift his axis. The follower, sensing the intention, first moves her free leg and keeps the presence of her upper body still with the leader. This difference should become so subtle that it would be picked up only by the most eagle-eyed observer; a casual onlooker would see simultaneous action on the part of the leader and follower.

I have been the follower many times in classes and it really helps to improve your tango skills when you learn to appreciate the problems the other member of the team can have. As a leader acting as follower, you really learn quickly how nasty it feels if your leader pulls you about, pushes you in the back or fails to indicate clearly enough what he wants. Worst of all is when he fails to allow you to complete a movement before changing direction. When, as a leader, you experience dancing as follower with a great leader you come to realise why those ladies who follow love it so much when you lead well.

Despite the fact that the leader is the captain of the ship, this should not be taken to mean that the follower merely does what she is told like a slave. It is wonderful as a leader to dance with a follower who is tuned in to the music and subtly pauses, within the sense of the music, before making the movement that has been suggested. The good leader gives a clear, unambiguous and thoughtfully timed indication of what he wants the follower to do. The good follower listens to the music and chooses the time to move. The leader, having given the suggestion, waits for the follower to initiate her movement and then accompanies her. This always sounds a bit highfalutin when described, broken down like this by teachers, but in the execution of a manoeuvre in one or two moments of music the 'indicate, wait, she goes, he follows' sequence is so fast that an observer might imagine it was all enacted simultaneously. It really does happen like this, and it feels so wonderful when it does that it is definitely worth practising it, particularly in slow motion, to grasp the feel.

The common model used to describe what I am talking about is this. The leader 'invites' the lady to enter a room. She accepts the invitation and, in her own time, enters, and he then follows. In a sense, therefore, the leader has become the follower.

I am sure this concept is very confusing for newcomers to tango. It certainly was to me when I first started, but after about 18 months of dancing tango I developed enough courage to dance socially with our teacher. Her inventiveness with the timing of her movements blew my mind and I could feel an entirely new dimension. Before that dance I had danced with partners who kept very strictly to a beat, so that their movements were somewhat predictable. Thank goodness they were so, since in the early days I would have been lost without this adherence to rigid form. Now I just love to dance with a follower who takes charge of her own rhythm and interprets the song her way, even if it throws the odd spanner in my works and obliges me to quickly rethink my plan. It's just like a game of chess, you see, with the added dimensions of laughter, physicality and flirtation. The thinking person's aerobics?

One really good exercise that I was taught did much to help me understand this concept of interactive decision taking. I now teach it to novice dancers within their first lesson or two. I get them to stand holding hands, side by side. One member of the couple is asked to indicate (or, should I say, invite) a forward movement. The other teases by holding on as long as he or she wants before committing to the step. The leader, whoever that is, tries to sense the very moment of the commitment and the couple go together. I find it so valuable when couples take turns to lead and follow in this so that they both experience the joy of the eventual unity. In any case, this exercise hones the body-listening skills of both leader and follower. The exercise can be done without music and this will enable a great deal of random choice of when the couple finally go. With music you would think it would be too predictable, but this is not so in practice. It is amazing how long you can reasonably wait, after the beat, and still make sense of the music and catch up by the next beat. That is to say that, however you take liberties with one beat of the music, you will both arrive at your next 'neutral' at the same time, balanced and ready for whatever comes next.

This exercise begins to get newcomers to grasp the level of mental activity required to dance fully improvised tango. They find it quite hard to begin with, even for a few minutes.

Tuning in so intently to the signals from my partner, whether I was leader or follower, took me months, if not years, to perfect. All this brain work during a tango song, lasting perhaps as little as two and a half minutes, can be very mentally exhausting because the concentration required is total. Many of us of the geriatric tendency manage three or four such dances in a row and need to stop for a brain break. There is no room for chat, and although it is not forbidden to talk during the dance it is so difficult to do the two things together that most people dance without speaking. After all, tango is a language in its own right, and you don't speak two languages at once. Even now, if I dance with someone who wants to chat, I risk losing concentration and, rather than be rude, I fall back on a dance style that is frankly simple, even banal, to be able to cope mentally. I know I am not alone in this.

I believe this intensity of mental focusing is a major difference between tango and most other dances. Just examine the faces of people tangoing. You see frowns of extreme concentration, glazed expressions as if 'spaced out', and – best of all – those beatific smiles of ecstasy on the faces of some followers. What you will never see are rows of flashing toothy grins or the synthetic facial contortions I used to detest so much on the faces of televised ballroom dancers. Here I have to confess to a personal weakness. I find that the look of rapt concentration on the face of a woman tangoing incredibly attractive. Take a look at the followers shown on the front cover of the book and see what I mean.

Leading, or 'shaping'?

Conventionally, leading is done by the man who is facing the line of dance. This means that he is on the perimeter of the dance floor travelling anticlockwise, so that he may safely navigate and not bump into other couples. As I have become more experienced and have introduced more turns into my dance I find I spend a significant amount of time travelling backwards to the line of dance. I do not possess eyes in the back of my head so there is always the potential for collision on a crowded dance floor, but this rarely happens and I think I know why this is. The reason is partly because the company I am in flows around the floor in a fairly even manner regardless, so that I am able to have a certain degree of confidence that the space that keeps opening up for me will continue to do so. In addition, those moments of 'blindness' are fairly brief in any case. Something else has happened to me over the years that may contribute to my safety zone. In the early days I used to worry about my feet and look down from time to time, and when I was not doing that I focused on the dancers around me. Nowadays I have noticed that I dance looking slightly to my left and I focus on nothing at all. My mind is not on visual things so much as on the music and the feeling coming back from the woman in my arms. I believe that this means that my field of vision is wide and general, not narrow and focused on one or two things in the room. I realise that I too have now acquired the glazed look I used to see on more experienced tangueros' faces. I never understood it, although, for reasons I simply cannot analyse, I always loved the look of it. Mind you, in comparison, I detest the phoney frown one famous tanguero adopts as a default.

The common instruction for couples, but most particularly the navigator, is that they should avoid the centre of the dance floor as if there were a poisonous snake there. This is the part of the dance floor where you are most likely to be kicked because it is inhabited by the more flamboyant, if not more skilled, dancers. The flow is different and less predictable. I was advised very early on in my dancing career that less experienced couples should stay in the slower, outside lane and refrain from overtaking and cutting across. I am sure this was sound advice.

The male leader may also be, on average, taller than his partner and have a reasonable view of the room ahead. My wife, who is almost a foot shorter than me, has all sorts of trouble leading me because, if we walk straight, she simply cannot see where we are going. The solution is to weave about and turn all the time. Being a tall leader also has its problems, however, and I usually went home after dancing with a backache in the novice days. This was because of adopting a self-conscious posture, and my eyes were opened to this by Alex Krebs, who is even taller than I am. He showed me that, if the leader is very much taller than his follower, he should not stoop, crouch or bow his head in an attempt to minimise the

Alex Krebs

difference in height, because that would alter his balance and, besides, he should be looking where he is going. Indeed, the greater the difference in heights the more determined the man should be to stand tall and be elegant and poised.

From a follower's point of view, it is most disagreeable to dance under a tall leader who behaves like a mantelpiece over her head. If my follower feels as if a wall is about to topple onto her this is bound to affect her posture, quite apart from being an unpleasant experience. Why would I want that feeling for the woman in my arms? When Alex demonstrated this to me, finally the penny dropped. I had heard the words and grasped the meaning but it took being led by a taller man than me to feel it. It may well be kind to a petite follower for the leader to reduce the length of pace to suit his partner's shorter leg length. It is remarkable, however, to see how a small but experienced follower can take a back step that is infinitely longer than any forward step the man will want to take. Whether this is because the lady has suffered a few crunched toes in the past I can only guess, but the physical reason is in the technique of taking back steps I describe in detail in the follower's section of this chapter.

We use the upper body to convey our leads to the follower. When we think of a tall leader dancing with a small follower, however, we can imagine that it would be possible for the lead to be 'over her head' in every sense if the leader restricts his lead to his shoulders. In this situation, in consideration of the height of focus of the follower, it is often best if the leader makes intentions with his whole upper body, including the pelvis. Not only that but, if we wish to make a lead crystal clear, we can also release arm pressure on one side to suggest a void for the follower to walk into. I wish to make it very clear that I am not referring to a pull here but, rather, a relaxation of presence.

The other important consideration for the tall man is the position his arms will need to adopt to accommodate the shorter partner, particularly his left arm, which holds the follower's hand. A comfortable compromise needs to be struck, but it is my belief that the follower's comfort and enjoyment of a dance is paramount. I know that one of my persistent sins as a leader is to hold my follower's right hand too high and to some extent cock her wrist backwards. One way I have found to get round this last bad habit is to adopt the hand hold I saw used by Pablo Verón in the film *The Tango Lesson*. He places his fingers above his partner's fingers and not around them. I find it more difficult but good for the shorter follower in my arms and well worth persevering with.

As I have indicated, I have done a good amount of following, and I enjoy it. I have been led by women who were shorter than me and, concentrating hard on giving a positive lead, pushed me into stationary traffic with abandon. Being stepped on is bad enough. Having a leader who encourages you to take a step backwards into some innocent dancer is worse because you have been the aggressor even though it was not your fault. It's good to practise following if you are normally a leader to experience how horrible it feels when the leader is insensitive.

The final responsibility for the leader is to take the blame at all times. A follower who keeps feeling the need to apologise all the while is being incompetently led. No 'ifs' and no 'buts'. How nice to discover an absolute law in a world that sometimes seems a little wishy-washy. The lady is never at fault. Believe me, leaders, if you accept this rule at the outset you will come to no harm. This is a social dance in which the follower is entertained as much as possible. There is no room in tango for bickering or postmortem.

Following

It goes without saying that the follower follows the indications given by the leader. The reality, however, is that, while it is relatively easy to teach someone to make decisions and to use their whole body (not their arms) and to show intention, I find that teaching the same person to trust another leader *not* make decisions and move where it feels right, from moment to moment, is hard. For some the two roles will not be easily interchanged; they will either be leaders or followers.

It may have been easier for the men and women in 1900s Argentina to simply drop into the traditional leader and follower roles since they were more akin to other models of male and female behaviour at that time. Men expected to be dominant and there were fewer propensities for women to challenge that. Even now there is a distinct difference between the attitude of tango teachers in Europe and those who visit us from Argentina.

In Europe, the idea seems to be that harmony in dance is arrived at by mutual consent and that men and women are equal partners. I get the distinct impression, however, that even today, in Buenos Aires, the idea is that the man is in complete control; every action has its lead and the progress of the dance is a series of well-established consequences. This is, I am assured, to ensure coordination and harmony between the dancers and to avoid things becoming messy. I can see how a system that insists that there is only one who chooses everything can ensure coordination. I'm not entirely sure, in the context of dancing with feisty European women, about the harmony element!

David and Celia at Cambridge. Surrender? I should think NOT!   *Photo DM*

Surrender!

Here is another example. A recent article from a tango web site in Argentina touched on the relationship between the man and the woman. It used the phrase "The woman's attitude of *surrender*". This caught my eye and set me thinking. I am not at all sure this notion would find much acceptability with the women I dance with. I can see how it might be interesting to look at the undoubtedly macho flavour in history of tango and perhaps derive some ideas from it for our dance-play today. I am less happy to accept this idea as the essential feeling of tango in the modern world.

I am more attracted to the idea that tango evolved out of a lucky fusion of multiple cultures, mostly European in origin. It seems that it received a transfusion of refinement in Paris in the 1920s, and it looks to me as if it is benefiting today from another shot in the arm all over Europe. Tango is growing apace here and is being distilled to meet the requirements of today's relationships. I believe it may be losing its narrow, even parochial feel and is becoming truly international in the hands of a new and more cohesive European people. We are not frustrated, homesick, stressed Europeans, seeking love miles from home with too few women to share. We are a new breed in a new world. Though the passions we bring as individuals to the dance will be the same basic feelings all men and women have shared since the beginning of time, the intensity must be different, and the balance between the sexes has altered most of all. It may also be the case that our societies in Europe are evolving at a different pace from that of Latin America, though not, I suspect, in a different direction. In the Europe of today women have immense power, status and influence and they express their needs very clearly.

The modern European woman is unlikely to respond too positively to macho posturing. I undertook a small opinion poll about this; well, I asked Judith, and she agreed. It seems women like their men to be positive but they also want finesse and thoughtfulness. Women hate to be bullied. They prefer to be invited and to feel that they are in full control to accept, or decline, as they feel.

Accepting an invitation is not 'surrender'. We all come to tango for so many different reasons. I'm sure some see it as a form of exercise; others imagine they might meet a life mate. All of us are there for connection with another human being at an intimate level. I feel sure that, for this to be fully enriching as an experience, at least in the circles I move in, mutuality of respect and status is important.

Walking backwards elegantly with a straight leading leg. Claire is well balanced on her supporting leg, the knee of which is 'soft' but not bent. Although she is moving away from Lachlan, she is giving a lot of presence to him. This is an extremely hard skill to learn.

Later in the same article the writer-I am guessing, a man- explained how the man guides the woman by pressing her back with his hand. "That says it all," said Judith; "he clearly has no idea how horrible that feels to the woman in his arms. Yucchh!" Perhaps women are different in Buenos Aires, but I suspect not.

The problems for followers seem to fall into two groups: balance; and feeling the lead.

Balance is the bigger problem. While the leader is able to walk forward, something he will have done for many years, the follower often has to step backwards. This is an unusual and infrequent movement at the best of times, but, unlike the fast backing out of danger we do instinctively, the backward step of tango is an elegant movement. It needs to be worked at simply because of the need to maintain balance at all times. The upper body stays upright; there is no leaning forward to counterbalance the weight of the leading leg. First we initiate the leg movement in the direction we wish to travel, then we shift the body mass in that same direction. Finally we allow our mass to resume normal balance on the new leg and collect our feet together.

The only reason walking backwards feels so awkward is that we rarely do it in normal life. I know we don't have eyes in the backs of our heads but we have all learned to walk forward with our eyes closed, even in childhood. Do you remember blind man's buff? Learning to walk backwards elegantly and comfortably and covering the same amount of ground as normal forward walking is bound to take a considerable amount of concentration and time when you consider how many years most of us have been practising walking forward. Most of us who want to enjoy following need, therefore, to practise this walking backwards for many hours until it feels natural. I certainly did. In tango, whatever is useful for one is just as useful for the other, so I would strongly advocate that leaders do the same. It is so good for balance skills. Try it wherever you are and ignore the stares. Do not, however, ignore the stairs! If you begin to feel frustrated because this skill seems to take such a long time to muster, pity the poor American football quarterback who has to learn to run backwards and read the play with huge, ugly tacklers bearing down on him. Wide receivers learn to do it even more rapidly, I am told.

If the follower maintains her balance so that she is poised at the end of each step, she will be able to respond to the indications as long as they are thoughtfully timed and positive. More importantly, she will not need to hang on to her leader for balance and spoil his dance and send him to the osteopath with a back condition. Having said this, a good, big leader who is demanding much of his follower can expect to absorb some holding on. Remember the rule about the leader always being responsible?

The follower's responsibility is to be able to read the lead. To do this properly, she needs to focus her attention intensely on the leader's chest. I have enjoyed dancing with followers who kept their eyes shut and relied completely on their tactile senses and others who stared, eyes glazed, away to my right. Each follower has to discover what works best for them. For me, it is always watching the chest. This can be a touch disconcerting when I dance with a certain Russian lady who has spectacular cleavage and is generous enough to share it. At least *I* know why I am staring with so much concentration, even if others doubt my motives. Look, I am trying to follow, alright? All I know is, if I become self-conscious about it and look somewhere else, I lose the indications because my tactile following senses are less well developed than my visual ones.

Put rather simplistically, the follower senses the lead coming from leader's body and responds appropriately in order to maintain the tango relationship, the feeling of togetherness in the embrace.

In general, the more physical contact there is between the dancers the stronger the connection is and the easier it is to feel the intentions of the leader. In an open embrace the hands and eyes are vital tools and the space between dancers, ideally about nine inches, allows for plenty of scope for fun manoeuvres. The 'close embrace', a sort of hug, allows the tiniest of signals to be transmitted and received. This would seem to be the point of it. When you think about tango being danced way back at the beginning of the 20th century by earthy men in bordellos, hungry for a woman's touch, closeness between a man and a woman was the business they were in. It was in the 'sanitising' of tango for the more genteel public and the wider world audience that the open embrace evolved.

Another way of helping a follower realise what the leader is asking her to do is if both of them consider that they are cradling a fragile balloon in the circle formed from their bodies and arms. This circle is sometimes referred to as the 'frame'. If, between them, both leader and follower dance in such a way as to never crush the balloon, nor drop it, then they will create the conditions in which the leader will be careful to indicate well and the follower will move to suit the need, which is the maintenance of the connection between the dancers. I have offered this simple concept because I think it helped me when I first started to tango, but I realise that as we progress we want other things. Learning to maintain the frame is good for beginners. Later on, we learn how to deliberately use distortion of the frame to gain more.

I have used a fairly simplistic model of leading and following for the same reason; we all need to start from some bedrock. In fact, if there is an overriding rule of tango, it might be "There are no rules". Experienced leaders can become fairly quickly bored with followers who do only as they are told. They find dancing with over-compliant followers as exciting as dancing with a tailor's dummy. Such leaders appreciated the follower who clearly feeds back her feelings from moment to moment and influences the leader. Think of it this way: it is fun to chat to a child at their level, but after a while it is human nature to crave the cut and thrust of an adult conversation. So it is in tango. Finding the connection to *the* tango companion, with whom you click for even the most fleeting of moments, is the 'Holy Grail' that all who love tango are continually seeking.

CHAPTER 4

The walk, including parallel and cross system

The basic element of tango is the walk, and I suppose the most important thing for a beginner to recognise about the walk is that, in common with ordinary walking, the vast majority of it is simply left-right-left, without any hops or skips. It is a level walk, without any rise or fall of the body. Since the basic rhythm of tango in its most classic form is a fairly simple, regular beat; at about 60 to the minute, like a relaxed, healthy heartbeat, then it is not a terribly difficult form of walking at all. There are some that would have you believe that there is some 'authentic' tango walk. For me, to begin with, this can be a needless complication and obstructive to the point of it all, which is

Tango in Italy   *Photo DM*

enjoyment. There are so many legitimate styles that, in walking forward, you may step onto your heel or your toe, or – perhaps more usefully and elegantly – onto the whole foot, skimming the sole near to the ground but not raising an audible swish. El Chino puts it poetically: "The foot caresses the floor." It does not scrape it. There are, however, a number of special features about the way we walk in tango, which add to the style for sure but, more importantly, help us dance more successfully.

The most important thing I have learned from several of the tango teachers I have been privileged to meet is how to move from one place to another in a relaxed, smooth and calm manner in harmony with the music. When I first started to dance tango I was surprised how many visiting teachers wanted us to concentrate on our simple walking skills when I had expected them to teach us step patterns. Now I understand why. They all asked us to dance for them to assess our needs and must have seen at a glance that we were fixated on the 'figures' at the expense of the vital issues of balance, self-control and a sense of the meaning of the music. It was only after thinking I could dance tango for a year or so that

I recognised the importance of keeping my weight forward on my toes, without raising the heel off the floor. This concept needed to be worked on before it came naturally to me, and, to some extent, I am pleased that my earliest teachers did not worry me about this. They were wise and kind and they just let me dance as best I could. They allowed me to have the fun that was possible for me at that stage and kept me enjoying tango. Later, as I wanted to progress, it became apparent that for me to do so I would have to improve my basic walking skills first.

When I am a leader, keeping my weight forward on my toes means that I am more able to impose my chest into the follower's airspace and lead positively. It enables me to give good presence of that part of me that leads. In addition, any anxiety about treading on a partner's toes is considerably reduced because, since I am more able to give good, early, clear leads, she steps with me. Keeping the foot low is also very important when stepping towards your partner to ensure that, if feet do bump against each, other little harm is done. It is also vital when stepping backwards from your partner into the unknown. As a leader, I have come to recognise the importance of maintaining a sense of stillness in my upper body because it is giving vital signals to my follower. In that context, when I walk forward I do not roll from side to side like a sailor, because that would offer a confusing message of intention. It would be a little like listening to instructions from two people at once. My walking style should allow one simple message at all times.

When I dance as a follower, since I have no idea what my leader will do next, maintaining my weight on the front of the foot allows me to pivot at any time to accommodate a change in direction. Being able to pivot in a balanced way is very important to tango walking, and I have devoted a great deal of attention to this in chapters 7 and 13.

By 'front of the foot' I mean the whole front of the foot, including the toes; not just the ball of the foot. The leader knows when he wants to pivot in advance, so he can – if he so wishes – step onto his heel first. In general, however, it is a great deal easier to pivot on the toes, and, given that it is best to dance with the weight a little forward and not rocked back on the heels, I favour walking onto the toes. In addition, it is more comfortable to dance for many hours with the weight forward of the heads of the metatarsal bones and not on them. Actually, for very long sessions I now find that I need to vary my footing considerably, but until I became more skilled at holding my weight forward my balance suffered. Lately, I realise that I have developed the habit of allowing my weight to rest on the outsides of my feet. I do have fairly high arches and have been obliged to have dance shoes made to measure. They have cork wedges built into the insteps to prevent my arch falling towards the end of the evening. This has helped a lot while being very expensive. I justify this as the only self-indulgence I allow myself. That, and telling lies, of course.

Once a tango friend made me aware of this tendency to carry my considerable weight on the outsides of my feet, I sought ways to remedy the problem. I could have shed a stone or so but that's easier said than done. I suspect a modest degree of obesity was probably the basic cause. The problem is resolving by perseverance with an exercise or so to strengthen the foot muscles and encourage the balance point to centre under the big toe. I stand on one foot, pressing down with my big toe, then when totally balanced rise up onto that toe. No, I don't mean 'en pointe', that would be going too far, not to say anatomically impossible. This is to strengthen my feet not break toe bones.

As you begin to develop the feel for tango, and once you have stopped being self-conscious about the walk, you ought to practise often, on your own, to perfect your balance. One good place I found to do so was when shopping in a supermarket, because the trolley makes a lovely partner. If you buy some of the excellent CDs of tango music now available you can combine perfecting your walk at home with some simple improvisation. It is important to imagine that you have a partner in your arms because every move needs to take a partner into account. What I mean is that, if you dance around your kitchen to the music, you might *think* you can perform a pirouette, but no real partner could keep up with the spin.

Many other dance disciplines are taught by considerable attention to the placing of the feet in certain preordained positions, and we must all be familiar with the sort of footprint maps used by some instruction books of dancing. There are tango books with such maps, but they cloud the real issues and encourage learners to concentrate on their feet when they ought to be thinking higher up. They really need to be thinking about the posture and balance of the whole body. I am sure we all find it very hard to imagine the whole body from floor maps of the feet.

Those beginners who suffer anxiety about where their feet ought to go tend to look downwards and break their body line at the neck and at the waist. When I do that it leads me into two problems. One is that I have moved part of my body mass in front of my natural centre of balance and tend to carry my weight too far forward. The other is that, sensing that I am always on the verge of toppling forward, I compensate by transferring my weight back onto my heels; that, or stick my bottom out. It looks inelegant and it interferes with my ability to rotate. The same fault is common when tall men dance with petite women. I am over 6 feet tall and this has always been a big problem for me. The tallest leader I know, Alex Krebs, has been an inspiration to me in this matter. He teaches that we tall men should at all times stand tall and be fully balanced in our own frame with all partners, whatever the height differential.

The other problem with worrying about your feet is that dancing tango takes all the concentration you can muster. As a leader, being fully aware of my partner's body position and which leg she has her weight on *and* listening to the music for inspiration, not to mention navigating a busy dance floor, takes all the brain I have. I can't be worrying about my feet as well. When I dance as a follower, the level of concentration I need to read the signals from my leader is no less total. I have to tune into the music and concentrate on the leads. I also need to keep an eye out for the potential for collision behind my leader so that I can put the emergency brakes on from time to time. Incidentally, most of us find we cannot dance tango and chat at the same time. There is just not enough human brain power to do that.

Footprint floor plans are helpful only when learning simple movements, but – in my view – in tango, which involves complex changes of the whole body, they have limited use. The reason for this is that the position of the feet should always be that natural place that you would want them to be in to maintain your balance at all times. Roughly speaking, and not just to raise a smile, this would be under your ears. This is particularly true for the follower because, after all, the leader has already decided where the couple is headed.

If the leader has made the lead obvious (known, by some, as "giving the mark", or 'la marca'), and has offered the appropriate space for the move, then the place the follower's footsteps should go to ought to be obvious as well. She steps where she can, in a style that the music dictates to her, and collects her balance at the new site.

Perhaps the only serious 'rule' about feet is that at no time should leader or follower stand toe-inwards, like a pigeon, when at rest. The reason for this is not just that it is unattractive, although that is true. More importantly, for the toes to point inwards towards each other, each whole leg would have to be rotated inwards from the hip joint, and this would significantly block our freedom to move.

I hesitate to refer to any 'rule' in tango because the truth is that we are allowed to make of tango what we will. One of the major beauties of this dance is that, to some extent, we find our own comfortable style; since we are all different in shape, this is just as well. Unless we have some injury that forbids it, however, when standing at rest in a neutral position it is most elegant if the heels and legs are together. It is so easy, when we begin to study our own movements, for us to become awkward and self-conscious and to stand oddly. The harder we try to relax, often the less comfortable and natural we become. Sometimes it is helpful to overcome this by fooling our bodies. I have discovered a good way to do this, and in the process discovered my own natural stance at rest. Try it for yourself. Just perform a small two-legged leap into the air and land on both feet equally. If you now glance downwards you find your feet where they ought to be for your own natural posture. The concept of moving elegantly from one fully balanced position to another cannot be overemphasised. It would be hard to think of tango without elegance.

I find it helpful to consider that each dancer's body as being divided into two parts: upper (above the waist), and lower. For the leader it is the upper body that dominates the airspace and gives the lead to the follower. For the follower the upper body tries to stay directly in front of the leader's upper body at all times. The lower bodies simply exist to cart the upper body about to allow these tasks to happen.

You may ask why I should bother to suggest this model at all. The answer is that, for competent leading and following in tango, we have to learn a new skill: how to 'dissociate' upper from lower body at will. By this I am not referring to some mystical concept of the paranormal, or to a stage conjuring trick! What I am referring to is the ability to walk in one direction while facing one's upper body in another. There are limits to this but most of us can manage 20 degrees without practice and a great deal more after a while. What is the point? When walking in an embrace, the follower will need to be to one side of the leader's feet or another, and not just directly in front of us, for us to achieve anything interesting at all.

This ability to dissociate at the waist is absolutely vital for the follower when she moves round the leader in the 'grapevine' manoeuvre, and for all dancers who wish to be able to pivot well. I have come to realise that the ability to dissociate well has been the central core of my personal growth in tango, and I strongly recommend all my readers to devote as much time to perfecting this as to any other element of controlling your own body.

It is fascinating to watch a group of people who have been asked to walk to a tango tune, all in the line of dance, around the room. For some reason, instead of walking naturally and – as they have been doing all their lives – without thought, they begin to concentrate on the process of walking. I know I do. We appear to concern ourselves with issues we gave up worrying about when toddlers, and sometimes appear to walk in a very odd way and even lose our balance. It feels awful.

One powerful image works for me every time and helps me bypass some of those theoretical barriers of self-consciousness. Just imagine that tango is like walking on a lovely summer's day, in the park, arm in arm with someone you love. You wouldn't be thinking of the technique of walking; you would be focused on your companion. Hey! That's tango! You would generally stay in step, without having to think about it at all, even if you had much longer legs than your companion. You might not be stepping with the same leg as each other at the same time. Bearing this in mind, an extremely helpful exercise for those just beginning to learn tango is to walk around the room, in step to the music, in the line of dance, hand in hand to begin with. It is good to come to a halt and restart from time to time, and both partners should take responsibility for initiating stopping and starting, changing from one partner to the other by agreement once in a while. Fairly soon it will become apparent that whoever is chosen to be the leader needs to give some sort of indication that the couple are to start walking.

Similarly, if the couple are to stay together when a halt is required, even if the music makes it very obvious, the chosen leader will be obliged to show in advance of the actual cessation of movement that a stop is about to happen. Of course, you could say: "Parade will come to a halt; three, two, one, HALT!" like a drill sergeant, but it is also possible to use subtle body language to suggest a deceleration sensation to the follower at the start of the step or even during the beat before last. It is remarkable how well most people who have walked arm in arm with someone else for a few circuits of a dance floor will pick up the signals.

I find, as a leader, that – when I want to start the movement again – even little signals of preparation, such as taking a deep breath, and the tiniest forward motion seem to be conveyed to the follower as indications of "Off we go" on the following beat. This preliminary signal we call 'intention', and what I am describing here is the basic, horizontal version of intention. A fun exercise I learned as a beginner is for the leader to send these little signals to the follower and make her commit herself to a move before the leader actually moves a foot. As we become more accomplished at sending and receiving these messages to each other, they can become smaller and thus less obvious to an outside observer. I have danced with followers who were so well tuned you might think they were telepathic.

Of course, the follower does not have to be completely passive in all this, just doing as he or she is told. Even more fun and another very useful exercise is for the chosen leader to indicate that the movement is to start but to be obliged to wait for the follower to show that she really is about to move. This tends to begin a little like two old gents at a revolving door: "After you"; "No, after you"; "No, no, I insist; after you". If, however, you are both standing together, side by side, holding hands and both transferring your weight forward, sooner or later one of you will have to step forward or fall over. When, as you perfect this exercise, you discover that moment when you both move simultaneously, it feels very nice. This is the complete togetherness, or 'oneness', we seek when we dance tango. This is the 'magic' of tango, and why we bother with it.

I now wish to consider the relationship of the walking, still side by side, to the music. Tango music from the old days was usually strict tempo and the beat was about 60 to the minute. If you ask the average person to walk to a faster beat of about, let us say, 100 to the minute, he or she will march, and the tendency will be for his or her heel to come down on each beat. If we were to freeze-frame a video of a soldier marching, we would notice therefore that, on the beat, the legs would be apart. Tango is a lot slower and very different, in that, on each beat, you can completely move from one fully balanced 'neutral' position, with knees and ankles together,

51

to the next. The difference is not just one of speed. Unlike the funereal, military slow march, however, where there is a distinct pause on the beat, in tango the walk is more fluid and the movement of the passing leg is continuous. Two freeze-frames from one side of two consecutive beats of music should look almost identical, and it should be almost impossible to discover that on the first beat the weight was on one leg and on the next beat the other. I offer this imagery in an attempt to be helpful to a beginner. As we grow in tango we develop our own personal style, and this is to be strongly encouraged. Many of us like to arrive in 'neutral' (the point at which our legs are collected together) with one leg slightly trailing. It feels nice and looks stylish, but it should develop organically, in my view; not be a learned trick.

It is vital that, when actually concentrating on walking, we do not focus on the leading leg, or get it into our heads, when trying to go from one position to another, that we are in any sense walking on stepping stones. If you were to cross a stream on stepping stones you would, of course, go from on balanced position to another, but the walk would tend to be very much about stretching forward the leading leg, searching for the next stone. On the contrary, if we must think about our legs at all, the leg we ought to be thinking about in the tango walk is the one that bears our weight during the step. The whole body advances in one piece. Actually, by far the best thing to be thinking about, particularly for the leaders among us, is that we are the 'tango eye', in the middle of our chests. Put another way, we dance better if our brains are at chest level and not at foot level.

Up to now, we have been considering the dynamics of the relationship between a couple moving together as a unit but in the familiar context of holding hands side by side. Of course, we dance facing each other; and this is where the problems begin.

To start with, I learned to walk 'in parallel'. This term means that, as the leader walks forward right-left-right, the follower goes backwards left-right-left. It is often useful to think of the tango couple as a basically very stable four-legged animal that sometimes, when they are attempting some difficult manoeuvre, comes to be a less stable two-legged one. Learning to become very stable as a united couple on two legs is the very essence of tango technique. Two-legged in this context usually refers to one leg from each partner, but you will see amazing things in tango stage shows, where the only two legs connected to the ground are the leader's!

Frank and Linda walking in parallel
Two sets of 'tracks in the snow'

Walking in the cross system, sometimes
now known in the |UK as 'opposite feet'

Thinking of the four-legged model, parallel walking is the way animals do *not* walk. They do not pick up both legs on the right side and move those forward, followed by both those on the left; but this is what we do when we walk 'in parallel' in tango.

As an inexperienced leader I often felt too inhibited to walk freely and naturally, because of a normal and reasonable fear of treading on my follower. As I became more confident it was common for me to discover that my knees connected with some followers' thighs, and it soon became clear that followers needed to walk backwards in a different way too. What worked best was when my follower learned to walk backwards in such a way that led with the foot and the whole leg, straight, hinging from the hip. Followers who were most comfortable to dance with kept their upper bodies still as they stretched their legs backwards. The most elegant of the more experienced followers had relaxed but not bent legs, and seemed to feel out the ground behind them with a toe. They did not lift their feet up and nor did they swing their shoulders. The most accomplished of the women seemed to have legs that went on for ever. As they stepped back they slightly relaxed the weight-bearing leg and allowed a little pelvic rotation, which, with relaxation of the ankle and softly pointed toe, added to the illusion of leg length and enhanced the elegance.

The year 2005 was a momentous one for Judith and me in terms of thinking about walking and in particular, walking backwards. We had become aware that we did not look as elegant as we wished. Up to then, how we felt in each other's arms mattered most and because we felt adequately comfortable, that was enough for us. Besides, had we felt more self-conscious at an earlier date, we would not have been confident enough to push for more advanced understanding of tango, let alone dare to teach it. As part of our learning process, we video'd ourselves dancing and were appalled at what we saw. We vowed to do something about it and sought the input of a feisty teacher in the UK with extensive knowledge of the old school of tango teaching. We went for lessons and much to our delight, found where we had gone wrong in our thinking. The key was in learning to walk backwards properly. The theory is that the good forward walk is in fact exactly the opposite of the good backwards walk. We were given simple but important exercises that enabled us to find the new foot position behind us and then to transfer weight onto that point sweetly.

It was such a simple idea. The point of tango is that we dance heart to heart. All our leads are designed to allow our followed to put her heart exactly in front of ours. Therefore our aim in moving is to shift our hearts about to be where we want them to be. If, as we step forward, we are carrying our free foot under our heart on a relaxed leg, then, when our hearts arrive at their destination, there is a foot and leg already there to hold us up. No more walking as if from one stepping stone to another. No more 'pendulum' ochos. In the backwards step, the leg goes to the new place and the heart is moved over it. The forward leg that used to carry the weight moves back under the heart. Once we have learned to do this with ease, the forward step is more elegant. To begin with it looks and feels like overbalancing. The more you do it, the sweeter it becomes. But there is no doubt that to begin with the back step is the way to achieve the good forward step. We bothered to practice every day and it really worked for us. I rate those lessons as the best money spent for the result achieved, ever.

I find walking backwards elegantly is quite difficult and I still practise it a lot in odd moments of my day. If I am obliged to stand and wait anywhere for a length of time I will often take a step backwards trying to keep my weight forward. Lord alone knows what people think, but I simply don't care. Over the years this silly little habit has paid off. I find that it helps if the knee of the weight-bearing leg bends a little, but there is no leaning forward to balance out this stretching back movement. By referring to a 'bend' I just mean to the extent of being soft and not locked out; not necessarily a bend that could be seen by an observer. This movement is nothing like any other movement in life. Normally, if we walk backwards, we lead with the top half of the body and the legs follow. It is very common for a person backing away from something disagreeable to overbalance and fall backwards.

The tango backwards walk feels quite an unnatural movement to a beginner, and I'm sorry but there is no help for it but to practise for many hours to make it feel second nature and make it look natural. Here the supermarket trolley can't really help, but all around the kitchen works well enough. There is one vital point that I cannot stress enough. It helped me to learn to break down the movement backwards into its parts.

1 Find a good upright balance on one leg, weight forward
2 Find the new place directly behind the old with the front third of the free foot well planted. Feel the ball of the big toe placed securely down.
3 Then and only then, move the heart back over the new foot.
4 Only when you can do that, wobble-free, increase number of steps.

Another important concept to master in connection with tango, when you are a beginner, is that, in general, there are no diagonal movements. This is partly because such movements would be rather difficult to indicate to the follower, compared to those simple backward, forward or side leads we started with. Once we have learned to be in simple control of simple movements, we can then stretch the boundaries as far as we like. I found it hard enough to control the position of my hips and use my torso to lead in two simple dimensions when I first started to learn tango. More importantly, only when we have learned to be in such control are we capable of more complex concepts that demand the precise positioning of hips. I refer to the movements involving intrusion of our legs between those of our partner, to achieve, for example, ganchos and sacadas.

Avoiding the use of diagonals, useful as it this 'rule' is for beginners, does not mean that the couple move about the floor like a knight on a chessboard; it is just that the leader attempts to place the follower in such a position of body rotation that her movement relative to her pelvis is always forward, squarely sideways, or back. If, therefore, the leader wants the follower to move diagonally to his right and against the line of dance, he first indicates a rotation of her body to her left by rotating his to the left. This works because the main logic of the couple in tango is that at all times they directly face each other, chest to chest, and attempt to maintain this same relationship at all times. The follower attempts to mirror any movement the leader makes with his upper body in an attempt to stay directly in front of him.

Consider just the simple steps forward, backwards and to the side for a moment. When a leader wants the couple to move to a forward position that is diagonally from where he now stands only using these steps, he is indeed obliged to make two right-angled movements to get there, and may not 'cut the corner' just by stepping across. A diagonal movement would be inelegant, and, besides, would confuse the follower completely. Whenever I tried to move diagonally as a newcomer to tango, there was always a collision. If I managed the manoeuvre in two steps – one forward and one side, for example – we maintained harmony.

Here I want to emphasise another very important feature of tango; that of moving from one balanced position, with knees and ankles together, to another identical position at every beat. If you accept that the knees and ankles must always collect at each step, then, should you wish to achieve

Neat feet   *Photo DM*

a diagonal move left and forward, the sequence will be as follows. The leader indicates a step to the left, steps left and brings right foot to close with left but not to bear weight. He then steps off with the right foot directly forward and closes with the left. The right foot did not go straight from its original position, diagonally across to the new position, but went via a neutral, closed position against the left foot. Insisting on this must sound very pedantic but it is absolutely central to the style of tango, and also has extremely important practical implications.

I find this such an important habit to get into because when I omit this element I become unbalanced and out of control for the beat between first and last, and cannot change my mind. I have become completely committed to the forward step. If the space I had planned for me and my partner to enter has suddenly become occupied by other dancers I have no ability to stop, because I have committed myself to two whole beats of music at once. The dancer who collects in neutral at each beat has full control at every beat. Furthermore, there is elegance in this way of dancing. To this day, my greatest style fault is walking as if I have just dismounted from my horse, and – believe me – I have tried very hard to correct this over the years. My friend the supermarket trolley has been a great help, and so has deliberately allowing my heels to click on each other as they pass. Granted, you don't do it when dancing, but it helps build the good habit of collection at every step. Walking like John Wayne has two major problems. One is elegance, of course, but the other is perhaps more important still. If, as we walk forward, we have our feet widely spaced we move forward and, at each step, from side to side. The poor follower is getting two signals instead of the one required, and even if she does not get confused she will certainly enjoy our company less. She might even get seasick.

When beginners first join a tango class they usually have to spend a good deal of time perfecting their ability to take these simple steps – forward, backwards and to the side – but, although it keeps brain usage modest, it is unnaturally restrictive. One giant leap forward for newcomers is when they encounter the 'pivot', which allows all points of the compass to be opened up to them. Now the problems of moving the whole partnership diagonally can be solved in one step.

To achieve the same goal – moving the couple together to a point 45 degrees from where they started, in one single step – the leader must first indicate a pivot to his left to allow both dancers to proceed in a straight line at 45 degrees. A 'pivot' is a little like what we do when we dance the twist, but in tango we do it without sticking our bottoms out, adopting a gorilla position and pumping our elbows. I trust that there are enough readers to remember the twist, though I do not expect anyone to admit it. As I have already mentioned, the pivot is so important it merits a lot more discussion later on.

Since tango is based on walking, for the beginner at least the length of step can be that which he or she would use in walking with a friend along the street. It would normally be about the width of the shoulders, about two feet, and does not have to vary too much for different heights of followers, as long as they have learned to walk backwards properly. Even the most petite of followers, if they use the correct way to walk backwards, should not be trodden on by a leader, however hard he might try to catch them! Leaders should therefore walk properly forward at all times and with all followers. As you gain experience it is great to learn how to extend more, and both vary the step and – at times – really travel.

I have found it very valuable to pay a great deal of attention to the business of transferring body weight from each 'neutral' position to the next. I use this expression 'neutral' to refer to a standing position that is balanced with head over shoulders over hips, and with knees and ankles together, though not necessarily with the weight evenly distributed on both feet. Indeed, we usually adopt the neutral position with the weight definitively kept on one foot or the other. A useful term to describe the position of the legs in this circumstance is 'collected'. The leader must learn not to initiate a new walking step until he is confident that his follower has arrived at a fully collected, neutral position and that she has not grounded both feet. On the beat in tango you should have achieved your full step; you have moved from one neutral position to another. The only difference between first neutral position and second is that the weight is now on the opposite foot. Remember that tango is a walk: left-right-left or right-left-right. There is no hop and, unlike ballroom dancing, there is no rise and fall in the body or any lift-up onto the toes. The shoulders and the eyes stay at the same level, albeit not so rigidly that you look scary. The knees are kept slightly relaxed or 'softened'; this means that they do not lock out, as in standing to attention, but it should *not* mean any position resembling a chimpanzee! The knees are merely 'softened'. I have seen lots of people dance tango like this, with knees very well bent, and for a while came to believe that this was a required position to attempt to adopt. It is not; it is merely a style adopted by some dancers. It will suit some and will look ridiculous with others. It is the correct posture for dancing a style called Canyengue which deserves a chapter for itself. I don't know if dancing in this style makes me look absurd but I love it so I don't care.

Before I leave the issue of the 'softness' of the knees, just to get a good idea of what I mean, stand up and move your knees forward and backwards as far as they will go without making yourself any shorter. You will find that there may be as much as 4 inches of travel. The idea is that, if our knees are relaxed, they will be forward from the fully locked-out position but not actually bent as in a crouch.

The most important thing is to develop your own style and dance for enjoyment, as comfortably as you can. There really is no single authentic style, so the thing to concentrate on is what works for you to become a competent leader or follower and be able to dance with practically anyone in any tango club in the world. What a fantastic prospect that opens up!

When we are talking about walking and being a little self-conscious about our body posture it is terribly easy to freeze the upper body, and perhaps raise the shoulders, and walk in an extremely unnatural way. Alex Krebs, a delightful tango teacher from the United States, always asks: "What would you think if somebody walked up to you in the street looking like this? Scary, man; right?" As with normal walking so, I find, with tango. It is more comfortable for me when I walk to allow my body some gentle extra movement, and when I began to learn tango I found that degree of relaxation very helpful to convey my inner sense of the music and rhythm to my follower. I found it helpful to use a little pivot at the hips and a little sway of the shoulders to produce a natural feel and a natural

A scary man   *Photo Samuel Kutter*

look. I am not talking about rock and roll here! The slight movements I refer to are those we associate with relaxed walking. More than that would be affected and unnecessary, and in any case would probably interfere with balance and certainly with our ability to communicate effectively. As I became more competent and more confident in my ability to lead I found I could reduce those movements to the minimum, and now I adopt a style that is more still but always relaxed (I hope), and is more in keeping with tango tradition.

Up to now the walking we have been discussing was parallel walking, in which, as the follower steps back with her right foot, the leader steps forward with his left. Logical, practical and safe enough. We can make it safer by good body indication so that the follower always removes the leg, and therefore the foot, before the leader steps. As a leader, keeping your feet close to the floor without actually making a swishing sound also means that, should there be a misunderstanding, feet will connect side to side or toe to toe, avoiding a bone-crunching experience. In addition, if we keep knees and ankles relaxed, any accidental contact produces nothing worse than mild surprise. Later we will learn how to deliberately touch our partner's feet for effect.

Now we ought to give a few moments' thought to 'cross system' walking, because it is a key that opens yet another door leading to more fun and variations in our dance. In this form of walking the couple actually walk with the same leg at the same time. As she steps back on her right leg, he steps forward on his right. How does he avoid stepping onto her left foot? One answer; the couple walk slightly offset. Think of a couple tangoing in virgin snow, walking one directly in front of the other. If they walk in parallel, the tracks will be fairly confusing but they will be in two lines. If they walk in cross system, the tracks will be in three lines. On the left will be the line made by his left foot; on the right the line made by her left foot, and, in the middle, one muddled track made by their combined right feet. This is assuming that the leader has his follower slightly to his right. This position is sometimes referred to as being 'in on a stroll'. It is the most comfortable position to adopt in cross system on a dance floor because it makes taking a left-hand, or anticlockwise, bend quite easy.

It is also possible for the leader to step with his right foot to his right of the follower's left, and for their left feet to be in the same line. This is known as being 'out on a stroll'. A very good exercise is to walk around the dance floor alternating between these two positions, and between parallel and cross system.

Here Frank has changed into the Cross System
but stayed in line.
The result?.........a clash of feet.

Walking to the side in parallel, making four 'tracks in the snow'. Note that Frank has 'dissociated' at the waist so that his chest continues to face Linda.

To initiate a walk in cross system from standing still, the leader places the follower's weight on one foot and indicates a step backwards for her, but this time he himself steps off on the same foot. To be exact, if she has her weight on her left foot, she must step back onto her right. Whereas in parallel he would step forward on his left, this time, though he may be leaning a little to his right to gain her weight shift, he actually steps off with his right foot, but makes sure to place it where her right foot had been. He then ensures that his next step with his left foot is outside her right. He also slightly rotates his upper body to the right to maintain the frame.

Another method of converting to and from these two systems of walking is if the follower keeps walking backwards but the leader allows his body to move forward to stay with the follower but does not take a step. This is quite hard to do and takes a good deal of practice. Easier is a small turn in which the leader stands still and allows the follower to take a step across him.

To recapitulate, then, the idea with the tango walk is that you move from one balanced position to another, in time with your partner, so that neither feels the need to lean on or pull at the other. Then the leader, at every beat, is in such a balanced position that he can make an instant decision of improvisation, based on the interpretation of the music and the room available on the dance floor. The follower arrives poised to react quickly and generously to any reasonable invitation her leader offers because each step is a finished product and she has not 'mortgaged' her next step.

We should not get lured into the notion that there is a single, special style of tango walk just because many people have deliberately copied some famous dancers' styles. There are as many different ways of walking in tango as there are in life. Do we walk the same way on ice as we do on rocky ground? When we are happy, do we walk the same way as when we are sad or angry? Some dancers find one style of walking that suits them and they stick with it for all seasons. Others alter their walking style to suit the music, their partner or their mood; and, of course, we are all obliged to adjust our walk to the conditions of the dance floor. Perhaps it is more reasonable to say what the proper tango walk is *not*. It is not bouncy, jerky, rolling or heavy on the heels. I try to think of a panther, not a guardsman.

There is no doubt in my mind that many Argentinian dancers have a particular style of walking and I have spent a considerable amount of time watching and attempting to analyse just precisely what it is that marks them out from most Europeans. Finally, I think I understand it. Unfortunately, I am not confident that I can mimic it. You may ask why I should want to? It is simply because it is attractive to me. First, you need a partner almost the same height as yourself. I'm sure there must be lanky Argentinians but I have yet to meet one. If I were a smaller man I might wear a big Cuban heel which would alter my posture and walk, just as a four inch stiletto alters a woman's. More significantly, I would have no desire to cave my chest and round my shoulders or stoop like a gorilla to conform to my partner. I would be much more likely to puff up my chest and strut. It is a hard discipline for a tall 'Anglo' to stand even taller but, if we think about it and reset our posture at strategic pauses in the dancing, surely even we can learn to overcome any natural gracelessness we have learned.

More important, it seems to me, is the timing of the foot transfer. Many Europeans learn to march in step to the beat from an early age and overcoming the deep, gut-driven compulsion to do that in tango is, for me at least, very hard.. I have noticed that if I keep my weight forward, it helps if I leave my trailing leg behind to counterbalance me. This means that bringing the back foot forward and through to its new position is later and therefore needs to be a little swifter. There you have it. The concept to get your head around is that of a swift and smooth passage from one pose to the next, rather than from one axis point to the next. When we concentrate on a mere axis shift from point A to point B, it is more likely to look like negotiating stepping stones, or marching.

The Argentinian leader appears to leave the transfer of his foot forward as late as possible without making the walk look stiff or staccato. In particular, it looks to me as if the very last movement of the walk is the straightening of the knee. In some dancers this even seems to lock out or almost hyper-extend the knee joint before the weight is fully transferred onto it. I only mention this because it has always intrigued me. Even now, I am unsure why the way they walk is so different.

Another serious postural thing most of us learning tango need to overcome is the burning desire to look at our feet. To begin with, faced with a woman in your arms, it is terribly tempting to watch her feet to avoid treading on them. Concentrating on her body, and learning how to read where her weight is from feel, solves that problem but it takes many hours, during which, most men develop an ingrained sense of anxiety.

A follower, for her part, can't be blamed for keeping an eagle eye on the man's feet as they advance towards hers so that she can skip out of the way in good time. The upshot of all this is, predictably, a joint anxiety that spoils any possible connection between the partners. Instead of listening to the music and focusing on the leads our novices minds are fully occupied on the toe hazard. The leader, in an attempt to spare his lady pain, drives her blindly into another couple. Worst of all, this weird posture leads to back and neck ache.

These are all reasons not to teach tango with any concentration on feet in my opinion. For novices, feet are simply those things that stop the legs fraying at the ends..

Most people learning to tango will have watched complex combinations of movements being danced by advanced dancers, and they will be very attracted to learning these 'figures', and there is no harm in that. Be warned, however, that you really cannot pull off a strikingly attractive figure until you have learned to balance yourself and enable your partner to dance freely. Even if you have learned a complex movement on your own it is quite another matter to fit it into a relevant place in a piece of music. After all, this is about responding to the music and connecting with your partner, not just showing off. It is great fun to learn to do something flash, but it is much more impressive if there is the odd flash from time to time in a background of solid, elegant, unified walking. A cherry cake is not made entirely of cherries. The other thing to realise is that tango is so popular that you will mostly be dancing on a pretty crowded dance floor, and the space available for fancy kicks and hot manoeuvres will be pretty limited – and we are not there to be injured. I am sorry to say that I have been rendered black and blue at some tango venues in the United Kingdom.

I strongly believe that we are there solely to communicate feelings to a partner, which can be done very nicely by walking well in each other's arms. When you have learned to walk well in the arms of a strange partner on a crowded floor without bumping and grinding, and still make something of the music, then you will have grasped much of the essence of Argentine tango. You would not feel out of place dancing with your partner at a 'salon de baile' in Buenos Aires, where the usual form is couples dancing in close embrace without showy figures.

Up to now, I have been referring to walking forward, which, for the leader (just to press the point home), is not merely sticking your foot out. First you lead with your body, conveying an intention so that you have already obliged the follower to remove her foot from the spot in which you would like to place yours. This brings me to the point where we make the whole business complicated and get into each other's arms.

CHAPTER 5

The embrace, the close embrace and variations

George Bernard Shaw famously wrote in 1962, in an article in the *Spectator* magazine, that dancing was "the perpendicular expression of a horizontal desire". El Chino tells me that the great tango teacher Carlos Copes said this many times too, but Shaw gets the credit in the *Dictionary of Quotations*. I wonder who said it first? Whatever the truth, there is no doubt that tango and sex have long been linked. It is salutary to remember, however, how aggressive the pope of the day was when the waltz first saw the light of day. This was because, for the first time, members of polite society danced in an embrace. Peasants had been enjoying such things long before that; the waltz was born of the ländler, an Austrian folk

Mandy and Anthony   *Photo DM*

dance. History is funny like that. Some things have to be acceptable to the ruling classes before they seem to matter much. I'm told that in 1816, when the waltz was first aired in polite society at Carlton House in London, it caused quite a sensation. The assembled company included the Prince of Wales and the Duke of Wellington, but history does not record what they thought of it. I would guess that their very presence stamped a seal of approval on the dance. Other notables were less accepting of the new fashion. Lord Byron, for example, was outraged at the sight of people dancing in an embrace. He wrote that it was like watching "two cockchafers spitted on the one bodkin"! I would love to see a discussion between Byron and Billy Connelly, who said: "Dancin' is foreplay!"

The tango was, of course, also denounced as lewd and unseemly, and I suspect that, human nature being what it is, this must have contributed greatly to its popularity. I would be surprised if very many people nowadays think of waltz in those terms, but tango still has its reputation. When you experience close embrace the reason is abundantly clear, but even in more open embraces the 'chemistry' of the dance is obvious.

Speaking as a mere male, and a happily married one at that, there are few things more pleasurable than being in the arms of a beautiful, fragrant woman. How many opportunities does the average man have to hold a woman in his arms during the day? I make the assumption from watching friends dancing that many women have similar feelings about men. What is more, the very nature of this thing called tango is that it is a form of flirtation between a man and a woman. How delightful that is!

When we attend our classes there are usually at least 12 couples, and it is a useful practice of many teachers to insist that we change partners regularly throughout the class. In that way you get to meet all the potential partners and get close enough to them physically to break down the barriers of shyness. I found that it was a great deal easier to ask them to dance socially after I had held them in my arms in a class.

This is not the only reason why, if we are to dance tango well, it is essential that we keep changing partners in classes. It is so important because, in one respect, learning to dance tango is a little like learning to drive a car. It is important to have lessons, but the thing that makes you a competent driver is the number of hours at the wheel. In tango, when you have connected at an intimate level with all the others in the class, it is much easier to dance with them socially afterwards, and that is where your growth as a dancer takes place: on the dance floor. This is not all. When we learn tango we learn about connecting with another person, and this is a skill that requires us to sense all that we can as quickly as possible about the way our partner feels about the music. Leaders need to learn how to judge whether followers have received the signal, or 'la marca', that precedes a move. Followers need to become increasingly sensitive to those signals. Because we all enjoy dancing in our own style it is far better to dance with many different partners as we learn. Let me return to the analogy of the language of tango. I could learn to speak English quite proficiently with my teacher from London, but be completely thrown by meeting someone from Scotland or the United States because of his accent. It can be just the same in tango. There are moves that work very well after I have practised them with Judith but never come off on the social dance floor with other women, however competent they are. It is often merely a question of accent. It is a polite custom to dance at least three dances with any partner before thanking them and moving on. Three seems to me to be the bare minimum for me to 'tune in' to a new partner. I have discovered the wisdom of dancing the first song very simply, trying to tune in to my new companion's vibrations. The greater the variety of people we dance with in the greatest number of different styles, including different types of embrace, the easier it becomes.

Actually, many useful exercises for learning tango can be carried out in what is referred to as the 'practice embrace'. This may be as unthreatening as standing in front of each other holding both hands, or – more commonly – holding arms with hands on our partner's biceps and wrapping arms around the other's arms to produce good feedback contact along the arms. The Aguerrodi philosophy frequently uses a much simpler embrace; the leader stands with hands by his side and the follower makes the connection by placing her hands flat onto the sides of his shoulders. She does not use the leader to hold her up; she maintains her own balance. In this position the leader learns to give indications with his chest without being tempted to use his arms. It works best when the leader keeps his weight towards his toes and, if the follower also does so, she gives a firm, clear feedback to the leader. The transmission of intention from the leader's upper body becomes very obvious to the follower with the connection that is possible in this hold.

Usually, once we have achieved enough success with an exercise to try the move for real, as it were, the teachers ask us to adopt the tango embrace.

The first embrace

Because Judith and I came to tango from a ballroom background, we assumed that when we joined a tango class the hold would be the same. After years of painfully building up all those arm and back muscles, we could readily assume the ballroom position, and so we did. You know what I mean? Hips together, upper bodies slightly leaning back, arms raised, elbows out. At least we had never perfected the silly facial expressions we used to see on *Come Dancing*, so we had no need to suck lemons for a week or so! We were surprised and delighted to discover that, in tango, the conventional embrace for beginners is totally different. In particular, the whole thing is completely relaxed.

We stand face to face, a few inches apart. I curve my right arm round the back of my partner so that my palm comes to rest below her shoulder blades and my elbow is down. This is rather different from the ballroom hold, where the right elbow is held outwards, and those dancers who come to tango from a background of ballroom dancing may find it hard at first to keep this right arm relaxed. I certainly did. The right hand is placed very lightly on the follower's back and is never, ever used to push or pull to lead a movement. Rather, the right arm cradles the follower, but is able to move from side to side to suit the dance position. It always provides a 'harbour wall' for the follower, who, if she accidentally backs into it, will find it firm and secure but no more than that. The idea is to keep in contact while at the same time allowing complete freedom of movement for the woman. This was another concept that caused me considerable pain in the arm to begin with, because I was trying to control my arm position instead of simply relaxing it. I found myself "working too hard at this relaxation business", thus defeating the object altogether.

My follower's left arm lies along the top of my right arm, maintaining as close contact with it as possible, because this forms one of the antennae for transmitting information between us. Her left hand may rest wherever she feels comfortable and this will vary with the different heights of my various partners. It is sometimes useful for beginners to cup the left hand to the outside of the leader's biceps, because that gives an extra indication of the forward movement of the leader's body in addition to the visual signal. Later, and with closer contact and greater degrees of intimacy, the follower may stretch her hand towards the back of the leader's neck. Speaking for myself, this is very enjoyable for the leader, but it may, of course, convey a somewhat warmer signal to him! The placing of the follower's left hand, therefore, will vary from partner to partner and also from moment to moment, depending on the feel of the music and the movements we make. It is a nice feature of the tango embrace that it is sufficiently flexible and relaxed to adjust continuously to the needs of each individual and the things we attempt to do as we play this game.

Thinking of the different signals we receive from the type of embrace, I shall never forget the first time I experienced something like a close embrace. I had been dancing tango for but a few months when I attended a class given in the Midlands by a very lovely young woman from London. After the class we had an informal milonga and she asked me to dance with her. That in itself was a first for me. I'm not ashamed to admit

The Embrace- some useful practice embraces

David and Jenny show a simple and effective practice hold that beginners find particularly helpful when they first discover tango.

This leader looks 'armless to me. We have found this to be a vital practice hold to ease leaders into the habit of leading from the chest, not the arms.

The 'unbreakable hold'. This excellent invention of Stephanie Gögelein is a marvellous way to help tango newcomers to get the feel of the principle of staying in front of each other, heart to heart, and of leading with the chest. In this hold, both dancers' arms are crossed with hands placed onto each other's opposite shoulder. When david rotates his chest, jenny has no option but to follow suit!

Of all the practice holds, this one shows beginners the vital business of 'chest mirroring'. Hands up all those who used to do that exactly the opposite way it ought to be. Me Guv? Guilty as charged!

My follower stays her distance and keeps me in my place by positioning her left hand firmly on my right biceps.
OK....I get the measage

My follower feels more relaxed and allows her left hand to rest more comfortably, higher up my right upper arm. We are closer and have more 'antenna' contact.

that I was scared, but not wishing to offend or seem to be a baby I took a deep breath and said, "Yes." She came into my arms, as it felt to me then, almost as a lover might and put her left hand softly round the back of my neck. I very nearly fell over. Up till then I had danced in a very ballroom-type open seemed safe and sufficiently decorous that I did not feel I had 'imposed' myself on anyone. Now here was a perfect stranger, half my age, nestling into me as if she was thoroughly enjoying herself. It blew my mind. I was unable to remember any of the things we had been taught, and just danced to the music. Little did I realise then that, for the first time in my life, I had actually danced tango as you should if you seek serious connection. At that time, for me, this embrace seemed very forward. For her it was simply close embrace – I assume her preferred style of dancing tango. I would hate to think that she holds any memory of that dance; I must have been a vile partner. It had a lasting effect on me nonetheless.

In general, though, when we begin to learn tango we are taught a much less exciting embrace, partly because cardiac arrest teams are rarely on hand. Having dealt with the leader's right side, or (as we think of it) the closed side of the embrace, let us consider the other, open side.

I hold my left hand outwards so that it is positioned with the palm

70

My follower is a close friend...Okay?!

facing both of us but turned a little more to my partner. My elbow is down, not sticking out. This left hand should be midway, or nearer to the leader, between the couple; I have heard this described as 'no man's land'. Our arms should be relaxed and not too extended outwards. The height of the hand should be where it would be comfortable for the follower, and, where there is considerable difference in height, a compromise can be found. A colourful image sometimes offered to us by teachers of tango is to imagine that the cup of the leader's left hand is a lamp shining on the face of the follower, or that it holds a mirror for her to see her reflection. There are some petite followers I dance with who positively prefer to hold their right hands high and I have come to be able to feel this preference soon enough. My follower takes hold of my outstretched thumb and I close my hand around hers with a light but positive grip. This hand clasp also serves as an antenna, allowing messages to flow between us. The hand grip can be very light, and I am attracted to the loose position I see adopted by Pablo Verón in the film *The Tango Lesson*, where his fingers do not actually encircle his followers' at all. This style of hold feels odd to begin with, but it certainly prevents any tendency towards bone-crushing, nervous gripping. It would also stop me using my arms to attempt to pull my follower around. Our arms, when we lead, should not inflict force; they do not function to pull or push. Where we touch at the arms allows us to communicate our body position to each other; the bigger the area of contact, the better the signal. I like the idea that this meeting of hands is where the two people's energies meet but do not conflict.

The frame

Between the two dancers is a space, which should be maintained throughout the dance. It is as if they are nursing a fragile balloon, or a soft toy, that must neither be crushed nor dropped. The idea is to keep facing each other, square on, as much as possible and maintain this 'frame'. Naturally, during certain manoeuvres, this will be impossible for a moment, but the aim should always be to restore the integrity of the frame as soon as possible. To be able to do this, we leaders must learn not to lead with movements of our arms but with chest movements, and the follower must try to stay in front of the leader's chest, whatever happens.

What I am describing here relates to a classic way to dance tango and has the overwhelming benefit for beginners that it fixes one simple logic that answers any question. If a follower has any doubt about her next move, it must be to restore the frame to its original default. For his part, the leader knows that he must not lead any movement so that his follower could not physically stay in front of him. At this juncture I must point out that, in the evolution of tango styles, both in the United States and Europe, this idea has been dropped in favour of greater flexibility of the frame. The newer styles go along with the development of another style of tango music; the so-called Tango Nuevo.

I believe that this 'no-rules, anything goes' movement detracts from the intensity of connection that maintaining the frame throughout the dance brings. I would therefore strongly suggest to any new couple starting to learn tango to accept the difficult discipline of dancing in front of each other, maintaining a strong notion of the frame. Once this technique has been solidly learned and the couple have found the stillness and oneness that maintaining a frame demands, then playing about with it can be a lot of fun. I have seen several couples quickly reject this discipline in favour of a more liberal approach, only to discover later that some of the moves they wished to perform were impossible because they had never grasped the tango-logic of leading and following from the stability and reference point of a stable frame.

The good leader must perfect his ability to ask the follower to make adjustments of her position to stay in front of him with sufficient clarity, coupled with a thoughtfulness that will allow her to achieve this easily and continuously. If the chest positions and the arm frame generally stay the same, as much as possible, it would seem obvious that the work to make this happen will have to be done by rotating at the waist and pivoting the feet. Later you will find a description of the 'grapevine' movement that both follower and leader should perfect so that they may rotate around each other elegantly, while keeping their bodies facing each other as much as is physically possible.

The Embrace- hand hold issues

The joined hands are being held in a comfortable compromise position for both dancers; at a good height and in no-man's (or woman's) land.

Joined hands are high but this may still be quite comfortable for taller followers because their right shoulders are free to move.

This position would be comfortable for Lachlan but not for Claire who finds herself cramped on her right side with her wrist cocked back. Small women often suffer this when dancing with taller men.

This is quite uncomfortable for Claire and would severely impede her ability to pivot left thus reducing her ability to stay close to Lachlan in the back step of a backward ocho to his left or any giro.

Quite a number of newcomers to tango discover that they experience pain in the muscles of their arms and upper backs after lessons, and even following social dancing. I know I did. Sometimes the reason is merely that they are unaccustomed to holding their arms up for long periods of time, but frequently the problem is tension in the embrace, which then feels unnatural.

A rather good way to find your own comfortable embrace position is to breathe in while stretching your arms skywards then exhale and lower your arms into the position you would imagine they would adopt to cuddle a giant toy panda. This way to find the correct position relaxes the shoulders and ensures that the arms are supported by those muscles attached to the shoulder blades known in body-building as the 'lats'.

The major advantage of this 'salon style' of the embrace, as it is sometimes called, is that there is more individual freedom within the embrace to perform complex movements. Sadly, particularly for the inexperienced, the serious disadvantage of the more open embrace is that connection is less easy, and giving and receiving 'la marca' is harder the further we are apart and the less contact we have with each other. The outcome is that we have more space to do fancy stuff and feel we ought to, but by definition reduce the competence. A recipe for disaster, you might think; and you would be quite correct. Big space raises expectations. One disappointing thing for a leader is to discover that the lady in his arms does not follow any subtle lead but is, in a sense, dancing her own dance. Similarly, how disappointing it is for a follower schooled to expect a lead, to find herself with a man whose idea of tango is merely to give her a big space to freak about in. For some people, tango is for showy stuff and that takes space. On a crowded dance floor, however, there may well be so little room that those movements are impossible in any case, and, with space at a premium, what is called for is a tighter style we refer to as close embrace.

Close embrace

It has been suggested that pressure of space on the dance floor led to the close embrace way of dancing. Well, excuse me, and far be it for me to argue, but I'm sure I remember dancing this way at the end of school dances in the 1960s, and we called it smooching. In fact, I remember thinking how sad it was that you had to waste so much of the evening showing everyone how well you had learned the ballroom stuff in dance classes before you got to the good bit. I refer, of course, to dancing in a hug.

There are subtle differences between just taking a girl into a clinch and shuffling about a bit, and dancing tango in the close embrace. For a start, the hug we do is the sort you would give your grandma. It's all at the top half of the body. Not only does this avoid grinding groins together but also, given that we are supposed to be dancing and interpreting the music, it frees the legs and hips up for the necessary step options. These are fairly few unless you are really comfortable with each other.

The advantage of the close embrace is that communication between the dancers is easier since the contact points are greater than just hands and forearms. Each body is one big antenna, in effect.

This is not for everyone, and when a leader moves to close an embrace – maybe where the music seems to suggest it – he must be pretty sensitive to the signals coming back from the follower. The follower should feel comfortable to melt her upper body into that of the leader and find whatever comfortable position she can for her left arm. Similarly, followers are perfectly at liberty to initiate a closer embrace. This is a mutual thing, and you either feel comfortable with it or leave it alone.

There are several ways a couple may learn to get the right feel for close embrace. I personally like the way Alex Krebs taught me. He pointed out that we are usually very protective of our personal space, other than with our family. We stand and talk to each other a foot or so apart, and many people are uncomfortable when those they are talking to reach out and touch them. Parts of the body people find least threatening to have touched are the shoulder and upper arm at the back. A touch on the front of the body would be most unusual in normal social interaction.

The way Alex taught us is that the dance couple should begin by standing in front of each other as for salon style, then shuffle their feet a little nearer to each other. They can then lean in towards each other, just a little, to impose their bodies on each other's body space but without touching or overbalancing. At this stage we found it useful to take turns to lead body reactions from one another. One member of the pair would lead a movement forward, backwards or to the side, and combinations of

75

these, while the other would try to follow. At this point we all discovered how far we could lean from the completely vertical, in any direction, and still stay balanced.

All the couples in the class then shuffled a little closer until they just touched. We were encouraged to take care to stand straight, holding our chests up and staying well balanced even though we were a little in towards each other. Our weight needed to be on the front of our feet but we were shown that this did not mean that we were dependent on the other for balance. If one dancer of the couple stepped back, the other would not topple over. Of course, we did to begin with, because we were too keen and tried too hard. Once we had become comfortable with this level of intimacy we were told to "melt into each other" from the waist up, but still not allowed to wrap our arms about each other. Even in this further position, if the opposite partner were to walk away the partner left behind should be able to stay in exactly the same position. The slight leaning is, therefore, still within the individual's balance.

Still without arms, each member of the couple took turns to lead body sway from side to side, concentrating on small subtle indications and subtle but positive responses. The next step was for a leader to indicate one forward step and stop. Once this had been successful, then some single sidesteps were tried and then single back steps, to demonstrate that the couple could stay together in the same positive connection wherever they went.

Finally, arms were joined in the usual hand hold, but the other arms needed to find their own comfortable home around the partner. It is vital to recognise that the arms do not keep the embrace together. The closeness is achieved by body posture, which should be as straight as usual, with no break at the waist; just slightly leaning towards the partner from the ankles up but within the full balance of each dancer's centre of gravity.

Learning the close embrace this way was valuable for me because it emphasised the need to continue to connect with the chest and not the arms. Interestingly, I would guess almost all of us have learned open-styled tango first and close embrace at a later stage, and, because of that perhaps, close embrace is seen by some as hard to do; they see it as an advanced extension of 'normal' tango. Nothing could be further from the truth. Given that the basic factor of tango is that we dance with connection, chest to chest, even

Close embrace. If one of us walked away, the other would be in perfect balance because we are still on our own axis.

Milonguero style. We are now so completely commited to each other that we must learn to stay together to survive the dance upright.

cheek to cheek, close embrace embodies all of tango. In reality, more open-style tango is the extension, is harder and requires more technique. They are the same dance, and it is odd that some beginners think of close embrace dancing as if it were another dance altogether. Having said that, I must point out some very important differences between dancing in close embrace and what is known as 'milonguero' style. Milonguero is another style of dancing tango characterised by the partners being chest to chest but appearing to lean in on each other from a greater distance apart. In close embrace we are able to do almost everything in tango because we are still individually balanced. If when dancing in close embrace your partner walks away, you ought to be able to stay in the same weight-forward position without toppling over. In milonguero style things are different because the dancers are leaning in towards each other and are out of axis. This sometimes causes confusion for beginners, who see milonguero style danced in shows and think it is close embrace. It certainly confused me.

I am indebted to Alex Krebs once more for this image for the leader to hold in mind when dancing milonguero. The leader should move his body like a refrigerator! How wonderful that image is, and how well it makes the vital point. For, you see, if we attempt the sorts of body movement in the milonguero style that we use in open style and close embrace, we become un-glued as a couple. Our follower simply cannot keep her legs where they need to be and stay in the hug if we dissociate.

Remember, we are still attempting to dance with each other voluntarily and the closeness must be mutually acceptable. The success of dancing closer together also depends to a great extent on the skills of both dancers in the different styles. If one of us can't dance close, then, as a couple, we cannot dance close. It is simply not acceptable for a leader to squeeze a follower to his bosom with an arm grip. In family life, hugs can be given and taken. In tango, close embrace is arrived at by mutual consent and held together throughout a dance only by the same mutual desire. To that end, the leader needs more feedback from the follower, and by this I refer to the pressure she exerts towards the leader. This is not leaning but a resistance from the feet up through the legs and body. Actually, the word 'pressure' is not quite right here. We should be thinking that the follower exerts her *presence* on the leader. It takes a while to grasp this concept, but there is an immensely different feel for the leader when a follower tries to resist the pressure to move backwards with her feet from when she leans on him like a dead weight. A very positive sense of presence from the follower assists the leader because it allows him to sense when the follower is ready to go, and they can move as one. Imagine that, in words, the follower might say, "Wait, wait, wait – now!" and change that idea into body language. The feeling is simply as different as alive and dead, and couples should experiment with this pressure, or sense of presence, until it feels good for them both.

To begin with, they should walk forward attempting to maintain exactly the same feeling all the time, then make that harder by varying the size of step and coming to a halt. More difficult is reversing the direction without coming apart. It stands to reason that, when a follower has committed herself forward into my arms and I step backwards, she gets the impression that she will fall on her face. It is quite an unpleasant sensation, as I have discovered myself following a huge guy. We had overcome our reluctance to cuddle rather well, I thought, mostly by giving back quite a bit of chest pressure to each other. I dare say we were attempting to be about as macho as two heterosexual men can get when hugging for considerable periods of time in a church hall in Cambridge. As he stepped backwards he took his chest away from me and I felt I was about to fall down a hole. It was very unpleasant indeed. So I learned the hard way that, should I wish to take a backward step, I should think 'chest forward' as I took my foot back. The mindset is always to protect the connection that is at the chest before the feet operate the axis shift. Of course, the axis shift is done gradually, not as a sudden jolt back, but you had guessed that already, hadn't you?

All these exercises should be done without using arms because that is harder to begin with, and if you use arms you come to believe you have grasped the idea because you have made it too easy. You then move on to the next exercise before you are ready to do so; the failing of all keen learners. I am a great rusher in this context but I have discovered that I always have to go back to the basic lesson to get it right in the end anyway, so I save no time by galloping onwards. For both dancers the weight should be well forward on the front of the foot and the ribcage should be held upwards and forward and not slumped down or back.

Al and Hannah. Note the added element of intimacy that this early hand hold represents

There are a number of variations of positions of the free hands that should always be held for maximal comfort and to permit free movement. Elbows must be down, not pointing outwards. In the 1920s the common hand hold was close in to the left side of the man's upper chest. Actually, this was simply a refinement of the position in which the woman might naturally find her right hand if she placed the palm onto the front of the man's chest with her fingers on his left collarbone. Some men danced with their left hands in their trouser pockets in this type of embrace but it is nicer, in my view, and more useful from a leading point of view to hold hands. To do this, the leader covers the follower's hand with his and curls his fingers under her palm so that his fingernails are touching his own chest. This means that the position of the hands in this close-to-the-chest style is not merely a matter of taking the usual hold and pulling it inwards. It is a different hold altogether. It so happens that we usually learn the outstretched hold first, but the reality is that this closer hold was probably the first and the outstretched hold developed from this.

After the close-to-the-chest hold came a lower version of the same thing, which I shall call the hip hold. In this position the woman's right hand rests with her palm to the man's left hip bone, her fingers curving horizontally round his flank. The man's left hand then cupped under her hand so that his fingers came to rest between her hand and his side. Again, this position is not achieved by merely bringing inwards and downwards the more modern hold. The relationship of the hands is unique to the position.

I like to think of these two early hand positions in this way. The high, close-to-the-chest position is affectionate and intimate, and the lower may look and feel a little more aggressive both from the man's and woman's point of view. Readers may have noticed that I have departed from my usual style of referring to the dancers as leader and follower in this section. This is quite deliberate. I believe that these two hand holds are significantly relevant to the gender differences of the couple. Whereas the modern, outstretched hand hold is neutral in terms of its power balance, these two intimate holds seem to me to be powerful gestures of a sexual nature between a man and a woman, and denote a level of intimacy beyond simple dance. The lower hold is often seen as more aggressive, or – at least – assertive, and even suggestive, particularly when there is a distinct backward and forward, pumping hand movement in a contra-body way, just as you swing your arms when marching. I realise that this is not very politically correct, but there it is.

The ocho in close embrace

Probably the next most useful thing to be able to do comfortably in the close embrace is the back ocho, and here the technique may be very different from the usual step-pivot-step that we use in the open embrace. The usual rules of dissociation and avoidance of thigh crossing may have to fly out of the window because, for some of us, there may be no alternative if we are to maintain a comfortable hug. That is not to suggest that it is impossible for a follower to pivot in close embrace, but to do so demands very good dissociation ability indeed. I for one prefer to dance with a lady who tends towards the minimalist and elegant in this respect than one who executes an ocho like an eel and loses her balance. Whatever turns you on, I say. For certain, pivots are nigh impossible in milonguero style because the chest relationship must stay very stable all the time – even down to the belt.

For a more cosy ocho, the follower slips her left foot around the back of her right heel, keeping her thighs together, and steps to her right and slightly backwards. To begin with this step need not be too big but all weight must be transferred onto the left foot. As the left foot passes behind the right heel, the right knee relaxes more and the right heel lifts off the floor. This enables the necessary pelvic adjustment to make this manoeuvre comfortable and readies the right foot for the return journey to the left. It is a zigzag walk backwards with pivots. At all times the upper body faces the same way – as nearly as possible – and there is no rise and fall. Remember that there is considerable forward and backward play in the knees without losing our height, and if we let our heels off the floor even more leeway is possible.

The aim is for the couple to stay bonded in the dance and the connection not to be spoiled by friction side to side, up and down, and separation and bumping back together. The leader plays his part in this. While it is just possible for the follower to manage the ocho on the spot, on one plane it is pretty uncomfortable. It requires the follower to take very tiny, even half steps. The leader accompanies the follower with sidesteps that both curve around the follower and progress along the line of dance. Each couple will find their own resonance in this. Some may need considerable procession and others less. What counts is that it feels good for them both. Leaders ought to realise that followers are performing a fairly strenuous set of movements while they – the leaders – are merely sauntering. Be kind, you guys! And, while I'm thinking about the leader in this ocho, he might try to ensure that he does not look as if he has spent a month in the saddle and bring his feet together with some semblance of elegance now and again.

The lead into the backward ocho may be the usual sidestep and weight change we are used to. An elegant alternative that works well comes from a position where the leader is backing down the line of dance, leads a simple turn and keeps the body rotation going, but stops his feet to lead the first pivot then steps into the accompanying step.

All sorts of neat variations are possible once I recognise that the ocho means that I have led my follower to a pivot position. I can produce a giro if I lengthen one sidestep around my follower and simply close my feet together for the second sidestep, staying in place thereafter. As long as we have good connection my follower adjusts her step in length and placement to stay bonded to me. This seems to me to be a lot easier to do to my left than to the right, probably because of the essential asymmetry of the embrace.

Instead of enabling my partner to continue her ocho, I can halt her at the point of her pivot, while she is balanced on one foot, and tease her with small, repeated changes of direction before allowing her onwards. This produces for the follower the opportunity for small boleos.

Another fun variation is to lead the ocho but check the follower's ability to transfer her weight onto the backward placing foot. Suppose she is stepping back on her left foot and I am accompanying with my left. If I am 'mean' with my accompanying step and stop it short of allowing her to pivot, then rotate to my left, she will lift the left foot and replace it to her right. If I then allow her to pivot she continues the ocho but we have produced a small change of direction to my left. This may be vital on the dance floor. Naturally, we can either tack these variations together, or we can repeat the last variation to produce a series of slightly jerky, syncopated movements if I feel that the music has been crying out for it.

Those who have been paying attention may have come to realise that this back ocho and my accompanying step mean that we have changed from parallel walking into cross system. This means that I must now remember to make a choice: either to convert back before ploughing on into forward walking, or to walk offset after a series of ochos. If I elect to change back into parallel this is not difficult. It can be done easily enough by a double step, or perhaps more elegantly by pausing for a beat on one foot. When dancing with a really competent follower, with great stillness between your chests, it may be hard to feel the ocho taking place. The beauty of the close embrace is that, for most of us, we are able to place our right hands under the follower's right shoulder blade and feel the different movements of the muscles that power her ocho. It's a personal thing, but I thought I would draw it to your attention.

The giro in close embrace

For a long time I had a great problem with this, particularly in turning to my right, the 'closed' side of the embrace. I was able to cope with the first elements because, after all, they were merely those of the forward ocho. I found adding the extra dimension of the follower side step to achieve the ocho Cortado not so much more demanding that I felt uncomfortable but I sensed that I had reached my end point. I would dissociate to my right and feel my body coming up against the buffers and be pleased to reverse the movement. Of course, part of my problem was the blindness we have to our right side when dancing in close, particularly with a tall woman. A full giro to the left felt more comfortable every time. Human nature being what it is, I soon capitulated to my sense of incompetence and gave up trying. What a wimp!

Homer Ladas sorted it out for me and I shall be eternally grateful. Homer is one of those wonderful characters you meet in tango. His philosophy of tango exactly matches mine, in that he agrees with me that tango is ours for the use we can make of it. He fusses less about style than about practicality, fun and comfort and his relaxed style of teaching rubs off on the entire class. As we relax, we enjoy our dancing more. Homer manages to combine energy with cool. I suppose living in San Francisco has a lot to do with it. I danced with him and he soon saw where the problem lay. As I felt anxious about losing contact in the embrace as we turned more to the right, I changed my posture. Instead of maintaining a strong upper body presence, I tended to retreat onto my own axis point while at the same time flexing at the waist in a vain attempt to stay with my partner. In an effort to stay in control of my balance, I was giving a powerful signal to my lady that this was no man to rely on, let alone lean into. In a situation

Homer and Christina

in which mutual trust was utterly vital, I was behaving as if I was a wet lettuce. Now, when I ask something more of my follower, I think of Homer and stand up, lift up my chest and offer a strong front top be relied on.

Incidentally, I have learned a number of things from Homer. He is one of those men I think of as a big small man. When you lead him he is the best follower you could imagine; gentle, quick and as responsive as a Ferrari. When he leads he is positive and powerful and has great presence. I don't suppose he is taller than 5 ft 6 but strong in the upper body and nimble. Most important of all, he is decisive. His big 'thing' is what he calls 'Organic Tango' and his website is worth a visit. He wants us, each and every one, to find our own way in tango and he deplores- as I do- the way some exponents of the dance have introduced negativity into it. We share the view that the tensions between stage and social dancing, past and present, Argentine and non-Argentine traditions stand to damage what is real in tango; the ability to reach and connect intimately with our fellow man and woman through another medium than language.

For me, Homer and Christina present the friendly face of Tango Nuevo. They dance musically in a calm rhythmic and measured style, often using the older instrumentals for inspiration rather than resorting to more modern drum and bass non tango. There is humour in Homer's style but the feature that stands out is elegance. Total balance control is often achieved by an unconventionally wide stance but it works beautifully for them as a couple. His timing is impeccable; nothing is ever rushed. Whilst he takes immense liberties with the frame, his skill is to borrow and pay back so that the tango logic is always clear.

Many tangueros dance in a variation of the close embrace that is best labelled the 'V' style. The follower is held closer to the right side of the leader's body but the left, hand-holding side is left open. If we were to look from above onto the couple, their bodies would make a 'V'. In this position, I find my right hand finds itself, more or less, in the armpit of my partner, which is more agreeable with some partners than others. Need I say more?

The whole issue of the leader's right hand becomes more important in these closer embraces because there is a greater potential for the leader to hold his hand too low down the follower's back. I suppose what counts most is that the hand on the back does not alter the follower's posture to give her backache. Ideally, it should rest at shoulder blade level to prevent that possibility. Different sizes and shapes of people in the past will have led to the different styles being seen. Not all of us are comfortable in all the styles and we are best finding what suits us, I believe. If it works and is comfortable, it's for me.

This 'V' style leads to several possibilities over and above those offered by close embrace but, naturally, also produces restrictions. A greater sense of intimacy is felt, without the legs being so close as to forbid all but the simplest movements. This would seem to be a very practical compromise, but there are problems associated with the 'V' style, not the least of which is that both dancers function in a situation of permanent dissociation at the waist and many of the movements available are only on the open side. Moreover, the leader's visibility is restricted, particularly if the couple dance head to head, both looking towards their clasped hands. I never used to like this style very much but somehow or other, Judith and I have gravitated more towards it over time. We find ourselves dropping into it more and more,

In the past there have been some interesting postings on the Tango-UK message boards on the subject of V style embrace. From them, it seems clear that people over here are polarised. Some love it; some hate it. Many feel it restricts their movements. In a sense it does. While it opens up the hand clasp side, it closes the other and it certainly restricts vision for navigation. On the plus side, it leaves you having to dance simply and focus on each other and the music at what feels like a higher level of intimacy. I think that's very tango.

One style that is definitely danced in V style is called Canyengue, pronounced "Can - jen-gay. I am increasingly attracted to it and we have a lot of fun dancing this way. Canyengue has been promoted as a very old fashioned way of dancing but, as with an awful lot of elements of tango, it seems possible that it was resurrected, perhaps even concocted for commercial reasons, not that long ago. When demonstrations of it are put on the dancers often wear period costume, which might make some cynics amongst us highly sceptical of its authenticity. Since nobody is alive to confirm or deny that Canyengue looked like this, I for one am prepared to believe it.

There is a delightful pair of DVDs called 'Así se baile Canyengue' (Canyengue is danced like this) with Martha Anton and Luis Grondona. They explain the style and teach some set steps but the best thing is their public performances. As I mentioned, it is danced in v style and close embrace with the follower's arm so round the leader's neck that her left hand comes to rest on his left shoulder. From the waist up there is close contact including at the side of the head and the feet are further apart in a style perhaps referred to as 'apilado' or piled up. Best of all from my point of view as a tall guy, both bend the knees considerably. That's the only way I get head to head with most of my dance partners as a rule. Naturally, in this very close and stylised embrace, movements are quite restricted and much of the fun is to adopt the swift almost jerky style to play and tease according to the music.

As danced by Martha and Luis, the underlying sexual tension of the era of Canyengue is quite apparent. Luis explains how guys went out to dance still wearing aprons and carrying knives, 'fresh' from work in the abattoirs! As we might expect the pieces of music best chosen for dancing Canyengue are the chippy, rhythmic early, strict tempo instrumentals such as those by Canaro or Carabelli.

I firmly believe that the most important issue for any couple dancing together is that of connection with each other. We ask ourselves: "Do we feel comfortable and relaxed in each other's arms?" Given the nature of social tango (which is that we dance with many different people in an evening), we need to learn very quickly how to adapt our embrace style to suit all partners to ensure comfort and practicality. We should always remember that tango is about how we feel and not so much how we look. There are no medals for elegant suffering! Whatever shape, size and level of technical competence our partner brings us we must be able to adapt, and the beauty of tango is that this ability to find our own style is inherent in the dance. We should understand and be able to use all the different types of embrace and then suit them to the partner of the moment. As I write this, I am thinking to myself: "What a truth this is for life, never mind about tango." Perhaps in this we can see why tango appeals to so many people; tango is life in dance form.

CHAPTER 6

Connecting with the partner

This concept of connection is at the very heart of tango. I dare suggest that it is the reason why tango is so popular and why in real terms – unlike any other dance discipline – in tango, anything goes. By this I mean that there are no wrong steps or wrong moves. There are *classic* moves (which work well) and classic 'figures' (which we can copy) but, since the dance is to be improvised, you are permitted – not to say encouraged – to experiment. You can make it up as you go along. After all, that's what the old school did to begin with. There are some things you won't get away with. For example, if you place your follower on her left foot, you cannot expect her to

Kicca and Juan Manuel   *Photo DM*

step squarely to her left on her left leg unless she is to hop. If you realise that her weight is on her left leg but you wish to invite her to move to her left, you must first enable her to pivot. Knowing for certain which foot the follower is standing on is essential for the leader. Central to the art of connection is for a leader to sense this *without* having a desire to look at her feet; an apparently instinctual compulsion for beginners faced with this concept. The biggest breakthrough for me was the concept of using my partner's shoulders as an indicator of where her feet had to be to stop her falling over. For a follower, often fixated on the chest of her leader, it can be helpful to think of their leader's feet being underneath his nipples. not hers, though in close embrace, they might well be!

The very simplest way to maintain connection is to attempt to stay directly in front of one another; or, at least, make it feel as if we are. This is a dance of the heart and, whether we choose to dance in an open embrace or touching at the chest, we are trying to keep our two hearts close to one another's. This is the nearest thing to a 'golden rule' in tango, because so many 'rules' seem to be there to be broken.

Dissociation

I think it is almost universally the case that, when we begin to learn tango, we are taught to walk directly in front of each other, in parallel. I am sure I am not the only one who found this difficult to begin with and was delighted to be taught something new. It has taken me years to begin to appreciate how important that first lesson would be in leading me to the pleasure I now experience when I dance. At the time, however, I could hardly wait to move on from it. I was, like anyone, excited to have found a new thing to learn and I wanted to get on with the fancy stuff. How naïve I was! But wait; what was the next element to learn? Walking to the side.

The concept seemed so simple. Instead of walking bang in front of each other, one of us would be offset. Instead of making two 'tracks in the snow' as we walked, we would make four. To help us understand this we were taught about the 'tango eye'. This is an imaginary, Cyclops-like eye in the centre of your breastbone. We were taught that both leader and follower should endeavour to look each other in the tango eye all the time. This concept was extremely helpful in forcing me to realise that tango was about connecting with my partner at the upper body, and deflecting my attention away from my feet.

The value of this was driven home for me when I joined a workshop in which the teachers attempted to teach walking to the side from a footprint point of view. The leaders were told to cut across the centre line from one side to the other, while the followers simply walked backwards. You have never seen such antics and contortions from a set of leaders! Petrified that they would crush a toe as they moved across, they all forgot all notions of self-balance and looked at their followers' feet. Worse than that were the body twisting and bottom waving they obviously felt were essential to be able to position their feet as they thought safe. At no time was the point of the change in alignment explained. Why is it useful to be out of line with our partner? It allows us the freedom to do more fun things. Besides, we are less likely to step on each other.

Being in a different alignment with our feet does not mean that we are less close. We still need to feel together 'upstairs', where our hearts and thoughts live. We want to be, as Christine Denniston – perhaps the doyenne of the London teachers – says (somewhat anatomically), "two hearts impaled on one dagger". That is at least more attractive than Lord

Byron's "two cockchafers on the same bodkin". To be able to do this and dance it is necessary for both partners to learn to dissociate the movements of their upper bodies from those of their legs. To ensure that our chests face our partners' chests we must be able to rotate at the waist as freely as we can. From here on I propose to refer to this by simply using the word 'dissociation'. I intend to rub this message home at this point because, for me, this has been the biggest single issue I needed to grasp before my dancing ability improved.

If a couple begin to walk in the embrace along a straight line the leader should be able to rotate his chest, let us say, to his right at least 20 degrees while not deviating from his original course. The follower responds by moving to the leader's right but, twisting to her own right at her waist, stays chest to chest with her leader. She continues on the same compass heading as before but is now on a separate track to the leader. If you are helped by a pictorial image, just imagine that the couple were dancing in snow. They have moved from making two tracks to four tracks with their feet but the tracks stay on the same heading as when they set off.

Should the leader now reverse the chest rotation, first to the centre and then to his left, the follower will end up to his left, rotating her chest to her left, to stay with the leader and keep 'tango eyes' looking at each other. As I write this, now, from a rather more experienced point of view, I am almost surprised to have taken up so much ink to do it. All I have to do to realise how vital this concept is is remember how many hours it took a group of us in a workshop to get this right. Like lots of things in tango, the simplest movements often seem to take so much work to perfect.

Clearly the leader needs to perform the rotations at a speed that is steady enough for the follower to stay with him at each step. Throughout this exercise it is not necessary to bother about foot positions just so long as the leader leads with his chest and not his feet. The follower needs to be active in her stepping to be able to move across while staying in front of her leader and, at the same time, maintain the relative distance between them. I think this is quite a difficult skill to learn, but so vital.

What is the point of all this? Well, walking to the music, leader forward and follower backwards, is all very well but it would be pretty boring after a while and, as a follower, my tolerance of walking backwards is fairly limited. After a long session of following I find I have muscles in my legs I never knew about! We followers want some fun and variety. We also want to change direction from time to time. As leaders, learning to switch our partners from side to side is the first element in permitting a whole range of further possibilities and gets us into the vital habit of giving and receiving rotational chest leads. Moreover, it reinforces the big message about staying in front of each other. I often think that we can dance many dance disciplines *next* to our chosen partner, but that tango is danced as an excuse to be really *close* to our partner. That's connection.

It didn't take too much thought for me to realise that, having learned to move my follower from one side of my body to the other, I could just as easily keep my follower on her same track and move myself from side to side. I discovered that if I dissociated as I did so she had no feeling that she ought to deviate from her track. Furthermore, it soon became apparent that, if I continued the rotation so that my partner now had her chest so rotated that she was facing at right angles to the line of dance (the direction of travel), we now had several new possibilities. This extreme degree of dissociation was pretty uncomfortable for the young and agile and positively impossible for those of us past the first flush. Something had to give. What feels completely natural is for both partners to release the tension by unwinding their waists and taking a sidestep along the line of dance with the leg that is further away from their companion.

I'll explain that another way. Assume the leader has led a left

Tom and Fernanda in 'V' Style   *Photo DM*

rotation and now has his follower on his left. As he increases his rotation he takes a left step forward into his most extremely rotated position, continues to rotate his body to the left but now sidesteps along the line of dance with his right foot. They are in parallel, so she steps along the same line of dance with her left foot. They have completed a half turn.

If the leader continues to rotate to his left but stays on the same course he is obliged to dissociate strongly at the waist to enable his next left step to go in the correct direction. I'm sure I don't need to point out that, within a step or two, the couple will have completed a full half turn and the leader will now be walking backwards. The point of this exercise is to emphasise that, if the couple observe the rule of full frontal facing and so long as the leader is kind, a movement as complex as a complete turn along the line of dance comes naturally without obsessive attention to the feet.

Many people who come to tango have done so from a background of other dances, particularly ballroom. Here the common way to learn a new dance is that the man learns the man's part, the woman learns her part, and then they try to put them together. Strict tempo is vital and there needs to be a great deal of concentration on the foot positions if you are to have any semblance of dancing together. With this method you are, of course, dancing together, but almost in the sense that you would be if you were marching in step in a squad of soldiers. Line dancing is dancing together within this meaning too. While each individual is dancing to the beat, or a recipe of prearranged steps, and while they are no doubt having fun together, they are not interacting in the sense of influencing each other's dance at all. They could well be in another room. Tango, really, ought not to be like this, but the only way it can avoid being so is if beginners spend a good deal of time concerning themselves with the art of connecting with each other, leading, following and – above all – improvising.

If you learn tango as a series of sequences you will end up with repetitive patterns because you simply won't be able to remember well enough to juggle the figures about. As a leader, if you learn to read your partner's body position and know where her weight is and sense when she is free to accept another invitation, you are completely free. If, as a follower, you have learned your own sequences but not how to read the signs offered by the leader, you will often guess wrongly what to do next. I mean to say; we walk – without thinking – left-right, etc. If when walking along the street I suddenly realise I have left my wallet in the car, I am quite able to whip round and reverse direction without going through a checklist. There is little danger of me falling over when I do so. When we walk, our minds are totally freed from the functioning of the legs, so that we can deal with avoiding the man who was walking behind us, and the lamp-post to his left.

As leaders, if we learn the skill to 'read' our partners and know what we can ask them to do, we will have more than enough time and brain space to give a good, well-timed indication to any of the options we feel the music suggests or the floor space allows. (I assume that we have learned the skill of walking with sufficient balance that we don't need to hang on to one another for support.)

If the follower makes a 'wrong' move it is very simply the case that the leader has failed to give the signal to the follower that would have made her move completely obvious. He may have thought he gave a good signal but, by definition, if this follower has not got the message then that message was not sent with adequate clarity. The connection has been lost. Restoring it is possible in a heartbeat, however. Part of the charm of tango is that, as a leader learns more and gains experience in improvising the dance, he can lead something useful, elegant or fun from wherever he and his partner find themselves. Much of the fun I experience in tango is wrapped up in that charming word 'serendipity': the joy of discovering an unexpected delight.

As a follower I am becoming more comfortable with the idea of clearly communicating my body position to my leader. I am even increasingly tolerant of being unsure of what I am being asked to do. I 'panic quietly' and wait for my leader to sort it out – unless, of course, I see we are heading for a collision. Then I apply the emergency brakes and avert the crisis, and I can't tell you how many times my own bacon has been saved by my follower in this way when I lead.

I have found over the years that, if I am dancing with a new follower, as long as I make my intentions plain she will oblige, more often than not, even when she has not been taught a particular movement. Occasionally, though, things do go wrong. Sometimes the error will have been in the magnitude of the indication, but – more frequently – the message will have been mistimed. No follower, let alone a new follower, can follow a message given so late that she is already committed to acting on the previous message.

So, my feeling is that a leader needs to tune in to the sort of follower he is dancing with to ensure the connection, and this may take a little time to begin with. The wise and thoughtful leader will not freak off into fancy footwork before finding the 'resonance' of his follower. Even before the feet move, the leader will try a few weight changes to the music to see how the follower moves and feels in his arms. He is testing the connection.

Similarly, the wise follower focuses on the leader's chest to be able to gain early signals of intention. Some followers, however, dance with their eyes shut and find that this enables them to feel the indications better using the arm contact as 'antennae'. This really works only when the leader has learned to keep his arms fairly still in relationship with his upper body. They then act as amplifiers of the chest lead. It is for each dancer to discover how best to tune into their partner; there is no right or wrong way to do it. One fairly universal agreement is, however, that the follower should 'try not to think'. This is not to be taken too literally, but refers to the fact that it works better in tango when one of you leads, plans and pilots using the brain constantly, and the other reacts spontaneously as an animal does; with the spinal cord.

A better motto than 'try not to think' would be 'feel where to move'. 'Tango heaven', for me as a leader (dare I suggest), is when I take a woman into my arms who has enough confidence in me and herself that she lets go and just listens to the music.

If a leader has learned to dance to the music, he 'opens the door' at the appropriate moment in the song and she enters with her own interpretation within the follower's role. Given the relatively small numbers of favourite classical tango songs to dance to you soon learn them, and it is good to dance alone to them around the kitchen to explore the feelings they induce. How wonderful it feels when you are dancing with a partner who shares your ideas about a piece. How frustrating it can be to dance to a romantic or sad song with a partner who clearly is unable to listen and appears to prefer to march!

The leader, having gained the confidence to know what the follower is able to do, decides quickly what he wants her to do and signals the intention early on. The follower should not be thinking: "What am I supposed to do?" but should move instinctively to the only sensible place that prevents her bottom from hitting the floor and keeps her upright and elegantly balanced and ready for whatever next is suggested.

What is lovely for the leader is to be able to take momentary breaks from brain effort by merely walking to the simple rhythm of the tune being played. Alternatively, he may just change weight from foot to foot a few times, without moving on for a few beats of music, which allows him to mentally catch his breath and plan forward. For this break he needs to be able to trust that his follower will stay still when he is still, move when he moves, and change weight in sympathy with his body movements. This does not represent a cessation of connection in any way.

Another way a leader can take a break for inspiration is to pause. This should be led as a deliberate event, not just a cessation of dancing, and it is best if both leader and follower maintain balance on one foot, mainly to enable a quick resumption of progress around the floor without dithering. At the very least, the wise – if inexperienced – leader does not allow the follower to equalise weight to both feet during a pause. He does this by transferring his own weight onto the foot opposite the one his follower has her weight on. I am not referring to maintaining an impersonation of the famous building in Pisa; merely a weight transfer, in fully collected balance for us both.

Pauses are often needed on a crowded floor but they may also be suggested by the music. The time during a pause is a good time for one or other, or both, to engage in an adornment or ornament – of which more later. Suffice it to say at this stage that adornments are extra movements of the feet and lower leg that look interesting to the onlooker, feel nice to the one who is executing them, and ought to feel good to the partner too. It is all very well to show off to an audience with an extra little flourish at the ankle but it should be in keeping with the mood of the dance. It should be a rare treat, like a cherry on a cake, and not interfere with the underlying interpretation of the music.

A leader whose follower is performing a little extra movement at a pause needs to be able to feel what is going on, allow space enough for it, sense when it has been accomplished and move on at just the right moment. This can happen only when partners are in true harmony with each other and the music, and, when it comes off, we feel a level of satisfaction that is at another plane altogether.

There are lots of useful exercises that a couple can perform to develop this sense of connection with each other, but it takes time to develop. Most importantly, if we learn to walk simply and well in each other's arms without rushing too far ahead with fancy stuff, it comes more quickly. The tendency is, however, for couples to want to do tricks, which to start with they will do badly and lose any sense of connection with each other. I know it is human nature to try all the fun things as soon as possible but they do not encourage connection in the early days.

I have found this to be helpful, so perhaps you can try it for yourself: standing together in tango hold. The leader leads a side-to-side weight change and lets it subside naturally. Think of the movement of a pendulum dying away. When the leader feels the very moment that his follower has become still, he leads a normal forward step. This Alex Krebs exercise taught me to tune into my follower very accurately for the minimal amount of signal. It is relatively easy for the leader to feel the follower's moves if the 'pendulum' is swinging well. Timing the move at the very moment the pendulum comes to rest requires a real feel for it.

It is my experience that all connection exercises should be done by both partners, be they leader or follower. Connection is a two-way thing.

In chapter 8 you will find a description of a movement that from here on, for convenience I shall refer to as the 'grapevine'. It is a word used more, I believe, in the United States but I like it and I think it merits a regular place in the jargon of tango. This movement is used in the giro (or turn) to allow a follower to travel elegantly in a circle around the leader, but it can equally well be used by the leader to circle a follower. Very briefly, it consists of sidestep, pivot, back step, pivot, sidestep, pivot, forward step. Actually, the true grapevine manoeuvre is done by both partners together to progress rapidly down the side of a dance floor, where space allows. They take the sidesteps together, but when the leader takes his forward step the follower takes a back step, and vice versa. The couple progress in a zigzag along the line of dance. I am sure I have seen this done in quickstep too. It lends itself to another excellent connection exercise I learned on a leader's course some years ago.

Couples stood facing each other in hand-to-hand hold. As is usually beneficial and always fun in such exercises, we took turns to lead. When I first encountered this exercise I was on an all-male course for leaders and spent many hours finding out just what it felt like to be led. It did me no end of good, I can tell you.

The idea is that the dancers perform a 'ring o' roses' using the grapevine movement, starting and stopping, reversing direction and varying the tempo. The leader should try two approaches. One is to try to fool the follower, which hones follower skills. The other is to concentrate very hard on giving such good indications of intent before every change that the follower always stays in touch and the movements of the couple are totally together. This is a great deal harder than it sounds, I find, because the follower is performing a movement that is the opposite of that which the leader is doing. As an exercise, it is the tango equivalent of rubbing your tummy and patting the top of your head at the same time!

While it is good for leaders to feel what it is like to be followers, and vice versa, in the practice situation it makes sense for the couple to tell each other what it feels like, verbally. "Was my lead clear enough?" "Did that feel nice to you?" Gradually, however, many of us develop a sort of sixth sense in tango. Golfers will know what I mean when I refer to that lovely sensation when you connect a driver to a golf ball 'on the meat', and you just know without looking that the ball has gone well. I expect footballers and tennis players have a similar experience. Well, this happens in tango after a while and it is a great feeling. We could call it 'oneness'. I gather that some think of it as being 'in the zone'. I feel very sure that the road to this feeling is by connection exercises and by hours of social dancing of the very simplest nature. By this, I mean dancing with dozens of different partners, avoiding complicated steps and listening to the music.

The music may well be the key to the whole connection thing because, if you dance simply for two and a half minutes and concentrate hard on the musical interpretation and your companion, you are forcing yourself to occupy your entire mind on connection skills. When I first grasped this notion I had got it into my head that my dancing must be boring for my partners because I used so few 'figures'. I simply could not remember them, though I had learned them well enough. My problem seemed to be that I could not switch off the music, which insisted that I danced in a particular way. I thought I ought to be performing certain 'tricks' but the music said otherwise. That was how I saw it then. I asked several partners if this was so. Was my dancing a bore, as I thought? They were universally of the opinion that I was wrong. They had enjoyed the dance and, more than that, appreciated the fact that I appeared to be tuned in to the music. The penny dropped. These followers were already free from my anxieties about doing figures, navigating and technical stuff. They were free to listen to the music and just be 'feelies' and enjoy the trip. When I danced in sympathy with the music and kept complications to the minimum, I had satisfied most of their requirements. We had connected. They would have been quite happy if I had been able to perform more fancy stuff but not at the expense of the connection between them and the music and me.

Speaking as a man who tries to be a good follower from time to time, I am quite certain of what I want from my leader. I shall place these wants in their order of importance to me.

1. Please listen to the music. I am, and if you don't it's hell to dance with you.
2. Please 'listen' to me. Where am I? How do I feel? What mood am I in?
3. Listen to the rest of the dance floor. Don't let me hurt someone else.
4. Maybe do some interesting movements. One per tune would be wonderful; the cherry on the cake.

Intention

When we watch experienced tango dancers, one thing that stands out is the togetherness, the sense of 'oneness' of the two people. When I first discovered tango I really had not grasped how fully improvised it was, so I thought, quite naturally, that the dancers simply *had* to be a well-established couple who practised for many hours perfecting their routine. After all, this was the model that I brought from my experience of ballroom dancing. Any insight into ballet and show business would reinforce this. If you attend a performance of a staged tango show you assume it is tightly choreographed. I now know that there are, indeed, many dancers who tango exactly like that on a social dance floor. What amazed me, though, was to see many tango dancers apparently dancing in synchrony with

Fig. 1 The follower's intention movement. At the merest forward movement of Lachlan's chest, Claire slips her free foot back. Her axis has not yet moved but Lachlan will be able to feel that she has responded. At the simplest level, his hand on her back muscles will tell him she has acknowledged his lead.

Fig. 2 Then the transfer of Claire's axis to the new position. Claire is such a well balanced follower with the most elegant backwards walk I have seen. Dancing with such a sensitive follower who understands how to respond to an intention lead with a leg movement before the axis shift is a delight.

several other partners in the same evening. How could this be? They could not have practised routines with all of them, surely? The answer, in part at least, is to be found in the understanding of the phenomenon we call 'intention'. To put intention into its proper context, let us analyse the sequence of events in improvised tango.

1. The leader thinks of a movement.
2. The leader finds a state in which such a movement is feasible.
3. The leader gives a signal of his intention.
4. The follower responds to his signal.
5. The leader senses that the signal has been received.
6. The leader leads the movement. This is sometimes referred to as an 'indication' of the movement, but in any case it usually means a clear movement of the leader's upper chest either in a linear or rotational manner. Advanced leaders also use hip movements to enhance the lead, but to begin with we learn to

lead from the chest.

7.   The couple move their entire axis, as if they are two halves of one animal, from one fully balanced position with weight on one foot to another.

The place that 'intention' comes into play is at phase 3.

There is another model you might consider for this if you drive a car. Let us think of the actions we are supposed to take when, as motorists, we wish to alter our vehicle's position on the road. We decide what to do and, well before we make any move, we indicate to other motorists our intention. At least, that is what we ought to do, though I suspect we all see motorists who just pull out without indicating and a few who, bizarrely, move into position and then indicate after the event, thus stating the blooming obvious. When I see a motorist in front of me begin to signal his intention to turn right, I also assume he will have to slow down and eventually halt, for a moment at least, before being able to turn. My reaction is to slow by taking my foot off the accelerator. I don't need to brake; that would be inappropriate at this stage. The other driver has not altered his speed yet but I know he will soon, and I really do not wish to respond to his red brake light. That would be too late.

If I am the driver who is indicating to turn right with traffic behind me, once I have signalled my intention to do so I check in my mirror to ensure that my indication has been received. I don't just indicate then move as if the fact of indicating made it safe to do so. Suppose a motorcyclist is overtaking me at speed, for example?

I want you to think of 'intention' this way. It is a subtle movement of the leader's body in the general direction that he plans to go but this movement is still well within the 'balance cone' of the leader. What do I mean by the term 'balance cone'? You know that, if you stand with your weight evenly distributed on both feet, it is possible to tilt from the ankles in any direction a few centimetres without feeling remotely unbalanced. It is possible to describe a complete circle with your head and thus discover what your own comfortable cone of balance is. If you tilt too far, outside this cone, you are obliged to step or else fall over. 'Intention' is a small but positive directional indication of intent, without any loss of balance and without any change of axis. Although the movement is positive enough to be sensed by the follower, it should be tiny enough to be hard to detect by an observer a few feet away. It is, clearly, a matter of degree.

The follower needs to learn to be sensitive enough to pick up such signals, but of course, by the same token, the leader must be able to give simple, positive and non-ambiguous signals.

It is not enough for the follower to recognise the intention. She must react to it, and she does so with a preliminary leg movement. This is not a big movement but it must be a positive one. The whole free leg should hinge in the direction suggested by the intention signal – forward, backwards or to the side – but, and this is crucial, there must be no shift of axis. To be clear, the follower's head and body mass stay put but the free leg, hinge-ing at the hip and held straight but relaxed, neither stiff nor crooked, moves to its comfortable position of expectation. It does not take weight. The heel of the free foot does not rise up. The foot merely shifts as it is by no more than half its length in the direction indicated by the leader. This is quite enough for the follower to feel committed to the movement and for the leader to sense that it has happened.

What is the point of it all? Well, at the very least the follower is more than prepared for the next step, but, more importantly, it is an

The leaning tower of Tony. See how far, within our own 'balance cone' we are able to move our chests forward to give an intention lead

Tony hinges at the ankle. Look at the scenery to see the considerable range we have to give an intention signal before we are obliged to step.

exercise in control and allows the leader to place the follower in a series of useful positions that will lead to more interesting movements for the couple. It is a finely tuned way of ensuring that the leader knows exactly where his follower's feet are and where her weight is. Let it not be thought that the follower is passive in this. By responding to the intention with a leg movement the follower is offering feedback to the leader, and by doing so is positively inviting the leader to follow up with something interesting. The leader senses the movement, assisted by the feel of the follower's back muscle tension with his right hand.

The natural tendency for all dancers is to collect their legs together in a resolution when there is any pause that enables them to do so. The benefit of knowing that the follower has her feet together is that the leader can lead a pivot. Many of the interesting and fun movements of tango depend, however, on having the follower's feet apart. This provides the necessary gap into which a leader may intrude with confidence to quite dramatic effect.

The best thing about finding yourself with a follower who feels and reacts to an intention is that the gap begins to open up when the leader has not yet moved his axis. Furthermore, if the follower has been taught to respond properly to intention, the leader can be sure that her weight is sufficiently grounded on one leg to enable a small, but positive, movement of the free one. He can have his own legs collected and therefore be able to pivot or to change weight, and this introduces a huge range of new possibilities that could not be so easily managed if the only time a follower parted her feet was when the leader took a step.

Intention offers a subtle tool for managing improvisation. Understanding and mastering it opens so many doors to new discoveries for leader and follower. For me, being taught to give an intention signal and sense when it had been responded to was one of those huge leaps forward in my ability to connect to a partner. I have to confess that it was one of the toughest workshops I can remember because the demand for concentration was immense. Now it is second nature and all the effort and frustration was well worth it.

I would go so far as to say that, as a peer group, those men and women who suffered those two evenings, collectively, reached a higher plane of enjoyment because of this one single key to tango. It is not merely a matter of technique, however. Another big issue is that of trust.

Tango trust

Tango is not just a dance form; it is a language and a way of life for very many people. You can go to any major city in the world and find a tango joint and, without being able to speak a word of the local language, join in fully with the activities and dance all night. I am not just speaking about good, experienced dancers. This applies to all levels of competence, since the challenge and rewards of dancing with someone entirely new to you are not about the techniques of the dance so much as the communication between the two of you. Naturally, the more skilled we are in a shared language, the more interesting and involved the conversation we can have. I feel sure, however, that all of us have enjoyed chatting to a child about this and that, avoiding using words we don't expect they know and staying on subjects that we judge would be likely to amuse them. So it is with tango. Higher skills are not for showing off; that would be odious. Higher skills are for the avoidance of embarrassment and the greater ability to pitch the 'conversation' at an appropriate level.

We ask someone to dance (and in the modern world it is as likely for a woman to approach a man as vice versa) and, should they accept

Christmas Ball at Belvoir Castle   *Photo GK*

our invitation, we enter an unspoken agreement of 'tango trust'. Both participants have given their consent to body bodily contact that might, and probably will, be well inside the usual socially accepted boundary that we all acknowledge when we meet a stranger. You know how it is. Usually, when people are first introduced, they talk standing about a metre apart and often at an angle to each other. They usually accept touch in the shape of the briefest handshake and often prefer limited, occasional eye contact for a while. Good friends may hug and kiss on meeting and stand closer. They may also touch each other from time to time, briefly and on the arm or back, but rarely on the front of the body. Men in more familiar relationships sometimes ruffle each other's hair and play-wrestle while women seem, in general, much more comfortable with a closer stance, gentler forms of touch and more intimacy.

Obviously, we go to a tango venue to dance and we expect and look for close contact, but it is still quite a departure for most people to take a stranger closely into their arms within moments of first meeting. It takes a big element of trust; the tango trust. Why do I bother to mention it? What is the relevance of this to tango and to connection? Well, let us consider the nature of the dance at its most basic. The man leads and improvises the movements of the couple and the woman follows. This is potentially a very unbalanced situation. It is not like a man and a woman playing chess or tennis together. Furthermore, the music and the lyrics speak of passion, anger, sadness, yearning and unrequited love. These feelings are communicated between the dancers, sometimes by very close contact indeed. It works only by mutual consent. At the safest level, dancing a tango is a harmless flirtation, but for some people it can be uncomfortably arousing. Like all powerful things it must be handled with care. I am sorry to say that not all tango dancers understand this. Remember that, just because you like the look of someone, it does not mean that they are a good or pleasant person to be with. Being a good dancer does not make you a nice person either. Just supposing both people are good people and wonderful dancers, it still does not mean that they will click on the dance floor. What makes that happen is usually a big helping of tango trust.

The tango world tends to attract people – men and women – who are seeking close contact with others in a safe environment. I suppose that a milonga would have something in common with a gay bar or a singles club. Human nature is such, however, that some people need others to lean on and others seek partners to dominate or control. Both these normal

103

extremes of behaviour represent an abuse of tango trust. Sadly, it is possible to encounter tango dancers who use their skill to impose themselves on others. Included in this group are those leaders who see their follower as an instrument that they can play as a drum to the music. There are those who need to believe in the caricatured macho image of historical tango for their own delight, quite forgetting the art of 'conversation'. These are the deaf who shout at you! I maintain that the essence of real macho is the self-confidence that allows a man to be sensitive as well as strong, skilled in the art of conversation and full of respect for the woman's strengths.

Thankfully, there are usually many available partners to dance with, and most of us find that we can easily avoid those who deny us our rights in the dance. There are several ways you might amend unacceptable behaviour on the dance floor, however.

The leader's death grip

Otherwise known as the bear-hug, this hold is very uncomfortable for the follower, leads to back pain and cramps the follower's style. The follower may amend it by the following strategies, in order of seriousness.

1. Relaxing your own arms and posture. You may be communicating tension yourself.
2. Being strong in your own axis, so that the leader loses any sensation that you need strength from him.
3. Being firm back. Specifically, you can press your forehead onto his head or chest (depending on your height differential), relaxing the pressure when he releases.
4. Telling him.
5. Walking away after one dance. Saying "thank you" and going swiftly.
6. Leaving in the middle of the dance.

Noodle arms.

The leader seems not to be aware of your presence and there is no sense of connection between you.

1. Remind your leader you are there by being more positive.

Move with a determination and exert your presence. Keep your weight forward on your toes and move with a crispness.
2. Stop guessing the lead. If nothing is being led, do nothing. If the lead would make you step on his toe, do so.

The toppler.

Your follower has poor balance skills and uses you as a Zimmer frame.

1. Let them go. More often than not, they hang on even more so.
2. Change the embrace to more open, allowing them more space.
3. Disconnect their hands.
4. Tell them, nicely.

Eager beaver, or the hyperactive.

The follower does not wait, and runs away with the movement despite the lead having stopped.

1. Dance more simply and reduce the number of moves that are learned in sequences, such as ochos.
2. Dance slowly.
3. Stop if your back is aching.

I do not approve of one suggestion a teacher once made, that, in the scenario where the lead has stopped and the follower continues to 'steal' ochos, over and over again, the leader waits for the fourth ocho then applauds admiringly and loudly. I'm sure he was joking. I think he was joking.

I have characterised these few points in terms of leaders and followers, drawn mostly from my personal experience. However...anyone who has danced tango will know that there are many, many more, and that what may be done by a leader can also be done by a follower, and vice versa.

Tango, a language

In the context of connection it seems to me that there are strong parallels between tango and any language. One's skill at communicating ideas and feelings verbally depends on two things. One is a reasonable grasp of words and their meanings, so that we can say things we want, but as important must be the ability to listen and respond appropriately. How many episodes of TV soaps do we see where the main thrust of the plot is when one character fails to communicate with another adequately and wrong conclusions are drawn? So it is with tango.

If there is one reason why the Aguerrodi system of learning to tango is for me, it is that at its hub there is always the business of both dancers of the couple learning to sense the position and intention of the other. Admittedly, the accent with 'el Chino' is always on control; mostly the control by the leader of the options of the follower, but also, and more vitally, the control of each individual dancer over his or her own balance. The good leader does not simply dominate the follower, though that is at least one practical solution to the problems of being a couple.

The good leader is constantly picking up the vibrations given off by his follower. A good conversationalist is not a lecturer but one who senses when the other person wants to speak and gives airspace. Similarly, the good leader finds out what his follower feels like, what she is capable of in a technical sense and what she wants at this precise moment, in this dance, on this evening. The good leader knows that for any given moment – even with the same partner – the mood will be different, and he must adjust to it.

I think it is both releasing and helpful for newcomers to tango to grasp at the outset that the skill they should seek is not one of clever footwork; this is to be the great raconteur. The skill they should seek at the lowest level of technical expertise is that of connection, and, to achieve that, they need the skill of listening.

CHAPTER 7
The ocho

The ocho is considered to be one of the most 'antique' original movements in tango. It has always seemed to me that it probably had the function in those early days of showing off the voluptuous nature of the woman's figure, although it may be performed by the man as well as the woman. I just like to envisage a man positioning his partner in front of a rival and inviting her to flaunt herself. I have known people who find this hard to accept, but I just wonder at their lack of imagination. The word 'ocho' is the Spanish for 'eight' and, superficially, the follower's body, most particularly the hips, describes a shape like an eight. A benefit for the leader of leading an ocho

Oscar   *Photo DM*

is that subtle, or – if needed – even dramatic, changes of alignment of the couple are simple to achieve. In this way it is often useful to turn a corner using an ocho, or even to complete a full turn with a series of them, so that the leader can get a good view of the whole surrounding dance floor. I shall explain how this is done at the end of this section.

Ochos are, at the most basic level, divided into forward ochos ('ochos adelante') and backward ochos ('ochos atrás').

Forward ochos

I suppose that the forward ocho is the very first of the set pieces you encounter as a beginner and it quickly adds an exciting new dimension to the dance. For the first time the leader is obliged to plan a complex set of movements in advance and the follower discovers a piece of the tango vocabulary that she may experiment with. The potential for fun and games and testing the power of the connection is enormous. I expect this is why the forward ocho is so frequently danced badly. At a casual glance it looks such a simple thing to do but, in keeping with so much that we do in tango, that simple thing needs understanding before it works well.

Put in its most simple terms, a forward ocho is a forward step, a 180-degree pivot, a second forward step, and another pivot without changing the weight in the pivot. The second pivot needs only to be a full 180 degrees if the ocho is to be repeated.

The forward ocho is the easier to describe and, for me, from a follower's point of view, also the easier to do. It may be led from absolutely any position because the follower is always able to take a forward step. I once went to a really dreadful tango workshop that was based on the basic eight teaching. There I was taught that the forward ocho may be led from step 2, or 3 or even 4. Indeed, you could lead it from the cross, and steps 6 and 7 and 8. To round the ridiculousness of this off, I was informed in all seriousness that the forward ocho could be led even from 'step zero', meaning actually *before* you step! Sadly, those teachers had not grasped the reason why a follower wishes to step into a forward ocho. They had been taught by a sequencing system, and their dance was technically sound because they could remember a fantastic number of sequences. I fear to say that, in addition, their dancing was sterile and totally lacking in heart and seemed to have no connection to any nuances that were sent from the musicians. How could they? The leader was not thinking at each moment but thinking several sequences forward. Even though they were saying that a forward ocho could be led from any position, they had not actually gathered that for themselves from the data they were using. Let us consider how it works best.

For me as the leader, the lead could not be simpler; having placed my follower on the appropriate foot, I rotate my torso in the direction I wish to invite the ocho to take. Which is the appropriate foot? The one that forbids the follower from taking another sidestep. I have heard that referred to by beginners as 'the wrong foot', as if there was any such thing in tango, but I know what they meant. They had picked up on the notion that we had insisted all along that you did not ask the follower to take a sidestep to the left when you had moved her onto her left foot. It's true; that would be unkind. But it bears a little thought once you have placed your follower in that position to consider this question: "Now she is here, where could she go?" For me, that is the true essence of the tango I want to dance.

108

One point is important for us leaders to consider when leading the forward ocho by rotating our upper bodies. The torso rotation works best, as far as I can see, if it does not take place using the centre of the body as the hub of the wheel but uses the opposite shoulder to the side of the ocho. For a moment, imagine that the leader's torso and right shoulder is a door, hinged at the left shoulder. If I want to make my follower feel free to step to my right I need to 'open the door' for her. This may seem a subtle difference but, if you are a follower who is offered a movement to the leader's right then, as you try it, you find his right shoulder in your face, you feel blocked and unable to step into the ocho. If, on the other hand, the leader creates a space for you to step into, you feel you want to go there. I have followed many men who failed to understand this. I have, for example, experienced the forward ocho 'lead', which began with leading me to the cross, then died completely. My leader wrongly assumed that he had done all that was needed to get me to step into the forward ocho. There I was, the good follower, patiently waiting for 'la marca' for something – anything – please! Nothing.

Another leader I know thinks that the lead involves tilting his shoulder downwards on the side he invites the ocho. More common would be the 'head lead', which involves the leader looking round to one side or the other. Bizarrely, one person who leads me from time to time accompanies the head lead with the entirely opposite chest lead! By far the worst lead for the forward ocho, however, is the 'head twitch'; the sort of movement you might make to your dog to send it scampering off or that silent gesture one might make to a mate in the pub to suggest we both leave now. When the 'head twitch' fails to produce the desired response it is always repeated, suitably amplified. After all, as most British people are prone to believe, if a foreigner has not understood you, just say the same thing louder. At least I have never experienced the 'head twitch' accompanied by a whistle.

For the sake of example, I shall take you through the steps of the forward ocho to the leader's right.

As a leader I place my follower's weight on her left leg and indicate a rotation of about 45 degrees by turning my upper body to my left. In effect I have led a small pivot to allow my follower's pelvis to face the appropriate way for the step. My follower maintains the frame by also rotating her body to her left so that we still face each other, though now

The forward ocho to the right

Fig. 1 Tony and Angela in start position. Note the position of his chest and compare this to Fig. 2 after he has led the pivot.

Fig. 2 Tony has led Angela to pivot to her left in anticipation of a forward step to his right. He has rotated his chest and Angela has responded by mirroring her upper body to his.

Fig. 5 Angela pivots through a full 180 degrees with her weight on her right leg. Notice that her legs are neatly collected throughout the entire pivot manoeuvre.

Fig. 6 The rotation of Tony's chest to his left leads Angela to step back onto her left leg. Notice that the step she takes is slightly curved towards Tony to maintain the frame.

Fig. 3 Angela steps forward onto her right foot, transferring her axis at the same time. She dissociates to keep her chest facing towards Tony which also sets up the tension in her body that will power her pivot. Tony likes to take a small step backwards here to accompany her.

Fig. 4 Angela arrives fully balanced on her right leg and is neatly collected in expectation of the lead for her to pivot to her right thus completing the ocho. At this point, she does not know if that will be Tony's intent so she should not assume that it will be.

Fig. 7 To complete the ocho, Angela collects her legs together and is here seen in the process of pivoting on her left foot to her left. Note a total absense of vulgarity.

Fig. 8 At the end of the ocho, Angela and Tony are back in exactly the same relationship to each other as they began.

slightly offset. Our feet have not moved. I then initiate the follower's next movement by a slight withdrawal of my right upper torso backwards. I think about the movement beginning in my right shoulder blade. In a sense, I 'open the door', and the follower steps directly forward on her right foot around me. She brings the left foot to the side of the right to arrive in neutral but, even before she does so, she begins to dissociate the upper half of her body at the waist, to face more towards the leader. This is an important point. The timing of the follower's upper body movement to her right must slightly precede the turn in order to set up a tension in the body, which is resolved as the follower pivots right, with her feet and knees still together and the knees relaxed. In one beat, therefore, the follower has pivoted about 180 degrees and is ready to step forward on her left foot, across to face me, back the way she came.

This issue of the dissociation of the follower's upper and lower body is absolutely vital for the successful ocho. The tension set up at the follower's waist powers the pivot. The upper body stays upright above the feet at all times, and begins to make the return journey possible even before the feet arrive at the pivot point. What follows is an excellent exercise taught to me by el Chino for perfecting the pivot, and made such a difference to me personally that I think it should be practised regularly by leader and follower alike.

The idea is to step in such a way as to map out a square on the floor. Because it may be quite tricky to visualise this, I shall use compass points in the hope of making it clearer. Imagine, then, we begin by facing north, with the weight on the left foot.

We start with a sidestep right, to the east, collect and – when fully balanced – take a forward step north on the left leg, and balance again. In the forward step, however, we allow the upper body to rotate to the left, or west. We have now described two sides of a square, and should now be standing with our weight mostly on the left foot; both feet and hips should be facing north. They still face the direction of the second step. When we arrive at the north-east point, however, our upper bodies should be facing to the left by 90 degrees. I found that it was important for me to pause and take stock after this second step and check that I really had arrived in the correct position. I could easily feel a sense of tension at the waist. When fully balanced, we release that tension using the waist muscles to rotate the feet through a full 180 degrees, allowing the entire body to finish facing exactly the way you came. The upper body has only to rotate another 90 degrees to achieve this but the feet will have pivoted fully, from both facing north to both facing south. El Chino insists that we do not accept anything other than a full 180-degree pivot under any circumstances, and I am sure this is vital.

Now we take a right side step towards the west and collect the legs with weight almost entirely on the right foot. As we take this step, we begin to rotate the upper body to the left, as before, to 'coil the spring'. At this north-west corner of the square we again pivot 180 degrees so that we are again facing north and can take a left back step to our starting position. We have negotiated an entire square.

Naturally we must complete the exercise by returning the way we came, so that we balance the skills to left and right. In any tango manoeuvre, I have discovered that it is vital to practise in both directions, to left and to right, whatever I am doing. In this context it is clearly good to reverse the process, in order to use the opposite pivots and therefore train those opposite abdominal muscles, as well as teaching ourselves perfect poise and balance at the completion of every step.

Well, that is all very beneficial, but we can take this exercise a step further. Once we have become competent at this particular square we ought to vary it by pivoting the opposite way. I mean by this that we were previously always pivoting left on the left foot and right on the right, but now we pivot right on the left foot. This has always seemed to me to be a harder option. I am sure that this is because, as I step forward on my left foot, I can easily produce a left chest movement because this is just an exaggeration of the movement we do in normal walking or marching. Now, instead of stepping forward on the left leg and pivoting left, we pivot right. When we step sideways in the square onto the right leg we pivot left.

The most important thing to remember to do in this new variation of the exercise is to try to keep the pelvis square as we step and dissociate. It is so easy when stepping forward to allow the pelvis to turn with the rotation of the chest. If I do this, I have reduced the tension at the waist and squandered the power for the pivot. This is one of those 'breakthrough' exercises that I found helped me take a giant leap forward, and that is why I have described it in detail; it's one that is worth doing over and over again, in my experience.

Unless the leader indicates a second forward ocho, the follower should end up standing directly in front of the leader, her weight still on the foot she stepped with last. As you now know, I like to imagine that, when I have led an ocho, I have induced my partner to wiggle her bottom at some unfortunate man sitting out this dance and grinding his teeth in anguish that I am dancing with this lovely woman and he is not! A wonderfully sexist and macho idea, totally in keeping with the older traditions of tango, as I understand them. The late and much missed tango teacher Miguel Gonzales once told me that the reason that the man held his right arm freely around the woman's waist was because he could never be sure that he would not be obliged to suddenly use this arm to draw his knife. Such were the levels of frustration and jealous rivalry expected at the birth of tango.

So, what does the leader do whilst the follower is performing her ocho? I find that it is sometimes nice for me to move to accompany the ocho. What is required is a body shift backwards and a little to my right. I can achieve this with a step backwards of either leg, with a little right rotation of the upper body. If I decide not to move I need to dissociate much more, and connection is better preserved if my follower takes her first step in a curve and closer to my right side.

This ocho can be performed to the left or the right. After all, what I have described as the recovery from the first right step of the follower is in fact the first half of the ocho in the opposite direction. It will feel different to us because the nature of the embrace is asymmetrical, with one side feeling open and the other closed.

It is a small point of style, but I believe it is more elegant if at all times the follower's feet are kept close to the ground and not flicked up behind, prior to stepping forward. I have attended a class and seen ochos taught with these flicks built in, and I disapprove immensely. A low foot carriage not only looks a great deal more elegant to my eye but also it is much safer during this manoeuvre, since the potential for kicking another dancer during the pivot is considerable if your foot is up. There is no harm in using the occasional ankle flourish as an adornment at the pivot when there is room, but its use every time is tedious and can look vulgar. It was not so very long ago that such a movement would lead to a couple being ejected from some dance venues in Buenos Aires by bouncers, simply because such a kick might lead to a serious fight breaking out.

Backward ocho (ocho atrás)

In the simplest possible terms, the backward ocho is a back step, a 180-degree pivot, another back step and a second pivot. The leg that steps is the one further from the partner, in comparison to the forward ocho, when it is the one nearest nearer. Only if the ocho is to be repeated need the second pivot also be 180 degrees. I for one find this ocho much more difficult when I am a follower, and this is mostly because I have the tendency to allow my weight to go backwards onto my heels. My other problem is that, like many others, I want to rush the movement and pivot before I have fully arrived at my balance point. Leading is easy enough in comparison to performing it.

The backward ocho seems to be most easily grasped when we begin to learn tango if it is led to the leader's left side. I lead a square step of both partners to my left. After we have both arrived I bring up my right foot to meet the left and transfer my weight onto it instantly, allowing me to take a second left step with my left foot on the next beat. My follower simply steps right, however, and is held with her weight on the right foot. The reasons she does not ground her left foot in anticipation of another right step are twofold. The first is that I do not convey my change of weight to my follower by any skip or bounce. In addition, I time my weight change while her feet are in motion; that is to say, when her legs are apart. If I delay the weight change until she has collected, she may well change weight herself and wreck my plans. More importantly than these reasons, as I do this weight change I lead a pivot by a leftward rotation of my upper body. This has the effect that the follower rotates her upper body to her left, and is prepared for a backward step with her left foot.

My follower pivots on her right foot with her left foot held beside it and steps backwards and to my left. I can facilitate her movement by accompanying it by stepping left. I soon found that I was able to ease the problem of us coming apart as a couple and losing the frame by taking this step with my left foot slightly forward to match my follower's movement. I step in a slight curve around her; enough to protect the frame. As she collects her right foot to the left I do the same. You will notice, by the way, that we are now stepping on the same foot as each other, right with

The backward ocho to the left

Fig. 1 Start point for a basic backward ocho to Tony's left.

Fig. 2 By turning his chest to the left, about his central axis, Tony leads Angela to pivot 90 degrees. Her hips and feet are still aligned to each other but she maintains her connection to Tony's chest by a dissociation at the waist.

Fig. 5 Angela has pivoted on her left leg a full 180 degrees to her right, keeping her weight on that leg. One of the hardest things for a beginner to learn is not to ground the free foot nor swing it out in the pivot

Fig. 6 Angela takes a back step onto her right leg. Notice that this is a true and full backward step, not a cross-legged one. Tony accompanies her with a side step to his right. Angel does not sit into her back step

Fig. 3 Angela takes a full and positive back step, accompanied by Tony who steps to his left and, to better assist the maintenance of connection, slighly forward.

Fig. 4 Angela arrives, fully collected and neatly balanced, her weight on the front of her left foot, ready to pivot if Tony leads it. He may lead a side step right, a forward or back step or even reverse the pivot. Who knows?

Fig. 7 Angela arrives after the back step, fully collected and balanced, her weight still held on her right leg in anticipation of a pivot to bring her back squarely in front of Tony.

Fig. 8 Angela pivots 90 degrees back to the basic starting position but she has still not transferred her weight onto her right leg. She is still, therefore, ready for any led move.

117

right, left with left. You will recall that this is often known as being in the 'cross system'. It may be arrived at in all sorts of ways, and opens up lots of nice possibilities for us.

The backward ocho is completed as the follower pivots right on her left foot, with her right foot, ideally, close to the left. As with the forward ocho, the follower starts her body twist in advance of the hips, and the feet and hips pivot last of all. Again, the idea is to set up a spring-like tension in the upper body, which is resolved as the hips come round. Imagine, if you can, that the follower is a puppet, suspended by a string from her head and with elastic bands between torso and pelvis. At first the feet are fixed to the ground by friction, so that as the top half of the body twists it winds up the elastic bands. If we were to lift the puppet off the floor, the lower half would twist round to face the same way as the top half. This is the sort of feeling the follower should experience in the pivot.

Once the follower has pivoted sufficiently so that her hips have completed a 180-degree turn, she steps backwards across her partner with her right foot. The follower should attempt to maintain the frame by keeping her upper body facing her leader as squarely as she can while stepping back. It is impossible for most mortals to avoid distorting the frame a little but if we both make an effort we can stay pretty close and connected.

The follower then brings her left foot to close to the right (but slightly in front) to prepare for the next step, then pivots slightly to her left to face her hips towards her partner again.

I pointed out earlier that, in order to accompany the follower in her ocho, I could quickly, even sneakily, change weight so that we both ended up stepping on the same foot. Remember that I referred to this as the 'cross system'. At the end of this ocho, both of us are still balanced on the same foot: the right. Naturally, if a leader wishes to return to parallel walking forward, he is obliged to perform a second quick weight transfer without letting his follower change her weight as well.

This transfer of weight from one foot to another is easily achieved by taking two small steps in one beat. The avoidance of doing this so obviously that the follower copies the movement is clearly important. If I change weight with a pronounced skip, any follower who is concentrating on my body might change weight too, and we would end up back at square one. I have been taught two ways of preventing this. One is to leave the two-step to the very last moment, after the follower has already committed herself to one full step. The other, which should probably always apply anyway, is to do the movement exclusively in the legs, giving no hint of it at the chest. In comparison, if I actually want to lead a double step, I find it works best if I use a slight body sway left and right on the two steps left and right. It is gratifying to discover how little of this 'contra-body motion' is needed to allow the follower to sense that a double-time step is required. When I follow, it feels very natural to me to take the extra step when this method is used. If I stay as the 'scary man', with the fixed chest, my follower will get no indication of a double step until too late to join me in it. The outcome is, of course, that we have a leg collision.

I used to worry a good deal about weight changing and because of this I practised it by stamping, almost like a guardsman coming to a halt. Really, all it takes to change weight is to close the feet together and relax the knee of the leg you want to release. No follower will feel that and copy it anyway. I should say here that sometimes it is useful to lead a change of weight, for instance when I want to lead a series of sidesteps in one direction. I find that the way this is conveyed best is if I sink down and 'ground' the new weight-bearing leg as it takes the weight. I find that even quite inexperienced followers seem to sense this is a weight change.

When do we use ochos? Well, they are convenient for the times when you have to pause in your space on a crowded dance floor, because they take only the space you have created by the last movement along the line of dance. They permit some change of direction and offer some breathing space for the leader. Beware, however, of this last reason. It is so easy to get trapped into repeated ochos this way. One ocho is nice; so are two. Three are just about acceptable, but four or more can be a bore for the follower. The key to the ocho ought to be the music. Sometimes the music positively cries out for an ocho. I am not quite sure what it is but sometimes a tune on a violin or bandoneon says 'ocho' to me, so, if I am able to, I lead it. Isn't that what this ought to be about? I have to accept, therefore, that, if the music says 'four ochos', then four ochos it will be.

Ochos can be enjoyed at different speeds, and, although any leader can indicate that he wants an ocho, it can be the prerogative of the follower to interpret the music and perform her ocho as she wishes. If she holds back for a fraction of a moment and completes the ocho with a 'whoosh', this sensation is extremely pleasurable for the leader as well as for the follower.

Probably the most important thing for a follower to consider in the ocho is that, during the pivots, the knees and ankles are snugly collected together, and that the body remains upright at all times. The head should be above the shoulders, which are above the hips, which are above the feet. This is so much easier if we carry the weight on the front of the foot.

So many followers I have danced with perform ochos with their feet in advance of their bodies. Not only is this ungainly but it also means that balance is precarious most of the time, and the poor leader notices that he is being used as a post to effect the pivot. Another problem I experience when I follow is that, when my upper body twist is left so late that I have to rush it, that makes it hard for me to reverse the direction for the second half of the ocho. By far the most useful advice I was given about performing the forward ocho as a follower was to forget my feet altogether and concentrate entirely on where my heart needed to go to maintain its regular relationship to my leader's. Once I had learned to sense the place my heart should arrive at, as long as I stepped with my free foot 'hanging' - as it were - under my heart. I could arrive at my comfortable pivot point, calm and collected.

I have found that it is a good idea to practise forward ochos, at least, in the kitchen, placing the hands palms down on a work surface or table. The idea is that my head and shoulders should always face the table and the movement should come from my hips. As the ocho is stepped, the hands should slide along the surface of the table, backwards and forward. I try to concentrate on anticipating the return movement by a twisting of my upper body even before the forward step is finished. This creates a twisting tension at the waist, which is released when I pivot.

Some teachers who draw their experience from the tango teachers they met in the 1980s have been very helpful in one respect. It was such a relief to be told that the very last thing I should ever think about as a leader was my feet. That same teacher who freed me as a leader from anxieties about my feet is much less reassuring to followers when teaching the forward ocho. The idea proposed is that, far from the forward ocho being a forward step, a pivot and another forward step, what the follower should be doing is

The kitchen ocho

Fig. 1 Forward step

Fig. 2 Collection before pivoting

Judith and I have found practising the forward ocho at the kitchen work surface very useful. It obliges you to pivot a full 180 degrees and encourages you to dissociate by attempting to keep your upper body squarely facing the surface while aligning your pelvis at right angles to it. Resting both hands on the surface - without actually leaning on it - helps to build confidence. If you try this, remember that, as you step, you allow your hands to slide along. It helps to keep your arms firmly in the same relationship as the body.

Fig. 3 Pivot completed

Fig. 4 Forward step, heart over foot.

ensuring that at all times her advancing foot points towards the centre of her leader. As he leads the rotation to indicate the first step of the ocho, she is supposed to carry her foot tracing a 'J' shape along the floor, rather than an 'I' shape. I think this is taking things one step too far along the road away from comfortable, unselfconscious dance and I have seen a class of quite competent followers rendered neurotic by an afternoon of such concentration. How much healthier would it have been to merely ask our followers to adapt their movements to naturally accommodate to curving round a leader with a stable axis.

I used to believe that it was for me, the leader to accompany my follower according to the length of her step in a forward ocho. That was because I danced with novice followers who were not actually following my heart. The skill here is to move the hearts as if connected together. We do it in simple walking. It's just harder to do in a circular lead.

The ocho is such a classic, characteristic and useful element of Argentine tango that it is worth perfecting so that it may be done effortlessly and with variety within it. There are several classic variations we can consider, too.

The ocho cortado

This is a classic variation on the basic forward ocho, and the term means a 'cut' ocho. Not that it matters a whole lot, but there is some confusion about the precise definition of this term in some minds. I must say that it seems very simple to me. Imagine that the leader has invited the follower to take a forward step into a forward ocho by leading with a chest rotation. He might abort the ocho by stopping the rotation before the pivot, or even on the point of pivot if he is dancing with a really tuned-in follower. So many followers I have danced with see the merest indication for an ocho and 'steal' it, regardless of what the leader had suggested, sometimes pulling both of us off balance in the necessary contortion for their move to succeed.

In the perfect world, however, the leader gives space and time for the pivot and the return so that the follower can complete the ocho. He has another option, which is to continue the chest rotation in the same direction as the first element of the ocho and convert the movement into a giro. So far so good. If the leader chooses, he may stop the action after the sidestep that would naturally follow the forward step. If he does so, then reverses the direction of rotation of his torso, he would normally expect the follower to return along the same path – which would mean that she would take a backward step. If, however, the leader should suggest a small internal pivot before the sidestep has progressed so far as to allow a change of weight, the follower will resume the forward ocho. Here is one of those tricky areas of leading that causes us a good deal of grief. I find that the best way to think about this variation is to return to the image of the leader's upper body being like a door with the hinge being one side or another. There is no doubt that, even when I'm dancing with a total beginner, if I place her so that she is ready for a diagonal step around me, as in a forward ocho, she will step instinctively if I remove the shoulder that appears to block her way. If I pretend that my left shoulder is the hinge and take my right one back, it feels as if I have opened the door. Imagine that she is stepping to my right side on her right foot. I have induced her to angle her body towards my right flank by rotating mine to my left. My right shoulder is actually in her way. If I want her to pivot on her right foot and complete the forward ocho, rather than reverse her step, I will now have to open the 'door' the other way by switching the hinge to the other side.

In this way the forward ocho has been cut into two sections by the insertion of a sidestep between the two forward steps. The normal 180-degree pivot that would allow the return of the forward ocho has been broken into two smaller pivots, adding up in the long run to 180 degrees. The result is the ocho cortado.

Ocho milonguero

This is another classic tango move, which can be confused with the ocho cortado, partly because the first elements are so similar. The follower takes a forward step into the forward ocho. To help illustrate this, let us say this step is to the leader's right side, and because the lead continues as for a giro she then also sidesteps to her left. As she does so the leader accompanies the sidestep so that both dancers arrive at a position, facing squarely towards each other, with their weight evenly distributed on both feet. The leader moves his mass swiftly and fully onto his right foot while at the same time leading a swift and very positive left chest and pelvis rotation to reverse the direction. This has the inevitable effect that the follower attempts to stay in front of the leader but has her weight on her right foot. She has little choice but to cross her left ankle in front of the right one, and is now in 'la cruzada', the cross position. This is the ocho milonguero.

In the ocho cortado the leader's movement is exclusively in the upper body. It may be gentler, and his weight is evenly balanced between his feet. I find that its greatest help to me is in close embrace, when it allows my follower to complete her pivot in two easy bites, which seems to feel more comfortable to us both.

Perhaps it is true that ochos are the most recognisable and commonly seen classic movements of tango. They can be enjoyed in a small space and add a very special flavour to the dance while posing just enough connection challenge for the dancers. This must be a strong reason why they are often the first complex movement taught to beginners. Because the ocho introduces the pivot, a major new skill to learn, it leads us out into a huge range of possibilities once we have mastered it. In addition, I find I discover all I want to know about any new partner after leading, for example, a set of moves called the 'media luna', or half-moon. I have even heard this referred to in England as a 'croissant'. I suppose this is 'media luna' is what Argentinians call a croissant, although what you eat in Buenos Aires bears only a passing resemblance to the Parisian model. It's sweeter and altogether less more-ish, as I recall. In any event, you get the idea of the shape the entire movement will take up on the dance floor.

This is a backward ocho linked to a forward ocho by an intervening single sidestep. The name reflects the fact that the follower travels in a semicircle around the central and essentially static axis of her leader. Actually, the true classical move also demands that the leader travels the entire crescent shape as well, but for the sake of this example I shall assume that the leader merely pivots, and I find that in social dancing to occupy a little less space is no bad thing. In this movement, we are now beginning to dance in a combination of linear and circular movements. In the media luna we may begin by sending our follower to the left, bring her back and then send her across the front of us to the forward ocho to the right, allowing her to return in the end to her original position. Suppose we did not allow her to complete her forward ocho but asked her to continue around us; she would eventually do a complete circuit, and we would have the 'full moon'. Actually, we do this in tango, and it is called the giro.

CHAPTER 8

The giro

Giros are simply turns, either to the right or to the left, and are commonly accomplished using the leader as the centre of the circle. As with most tango terms the Spanish word is used, and you will find two distinct pronunciations that may fox the newcomer. In Spanish the letter 'g' is not sounded hard or soft, as in either of the 'g's of the word 'garage', but more as a Scotsman would pronounce the 'ch' in 'loch'. This soft, guttural sound is alien to the English ear, so many people talk about 'heroes'. You will be glad to learn that there is nothing really heroic about doing this step, but it can be tricky for beginners.

Audrey and Fernando   *Photo DM*

Another name once given to this sort of turn is 'el molinete', or the little mill, referring to the action of a horse turning the hub of a millstone used for grinding corn. Of course, it is perfectly possible for the follower to be the centre of the wheel and for the leader to travel around her, and this is also a giro, but it tends to travel under the descriptive name of 'la calesita' (merry-go-round or carousel) and is less often seen. I could, of course, drop all the Spanish terms and simply refer to 'turns', but some of the flavour of tango would be lost, and – besides – I would have to invent an English word to replace 'ochos', and 'eights' would make some of my generation think of after-dinner, 'waffer-thin' confectionery too much!

To manage the giro, the leader needs to learn how to indicate its beginning, be a good solid centre of the circle, and also decide how and when to stop it. It helps to be able to pivot with good balance skills but a good giro is quite possible even without this. The follower needs to be able to move in a close circle around the leader without interfering with the frame to the detriment of the connection. Remember the fragile balloon we imagine we are holding between us in our arms?

The follower could simply shuffle round the leader with her body turned to face him, but there is an elegant way for her to move round which is occasionally referred to as the 'grapevine'. I know there are some who might object to the use of this word in this context and would prefer that I simply called the series of follower steps that I am about to describe a 'giro'. However...I actually think that it is useful to be able to have a separate, recognisable term for this classic piece of tango vocabulary, performed so often by followers, though not exclusively by them. It frees me to use the word 'giro' to mean the entire manoeuvre of the whole couple. The term 'grapevine' does not have a Spanish-language or historical connection as far as I know and I believe it is more commonly used in the United States. I do not think it is used in Buenos Aires, and since it is a very ancient movement, seen in so many dances done in a ring in Spain, Israel and Greece, my guess is that the name 'grapevine' may even pre-date tango itself. When I trawled the Internet using a search that included the words 'tango' and 'grapevine' I found thousands of references, mostly within North America but also including Australia, Russia, Sweden and Germany. One article attempted to explain how the term derived from the notion that one leg was the main stem of the grape plant and the other leg was a subsidiary branch winding round it. I can't say the image worked for me, but, short of coining an entirely new word, since so many people all over the English-speaking world use this term I think it is worth using.

The movements of the grapevine are broken down into a pattern of one sidestep, one backward step, another sidestep and then one forward step. I suppose you could think of it in almost any order but my friendly follower here tells me that this particular sequence is the best for her. The group of tango enthusiasts that meet in Leicester always used to do a very useful warm-up exercise as a group before lessons. They would join hands in a large circle and, to a piece of Jewish Klezmer music, perform a grapevine both clockwise and anticlockwise. The music would start very slowly and become extremely fast at the end. It was immense fun and very valuable as an 'ice-breaker'. I admit I have pinched the idea for my classes now.

Imagine therefore, if you will, a group of 12 people holding hands in a ring. They try to keep their heads and chests facing to the centre all the time. They step right to the side, turn their hips leftwards, pivoting on their right feet, then they take a backwards step onto the left foot, as close to the circumference of the circle they are travelling on as they can. They then pivot on this left foot, their hips coming to face the centre of the circle again, and they take another sidestep with the right foot.

This circle dance is not just a great warm-up for any class but is also a good time to underline the importance of the pivot in tango. The concept that underlines the need for pivots is that, in general, all steps are taken with the simplest relationship to the pelvic axis. They are directly forward, directly sideways or directly backwards from the pelvis; never diagonally with the thighs crossing. Ideally, steps and pivots should be clearly defined and separate. For example, in the sidestep preceding the back step, followers should not, in their anxiety about the back step, start to pivot as they step to the side. All sidesteps in the giro should start and finish with the follower's hips square to the leader. All pivots should be done under fully balanced conditions, and I personally found that I learned to pivot most quickly when my legs were collected and my knees relaxed. Pivots are, of course, perfectly possible with the legs apart but I very soon learned that the more tidy my body was the easier the pivot was; later, I could take more risks with my balance point and still pivot well.

This dance in the ring must be one of the most ancient dances ever invented and I always used to imagine that it would be done around a campfire. We should not be too surprised to find this sequence of movements incorporated into tango when you consider how many Jewish immigrants there were into Argentina. I believe the Greeks still dance this way today, and I understand it was a custom of the indigenous people of Argentina to dance around open fires on the pampas.

Dancing these steps in a wide circle is good because, by holding hands, you restrict the side-to-side movements of the upper body, and the whole thing works at all only if you are all in synchrony and pivoting very well, with good dissociation of the upper body from the lower. When two of us come to dance a circular movement in the tango embrace the circle is very much tighter and the skill needed is that much greater.

Both leader and follower should study and practice the grapevine movements since they are extremely useful for so many moves in tango. Judith has discovered that a very good way to become really accomplished at the grapevine is to try and do it around a broomstick held in one hand. She figures that, once you have become proficient at circling an object as thin as a house broom and staying the same distance from it,

1. Start position

2. Forward step

3. Side step right.

4. Back pivot. The tricky bit. Take time

Another kitchen aid to tango technique, the common broomstick. This really does focus the mind and train the body to perform a good, reliable and well-balanced grapevine manoeuvre. In particular, centring about such a slender partner you are obliged to perform a really good back pivot prior to your back step. It is worthwhile learning to do this without thinking and, better still, if you can vary steps with the music. After all, if the leader is central and therefore essentially static, it's the follower that interprets the music, isn't it?

5. Back step.   *6. Side step right*

performing a giro around a portly leader such as me is relatively easy. She stands the broom upright on its bristles in the kitchen and whirls round it. Just very occasionally the cat gets very sick and falls off!

The sidesteps and the forward steps offer no real problem but the back step needs to be done carefully lest the follower step away from the leader and out of the circle. The best thing to consider about the back step is to take a good deal of time completing the pivot before stepping straight backwards. It helps, to begin with at least, to make a conscious effort to place the backward stepping foot just as close to the leader as it was in its last position. We want the radius of the circle made by the follower to stay the same. This is why the backward pivot is so important. If the pivot is too mean, the follower will tend to step back away from the leader and the frame will be lost. Any time taken in the pivot can always be made up in the following sidestep, which can be done with a 'whoosh'.

As a follower I don't find this manoeuvre at all easy, particularly anticlockwise, for reasons I struggle to explain. I assume that it is because of the asymmetry of the embrace. It feels a great deal easier if I remember to hold my head up. The moment I begin to look down my balance goes, my pivots suffer and the whole thing feels uncomfortable – and probably looks awful, too.

When I lead a giro I realise that I must be positive enough to make my intention abundantly clear. You may say: "But this is true in all of tango." Of course, but I say nowhere is it more true than in the giro, because of the need for the follower to drop into the grapevine step pattern I have described. Once she is in the pattern she should be able to keep it up all night, until all the corn was ground in that old molinete! This grapevine manoeuvre is a sequence that is worth learning so that it becomes second nature for both leader and follower, because it is so useful. We need to be able to do it without conscious thought whenever it is led so that we free our minds up for more useful things, such as listening to the music. In this respect, the grapevine movement may be the one sequence we should hone to perfection, in my view.

In the giro, the basic element of the lead is simply the continuing rotation of the leader's trunk. Therefore it is quite feasible to initiate a giro from a stationary position, but leaders beginning to play with the giro may find it useful to consider the follower in two important ways.

The first is to begin the lead in such a way as to enable the follower to start her giro with a sidestep in the appropriate direction. As ever, this will necessitate the leader having a full awareness of which foot the follower is standing on. If you want her to sidestep to her right, for pity's sake, start when her weight is on her left. Secondly, though the follower will want a good, clear indication, she will not appreciate it if you spin with reckless abandon, particularly since her second step is a back step, which needs a substantial pivot before it can be done. Often the giros that feel the sweetest begin quite slowly and accelerate from the back step onwards.

A similar thoughtfulness is required at the resolution of a giro. The good leader already has a clear idea about the purpose of the giro and how far round the follower will go. Sadly, most of us get into a giro and try and fudge our way out of it as best we can. How do we stop it before we are both so dizzy we can barely stand? Ideally, we give our follower notice by slowing down the lead to rotate. If we then come to a halt in a sidestep, the follower simply halts in a fairly useful neutral position in front of us. If, however, we stop dead in this position without warning, she is likely to try to continue as she was and stop halfway on to her next comfortable position. In any event she will feel uncomfortable, and that is the last thing we want our follower to feel.

By far the easiest way to exit from a giro is to realise that the follower is taking sidesteps every other step and grasp the opportunity to accompany her in any one of those. As Stephanie Gögelein, a dear friend and the very first person to show me the true face of tango, puts it, "The follower's boat is going that way. Get on the boat." This is a good image for the leader. If a boat was moving along a bank and you wished to leap aboard without grief, you would need to plan the leap and time it to perfection, with your own body motion matching that of the boat exactly.

A much more interesting way to end a giro is to lead an ocho from it. This makes sense because, in a giro, the follower is performing forward and backward steps around the leader, each one of which is identical to the first element of an ocho. Therefore, either ocho is possible, but I find that the forward ocho is by far the easier, from a leader's point of view. If I want to lead the follower out of a left giro into a forward ocho I have realised that I must first decelerate my leftward rotation at least at the beginning of her forward step. Just to orientate you clearly, in the left giro the forward step is done with the follower's left foot, as is the backward step, because – of course – all the sidesteps are to the follower's right and must be onto her right foot.

If the follower is to end the giro on her left foot and pivot completely to her left to reverse the movement, she needs time in which to do this. The clearest lead will be a small reversal of the leader's rotation as soon as she has committed herself to the forward step but before it has grounded. This is, after all, the equivalent of the 'door opening' movement of the leader's right shoulder that encourages the first step of the right forward ocho.

From the time that the follower has accepted the lead and commenced her pivot, all the leader has to think about is whether he has led a forward ocho or simply reversed the giro, for if he continues to rotate now to his right that is what he will get.

Converting the backward step to a backward ocho may be trickier, simply because of the time the follower needs to recognise the lead and perform the harder backward pivot.

Another way to resolve the giro is to bring it to a halt with a

Giro to the left

Fig. 1 David has already led Christina to take a side step to her right and she now arrives, collected and balanced for a tiny pivot to her right before a forward step around him.

Fig. 2 Forward step. Notice that Christina has anticipated a curving step around David by the slightly angled placement of her left foot. Christina's pelvis is at right angles to David's.

Fig. 5 Christina collects neatly before the back pivot. This is vital. For balance, elegance and a satisfactory amount of pivot, the follower must arrive collected at the pivot point before pivoting.

Fig. 6 Christina now pivots so that her pelvis is 90 degrees to the alignment of David's before she takes her back step. This back pivot is the key to a good, connected giro and must not be rushed nor skimped.

Fig. 3 A brief, in passing, collection of her legs and a small pivot before taking a side step, but a curving one around him to stay connected.

Fig. 4 Side step. David has pivoted and both dancers are now squarely facing each other once more. The frame, briefly distorted by the forward step, has been restored.

Fig. 7 The back step, where most of the problems of the giro occur. Note that it is a real back step, not a 'cross-legger'. Christina's feet are equidistant from David's centre, making ganchos, sacadas and barridas all possible.

Health and Safety Warning

If the follower fails to back pivot correctly, her back step is likely to be away from her leader. This may have the effect of compromising connection and, particularly in close embrace, the leader may feel obliged to follow her by bending forward at the waist. This will inevitably lead to back pain or even worse.

In a closer embrace, it helps connection if, rather than 'sit' into the backstep, the follower actively thinks 'up' and attempts as she steps backwards to increase her presence towards her leader. If a giro is taken at speed the problem is worsened by a natural centrifugal force on the follower, tending to spin her out of the circle.

Time offered to the follower at back pivot time is easily regained by the speed with which the next three steps can be taken. Therefore, it makes no sense to rush the back pivot in the name of rhythm or musicality.

133

gancho. I describe how this is done in chapter 9. Suffice it to say at this stage that the giro is stopped on the follower's backward step and reversed simply because the leader's leg gets in the way. The follower, finding her movement blocked, retraces her steps. I like to think of this as a 'giro check'! Ouch! As in hospital, when in need, any bad pun will do. Sorry!

Leading the giro can be as simple as rotating the chest in the required direction, but – I repeat – it is kinder to attempt to allow the follower to start on a sidestep. The leader can follow the circular motion about him in a number of ways. At the simplest he may shuffle around trying to keep the speed of rotation under control, and perhaps allowing a little more time for the follower's back pivot (the one before her back step) before he moves. A much more elegant way to keep with the follower, and so maintain the frame and control, is to place most of the weight on the foot that relates to the giro. By this I mean that, if the giro is to the leader's right, he keeps his weight mostly on his right foot. The leader pivots on this foot and it is in the centre of the giro; it is the hub of the wheel. To begin with the leader indicates the giro by rotating his upper body just about as far as he can twist, keeping his feet still. The technical name for this rotation is 'dissociation'. We have dissociated the upper half of the body, which gives the leads, from the lower half, which carries the upper half from place to place.

If the leader wants to continue the rotation, the coil tension in his body can then be released, allowing his feet to pivot. Now you see why learning to pivot well is so important for leaders as well as followers. Pivoting will be a lot easier if his weight is just on one foot and well forward onto the toes, but the other foot should not actually leave the ground.

A very good exercise for the leader, therefore, is to practise rotating in this way on his own. To begin with he may find himself hotching himself round with his arms, but soon the ability to tighten the coil far enough and release the floor friction and progress round will become more natural. Many of us discover that this is easier if we relax the knees a little more than usual, but this should not become a half-seated position under any circumstance. We are, after all, not dancing the twist here!

How should a leader accompany the giro? Well, he has to be a calm centre point. How is that achieved? Most importantly, at least to begin with, by pivoting on one foot to ensure the centre hub of the circle is on the same spot all the time. It really does not matter which foot we choose. I find it convenient to stay on one foot and simply reposition the other one from time to time, rather than end up with my legs twisted together. There is a movement called the 'enrosque', or corkscrew, which is sometimes taught to beginners, but despite its seeming simplicity I find it more capable of fouling my balance than simple pivoting. As soon as we cross our legs, it seems to me, we are in difficult balance territory. (I only mention the enrosque because it exists.)

As leaders we can accompany the giro in a way that makes balance so much easier, and that is with the feet wider apart. This is often not very elegant and those of us who solve our balance problems this way have some work to do. I speak from the heart here. Being able to pivot well is so worth the practice time.

Those of us who are right leg dominant will be more or less comfortable with the right giro. I know I am. I suspect that the asymmetry of the embrace has a lot to do with it too. We need an easier way to lead the left side, at least to begin with. In my novice days I found the following method best. I learned quite easily to lead the left giro after I had taken a forward step on my right leg and my follower had stepped back on her left, in parallel walking. This allowed my follower to start her grapevine to her right with a comfortable right sidestep. As I had taken a full forward step my feet were well apart, so I felt secure and I kept my weight well on the right foot as I rotated to the left with the knee a little relaxed. I did not bring the left foot up but left it exactly where it was. In those 'dangerous' early days, I found this very comforting.

When my follower had done half of the circle around me, my body had rotated to the left so far that it came to face the opposite way. My weight was still on my right foot and my left foot was now pointing out in front of me. I discovered to my delight that I could, at this stage, step forward onto this left foot and end the giro. If, however, I wanted the giro to continue I found I had two problems in this position. One was that I could twist round no further with my body unless I did something with my left leg. The other was that this left foot now impeded the progress of my follower. At this time in my tango learning curve I was unaware of the fun things that we might get into because of this; I simply saw it as a problem – and I don't think I was alone in that. My novice follower often found it a real impediment to joy. There were solutions to this leg barrier, however. I could simply sweep it around to my left into 'neutral', or even into a corkscrew position, to allow further rotation to my left. I could even perform a double, anticlockwise circle with this foot, like the adornment known as the 'lapiz', or pencil, referred to in more detail in chapter 17. I very soon became addicted to this sequence, but I am pleased to say I am now almost cured.

I have described this method of dealing with a left giro for two reasons. It has a nice feel to it and I still enjoy it from time to time. More importantly, it illustrates how I, a complete novice, came very swiftly to engage in quite a complex movement by learning a sequence, but without ever actually understanding the principles of underlying it. If only I had been taught the reason why the giro needed a stable centre and how to pivot in the first place, so many doors would have been opened to me. As it was, I practised one tiny section of repertoire and failed to see that it merely led me to another problem; what do I do now? It was an example of how I was often taught to run before I had learned to walk. It was fun, of course, and kept my interest in tango high, but I must have looked totally ridiculous.

There are some more things to say on the subject of the 'grapevine' sequence of movements for the follower. It is a sequence, and some followers have considerable difficulty learning it. Quite a number of them become confused about whether the next step is a forward step or a back step. I have danced with some who preferred to twist themselves into all manner of contortions to keep to the set pattern, and others who would rather tie their legs in knots than step where their bodies felt most comfortable. Somehow, they have developed a 'thing' about it. It is merely a convenient convention to allow the follower to step elegantly around the leader while maintaining the frame. The frame is fine for the sidestep but we deform it a little in one direction for the forward crossing step and the same amount the other way for the backward. The frame is passing to and fro, through its perfect middle, so that – on average – we are together.

Some teachers disapprove of the grapevine being a sequence and teach it so that the leader is obliged to lead every pivot. I guess that there are some advantages to that, because it means the follower is less likely to go ramping off in her own little world when we try to exit from the giro. On the other hand, I don't want to give the impression that the follower is not in control in the giro. Actually, the follower drives the giro; she is the engine that revs to the flow of the music she is listening to. From a leader's perspective it is very tedious to have to lead absolutely everything for the follower, and it tends to melt my brain, so I, for one, support the teaching of the whole grapevine as a sequence. I just wish some of the followers would take the time to perfect it so that they kept the same distance from me all the way round and neither cut in closer during the forward step nor back out during the backward one. It all hinges on the pivot and the ability to disassociate at the waist, so that you can step straight forward or back while your upper body is facing almost 90 degrees to the line of movement. This is not a mechanical thing; the notion to grasp is that our upper body orientation *is* capable of being different from that of our undercarriage.

The key to the grapevine seems to be to ensure that, in the sidesteps, the follower's pelvis is facing squarely to that of the leader and that the pivots are not done until body weight has been fully transferred. It needs to be step-pivot-step-pivot, and not step with pivot at the same time. The pivot is essential, particularly in the back step, because it permits the follower to take the back step straight backwards without needing to cross her legs in an effort to stay close to the leader. It relies on the follower being able to dissociate at the waist to keep her upper body facing the leader as much as possible. Just to rub this vital point home to followers, it really does mean that, whereas in the sidesteps the pelvis faces the leader, in the backward and forward crossing steps the follower's pelvis is aligned in the direction of her step.

Why is this so vital? The reason is that, when the gaps left between the follower's legs are predictable, of reasonable width and equally placed, irrespective of the type of step she takes, the leader has greater ability to interfere with those gaps and introduce more fun to our dance in the shape of ganchos, barridas and sacadas.

Ultimately, we ought to see this learned sequence, the grapevine, as a potential benefit, which we can live without if we want to. How nice it is to lead and follow a giro without having to think about the steps. How wonderful it feels to maintain the relationship with the partner without pushing and pulling. I know this seems to contradict my usual antagonism towards sequences, but I see the ability to perform a really crisp grapevine in the same light that I view that equally valuable ability of well-balanced, elegant walking. We should do it without having to think about it; so we need to practise it. When both leader and follower are able to do this as second nature, we free our minds for more interesting things in the dance; each other and the music.

The giro in close embrace

Before leaving the subject of the giro, I think it would be kind to restate the difference between the way we dance a giro in an open embrace to the way we do in close embrace. I know I dealt with this in Chapter 5 but it makes sense to cover it again in this chapter. The thing that always made it hard for Judith and me to cope with a giro more than a quarter of a turn was that we had failed to realise that we were allowed to change the way we danced to suit the prevailing circumstances. I suppose we had thought we had learned the 'rules' and assumed they had to apply at all costs. This was despite the fact that we had both watched a lovely video of Tete and Sylvia, dancing vals in close embrace. Actually, we didn't quite know what to make of what we saw because, to be truthful, it looked nothing like anything we had ever been taught. "Fascinating, but not tango as we know it, Jim".

The biggest problem arose because we both assumed that a follower could pivot in close embrace much as she could in open embrace. Well, I expect that to prove me wrong, somewhere out there is a slim, svelte, young female contortionist who can. All I can say is that, in my estimation, a normal woman with average flexibility and width across the hips- and I dance with a lot of those- would have a problem with me.

The big breakthrough was to be told that it was perfectly acceptable for the woman to perform the grapevine manoeuvre minimally. This meant practically no pivots. The same formula of side, back, side, front was required. The difference was that these could be crossed steps, almost like a series of side steps alternating with la cruzada but with the replacing crossing foot travelling alternately in front of the opposite ankle and behind. How simple, how delightful? How effective!

At last, no more backache and no more nipple rash.

CHAPTER 9

Ganchos, paradas and barridas

The gancho, or 'hook'

"A gancho is an interruption of the collection of the legs," says el Chino. This is the simple, elemental truth about the gancho, but, as with so many distillations, it needs explanation and discussion. What, for example, do we mean by "collection of the legs"? Well, when we take a single step we move one leg from one point to another, and as the moving leg passes the weight-bearing leg this is the moment of collection. This moment is the thing that the gancho prevents.

Giraldo and Lee　　　　*Photo DM*

If we analyse any gancho we find that the reason it happens is that one dancer tries to bring the moving leg to a point of collection and is unable to do so because of an intrusion by the leg of their partner. Now, this next point is the critical extra requirement. The intrusion that interrupts the collection must be above the knee of the moving, collecting leg. If the intrusion is below the moving knee, it will be impossible for the intruding leg to be 'wrapped' by the collecting leg; but it will most certainly be 'rapped' by it!

Of all the moves in tango, surely the gancho is the one that looks the most exotic and excites the onlooker. When we do it well it feels great too. I am sad to report that the desire to perform the gancho exceeds by far the competence to make it work as it should. We love it to death! Only rarely does it love us. I think of the gancho not just as the cherry on the cake but, perhaps more accurately, as the cream on the chocolate on the icing on the cake. It can make you sick.

Lots of people, particularly newcomers to tango, see the gancho as a kick, failing to realise that this is one of many tango illusions; it is just supposed to look like one. The word 'gancho' means a hook, and if you visualise it as such you get a better idea of it. In the gancho, which can be performed either by leader or follower, one leg is hooked around one of the partner's legs, or even other parts of the body. The first gancho I was taught was a follower's gancho, of a variety that lends itself to quite simple teaching. Because of this, and because it was such fun to do, I found myself doing it all the time. This was long before I could walk properly. I must have looked dreadful, because I just thought it was about sticking my leg out and my follower thought it was about kicking. I will describe the gancho to give you a mental image of it.

In the process of a giro, the follower attempts to take the usual step backwards, to collect her legs, and finds her thigh blocked by an intrusion of the leader's thigh. Her momentum causes her leg to wrap around the intrusion. This sounds dangerous enough, and it can be so if not very carefully executed. Of all the movements that cause a pair of dancers to come to grief, this is surely it. What I am referring to here is the sort of dynamic gancho most of us learn in the early stages of tango, and I suppose that the reason we learn this way is simple.

In the beginning, our skills are limited and our ability to grasp the concepts even more so. We can understand the business of the arrested limb wrapping about the intrusion quite easily and manage the manoeuvre well enough. We like it so much we almost do it to death. Much later, we begin to appreciate that it is quite possible to lead a gancho without all this momentum, but when I first learned the gancho the feeling appeared to be akin to placing your finger into a rapidly closing door! I am now able to lead a gancho quite well from an entirely static position using contra-movement, which is a body movement against the natural trend. I find that I can even lead a gancho by intention alone. What links all these methods of achieving a similar objective is the position of the intruding limb.

I very soon learned that the basic 'health and safety' essential of the gancho is the relaxed leg, which should be free to swing from the hip and hinge freely at the knee. If you stand on one leg, supported by a wall, or your partner, and swing your free leg forward and back, when you relax the knee you will notice that on the back swing the foot will tend to go further than the rest of the leg. The momentum of the back swing has allowed a relaxed, if only slight, flexion at the knee. This is the comfortable feeling we want to achieve; one of freedom of the whole leg, neither stiff and tense nor flailing about. I find that it is an extremely good exercise for leaders and followers beginning to learn ganchos if they spend some time on their own balancing on one leg or the other and performing as many bizarre movements in the air with the free leg as possible. This is one of the many valuable teaching and learning tools I have acquired over the years from Alex Krebs. Can you visualise this very tall, almost gangly man, complete with goatee beard and black beret, stomping about the room waving each leg about him alternately? Hilarious – but it works! The reason this is such a useful exercise is that, for the successful gancho, both leader and follower must be able to balance well on one leg while the other moves away from his or her axis, free and relaxed. Of all the exercises I do on my own, even in the kitchen making breakfast, or minimally while waiting for a train, this is the one that has the most benefit over time. It has so many other applications for tango too.

On occasion one exercise in a class, or one brief pearl of wisdom from a teacher, has helped me break through a sort of barrier and allowed me onto a new plain of competence. In this context I am indebted to Stephanie Gögelein for one memorable sentence, which assists my mental focusing and prevents vagueness or negativity on my part. She says: "I concentrate on my standing leg." It seems to me that so much of tango is based not only on tiny, almost subliminal messages between two dancers but also important messages from our conscious minds to our unconscious. I have come to realise that tango is one of those areas of mind over matter. If I think of a movement positively, it is more likely to come off. I can also think of two other experiences here. One was when I was being trained in showjumping. My teacher told me: "If you don't think you will clear the fence, the horse will feel that negativity through your hands and your bum, and he figures, 'If the boss is afraid, so am I!'"

The other was when I went to cello lessons. My teacher showed me how to sing the note I wanted in my head before placing my finger on the string and bowing. It really worked. So, in tango, when I want to free a leg for an action I don't think about that leg at all. I concentrate on my standing, or weight-bearing, leg.

The other salient point about the gancho that followers might consider is that, although the gancho looks spectacular to an audience, it is supposed to feel pleasurable for both leader and follower. After all, when otherwise do you get to have your thigh squeezed?! If we continue

141

The backward gancho - one simple example for illustration

Fig. 1 James leads Frederique into the back step of a giro to his left. Notice how well she has pivoted and that her back step is true, not scissored and is near to James. Her connection is outstandingly good because she is able to dissociate so well.

Fig. 2 James intrudes his left leg without weight and in such a way that Frederique is aware of his contact on the instep of her left foot. This gives her an early signal to expect a gancho lead and allows her confidence about where to wrap the thigh that her own right thigh is about to meet.

Fig. 5 If we take Frederique away, we can now easily see that James's intruding leg is bent in (as el Chino would say it) 'one S' shape with his heel raised. His left hip is turned out so that his left knee faces the direction in which Frederiques's connecting thigh will travel. This is absolutely vital because it protects James from the possibility of damage to his intruding knee from side impact.

This posture also ensures that the connecting portions of the two dancers' legs is the soft thigh muscle, making for a safer and more pleasant encounter for them both.

Notice that James's intruding left leg is bearing no weight

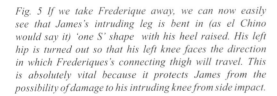

Fig. 3 James now leads a continuation of the giro to his left. That is the primary matter. The inevitable logic of the gancho is that, with or without the intrusion of James's leg, Frederique will respond to the leading of the giro by moving her weight onto her left foot and collecting her left leg to her right.

Fig. 4 Because James's thigh is now in the way Frederique is unable to collect her legs, nor can she take the next step of the giro which would be a side step to her right. James, however, is still leading the giro. Soft thigh meets soft thigh and...

........GANCHO!

Fig. 6 The same gancho, this time viewed from the opposite direction. In particular, notice that James has freed Frederique's right shoulder so that her pivot was good and her back step was truly around him. This is vital to this gancho because it means that Frederique's weight bearing left foot is easily within the reach of James's free leg. He is then able to intrude his leg without shifting his weight onto it.

Both dancers are fully balanced, supporting themselves, upright and on one leg each but also in complete connection with each other. Their chests are facing each other although their hips are approximately 90 degrees to one another.

thinking about tango as a conversation between a man and a woman, let us think of the gancho as a joke that we both enjoy, rather than a practical joke played about tango as a conversation between a man and a woman, let us think of the gancho as a joke that we both enjoy, rather than a practical joke played by one on the other. The gancho must not be taken or forced but invited. It should find its moment when the music calls for it and it should reflect the music. It may be gentle, tentative or teasing, or it may be swift and crisp, but – in my opinion – never violent.

The gancho may be led from a whole number of different positions and it is perfectly within the traditions of tango for you to work these out for yourself. Just think of all the situations where one dancer is in the process of collection and then ask how their partner could interrupt that with a thigh.

Forward ganchos (sometimes thought of as lateral ganchos) occurring in the follower's sidestep

Because forward ganchos can be done within the frame of the dancers and have less potential to interfere with others on the dance floor I propose to describe them first, although it was only after almost two years of learning tango that I was taught them. Let us consider the forward gancho to the leader's right to begin with. The follower is invited to take a sidestep of reasonable size and slightly around the leader. Once the follower has securely placed her left foot to the leader's right the leader intrudes his right leg. I have come to realise how important the placing of the leg is, so I want to drive home this point. If I am to intrude my *thigh*, my foot must end up past my follower's leading foot but be as close to it as I can manage. This 'leading foot' happens to be the follower's left foot, which is about to bear her entire weight. I find that, to be positioned correctly, I need to hold my right leg slightly bent at the knee, hip slightly rotated to the right, and it helps if I raise my heel off the floor. Naturally, under these conditions this leg does not bear any weight. If the leader keeps his heel raised, he offers the additional benefit of angling his thigh towards the horizontal just a little more.

As a tall man who frequently dances with smaller women, this seems to matter that much more, and I need to ensure that my foot intrudes well past her foot to get good thigh-to-thigh contact. I do have to be careful not to get thigh-to-groin contact, I must hasten to say. At one of the places in

The forward (or lateral) gancho

Fig. 1 James intrudes a free leg as Isabelle tries to side step right and collect. The intrusion is near to the leg about to move. The touch is at or below the knee so the outcome will be a sacada, not a gancho.

Fig. 2 Isabelle steps left and tries to collect. James has intruded deeper and nearer to her weight bearing leg, briefly transferring weight forward and giving a firm lead to his left. Contact is now thigh to thigh.

Fig. 3 Forward gancho completed. Note that James's intruding foot now bears no weight and that his left leg is safely bent and his heel is raised. At the end of the movement, all the usual gancho requirements are met.

Fig. 4 The same gancho seen from behind the leader. This shows why some call this the lateral gancho because the woman's leg movement is side to side as well as forward of her body line.

which I like to dance, a new leader arrived and was 'test-driven' by a few of the followers. Within an hour the word went about that he was a groin contact specialist, and he found himself sitting and watching for the rest of the evening.

After this sidestep I notice that many followers attempt a pivot and a back step to continue their grapevine because this is what they assume is being led. If they do so, they avoid the collection and the intrusion and miss the gancho. They perform a sacada instead. Since I now understand that the gancho is an interruption of the collection, I need to ensure the collection happens as well as concern myself with the intrusion. It is not just about sticking a leg in a gap. How can I stop a pivot? For a start I can ensure I don't lead it until I want it. I can arrest my upper body rotation and allow us to come closer to my right upper body. In addition, I need to consider what signals are coming from my left arm. If I have allowed my left hand to encroach on my partner's space and twisted her right wrist back, she will be very keen to continue to pivot to get away from the discomfort.

This is a problem I have been pulled up on in classes so many times. As you concentrate on one issue, bad habits sneak back somewhere else. If my partner's right arm is extended comfortably, she is much more likely to stop and try to collect. The collection fails, my thigh is in the way and the momentum of her leg allows the gancho to happen. I want you to be very clear about one thing here: the follower's moving foot, that of the ganchoing leg, passes *in front* of her weight-bearing leg. This is quite a different feel from the backward gancho most of us learn first.

At this time I stand still with a silly grin on my face wondering what to do next. By rotating my chest back to my left and moving my intruding leg to touch my partner's other thigh I can lead her to replace her weight onto the leg that ganchoed. Then, since she is unable to collect, the gancho is possible on the other leg. Well, if the first gancho has been a success we might do that, but perhaps better is to release the gancho position by leading a pivot to my right. This works well and this action frees the follower's gancho leg, just as long as she has held it relaxed and free and not clamped it to my thigh in a vain attempt to stop herself falling over. Oh, yes; they do that! As the follower pivots to her right, therefore, she disengages her right leg and is able to place it to the floor in a collected position. At this point the leader may continue leading the right giro, or he may step forward onto his right foot, pivoting to his right as he does so. Both dancers are now facing squarely towards each other in a full, collected position, but have rotated fully 180 degrees.

Perhaps it is more useful to consider the forward gancho to the leader's left as exactly the opposite of the one to the right that I described above. The follower steps to her right with a curve around the leader and tries to collect with the left leg, assuming it will be followed by a back step. The leader intrudes the left leg, again with a well-relaxed knee and bearing no weight, near (but also past) the follower's weight-bearing right foot, so that the back and right side of his left thigh causes the gancho to happen.

I don't think I am the only leader who finds that it is a little more difficult to bring off a forward gancho to the left than to the right, because of the asymmetry of the embrace. The reverse seems to be true of the backward gancho.

Backward ganchos

For me, the easiest way to bring off a safe backward gancho is during the giro by interrupting the collection of my follower's legs after her backward step. I personally find it easier to manage this to my left than to the right, and – as usual – I believe that this is mainly because of the asymmetry of the embrace, since I am neither strongly right- nor left-footed, as far as I can tell. Its success also depends on the competence of my partner to perform her steps in the giro, and in particular her backward pivot and back step. If her pivot is mean and her back step takes her away from me, I simply cannot reach to get my thigh into the correct safe place. If her idea of a pivot is to cross one leg behind the other, in a 'scissor' movement, to get the foot to the appropriate place the gap between her legs will be so small that I am more likely to kick her than not. When I dance with such partners, I expect they wonder why they get no ganchos. It is better that they are bored than we fall over, I think.

This is one important reason why it is so valuable for those of us who like to follow to practise that backward pivot and back step. We need to feel comfortable to take time over the pivot, irrespective of the pressure from our leader or the insistence of the music. Any lost time may be easily made up with the next sidestep, and this produces another of those enjoyable 'whooshes'.

The good pivot is a function of our ability to dissociate so that we can easily keep our upper body with its tango eye facing our leader while actually positioning our pelvis along the radius from the leader's axis. By radius, I mean an imaginary line from the centre of the leader's body outwards. A full pivot brings the follower's pelvis from a position squarely parallel to her leader's pelvis to 90 degrees to it. If we do this properly, our back step is square across our leader and our thighs are not crossed because we have taken no more than a simple back step. If there is one reason why I, and many men like me, make such rotten followers (apart from always wanting to be in charge, that is), it is that we are lousy pivoters and poor back-steppers. It's in the hips, I keep telling myself; I'm just not built for this. Actually, we can all do it well enough if we practise at it.

One of the problems I encountered with this gancho, even when the follower's back step was perfect, was that I failed to grasp the notion that it was my thigh that was to be the intruding article. I kept thinking it was about where my foot went. This meant that my brain was too far in advance of my body. My brain was thinking about getting my foot through a gap and making me anxious about whether I would kick my partner, when it should have been focusing on the position I would need to adopt to allow my thigh to do the work. I should have thought something along the lines of: "If I want to block the flow of water from that pipe with the back of my thigh, where will I need to stand to allow me to put the back of my thigh there?" I realise that is an odd idea, but it does work. Where would your left foot need to be and which way would your left foot be pointing if you wanted to advance the back of your right thigh into some space whilst bearing weight on your left leg? You would need to pivot to your left so that you could stretch your thigh out sideways, wouldn't you? When I simply sidestepped, the thigh could go only half the distance I wanted it to. Once I pivoted, I could get so much more length and the toe could curl round the weight-bearing instep of my partner, and she knew it was there.

Because I had failed to pivot adequately and was lacking in thigh length I then found myself making the next error. In an attempt to get more length I moved my weight forward towards my partner. Disaster! I was now dancing in her space, and we collided at the hip while I tried to gain balance by leaning back and we came un-glued at the upper body.

Common problems with ganchos

Fig. 1 This is the most common problem. Because Frederique has failed to pivot well her back step is too far away from James for there to be any possibility of an intrusion. He could of course lunge out but that would mean transferring his weight forward onto his intruding leg. A mean, scissored-legged back step would mean no gap for an intrusion at all

Fig. 2 So many new followers respond to a gancho lead by arching their backs. The reason appears to be their misconception that a gancho is a kick. The huge effort expended below the waist must be counterbalanced by a dangerous lunge backwards above. This is dangerous for both their backs and, besides, it's thoroughly ugly to watch.

Health and Safety Warning

Fig. 3 Followers who have not had the logic of the gancho explained to them may, after watching more advanced dancers, come to believe that they are required to kick through the leader's legs. After all, when you first see a gancho, particularly in a stage show, you could easily be forgiven for assuming that was what was happening. It's one of those tango illusions.

The reality is that, in the follower's gancho, the leader is inviting the follower to squeeze his thigh between her thigh and her calf. Whether she accepts this invitation or not is entirely up to her. If she does, the manner in which she ganchos depends on her feelings and the musical cues.

For a safe, elegant and satisfying gancho a follower should wait to feel her leader's thigh in firm contact with hers. She should always keep her thighs vertical and not lift her knee. The sole of her shoe should stay close to the ground until the very last moment. All the effort for the gancho should come from the travelling thigh and the foot should only fly when its momentum has been developed but the thigh movement has been arrested. I speak from the heart here!

Eventually, when I was able to grasp the concept, I was able to lead a giro so well balanced that I could choose whether or not to interrupt the collection, wherever it occurred and with whichever leg of mine I chose. However...I still need to pick my moment and be sensitive to the way my particular partner dances. After a few giros it becomes clear enough to me whether a back gancho will be possible or not. Frequently it is not, purely because of the follower's back step problem, so I let discretion be the better part of valour and don't even try. If there is no space to insinuate a thigh, best not do it at all.

I have laid a lot of emphasis on the intruding thigh because it is such a vital concept, but I think it would be sensible here to think a little about the poor old knee of this brave limb. Another vital point about this leg insinuation is that the knee of the leader's intruding leg must be slightly bent insinuation is that the knee of the leader's intruding leg must be slightly bent so that it is capable of further flexing as the two thighs meet. In addition, I have discovered to my cost that the point of the knee should always face the direction in which the follower is moving. Inserting a locked-out knee into a closing gap and facing the wrong way is the sure recipe for injury, even by a soft follower's thigh.

The follower attempts to collect her feet before taking the next step, which for her will be the right foot to the side. After all, with this big leftward body rotation of the leader, the indication is of a continuation of the giro to his left. As her right leg moves backwards, the right leg of the leader impedes its progress. The connection is with the outsides and backs of both their thighs. The thigh is stopped but the foot continues so that the follower's right leg hooks around the leader's right leg. It is a good image for the follower to hold in mind that she is wrapping her leg around the leader's as you might wrap a scarf. By this I mean that the wrapping motion is progressive, not like a 'nutcracker'. OK, I accept that the knee is a hinge joint like a nutcracker, but our thighs are well padded and the feeling we want to give and receive is one of massage, not fisticuffs. That should not be construed as meaning that I don't like a gancho that goes off with some spirit. I do – very much. It's the difference between a firm handshake and a bone-cruncher, that's all.

For me, the gancho can either be slow and controlled or quite brisk, as the music suggests it. What really matters most is that the thigh contact is made before any foot flies at all, and, when in doubt, followers should take it easy. The action of the follower's leg is led from the thigh, with the knee down and the lower leg loose. It is not an action where there is any focus on the foot as if attempting to flick it through a gap. If you must think about the foot then imagine that it should be scraped backwards along the floor as long as possible, as if you are trying to wipe something off it onto a doormat. I hope that doesn't sound too disgusting!

I have just described a very safe gancho but there are many others. I particularly like leading my follower to my right side and inviting her to step close to and outside my right leg with her right leg and well past my right foot. I need a generous forward step from her so I must lead her to make one. It is my experience that this is more likely as she vacates the cross (cruzada) position, but this may well be a feature of my particular way of leading more than a follower tendency in itself. The aim of inviting her to take this step is that our right thighs should be touching at the end of it.

This is similar to the position she takes when stepping into a forward ocho to my right, but we need to be much closer together. The difference is that I do not facilitate a forward ocho but actually 'close the door' on her by staying forward and maintaining a slight left-facing torso. I then invite her to reverse her right leg back to where she came from, but as she does so I place my right thigh behind hers and she performs a gancho against my right leg up from behind to in front of me. If I were to look down, I should be able to read the price ticket on the sole of her shoe, rising between my legs. Very safe, this. She can't make contact with me (or anyone else) with the gancho foot, which stays within the safety zone created by our embrace. In this situation, where, from a leg point of view, she is positioned a little behind me and to my right, I can gancho between her legs too, knowing from the firm feel of our thighs where her leg is. In fact, in almost any position where you end up with the backs of your thighs touching each other, either of you could gancho.

Leader ganchos

Thinking about the leader's gancho, a fairly easy variety can be achieved from what I shall call the 'up close sandwich'. From any sidestep the leader can introduce his free foot to the inside of the follower's weight-bearing foot. As the follower closes, she sandwiches the leader's foot. At the same time as he positions his foot to be sandwiched, the leader closes the gap between his partner and himself by placing his weight forward onto the intruding foot. In this single movement the leader has acquired considerable control, and he is able to capitalise on it. Leaving the intruded foot next to the follower's weight-bearing foot, the leader steps back, obliging the follower to step forward on her free foot to maintain connection. The couple are in a slightly overlapped cross system here, and the leader has complete control and knows with pinpoint certainty where his follower's forward leg is placed and that it must stay put until he moves forward. The leader, therefore, knows where the gap is between the follower's legs, and freeing his forward foot he may rotate his pelvis to gancho through that gap.

A rather trickier leader gancho that I like is possible if the leader simply induces the follower to take a good-sized forward step towards him. As he releases his weight from one leg, the other can be left forward and curl carefully behind the follower's advancing leg, which should be fixed and slightly bent as she comes forward. This is quite a cheeky little move, requiring a bit of care, and you have to commit yourself to it quite boldly, in my experience. Any delay and you are quite likely to be caught by the advancing back leg. The move to insinuate your leg behind the follower's must be quick and accompanied by a slight forward movement of the torso to arrest her forward movement. Placing the follower into the 'up close sandwich' position is a great deal safer, and there are several other possibilities of variations from that position too. After all, we really do not want our followers to feel the up close sandwich and know it is always followed by the leader gancho.

The leader gancho I have just described is very safe because it arises from a stable, static position that is entirely in the leader's control. More exciting possibilities are offered whenever the follower offers a predictable gap in, for example, the giro or the ocho. In a forward ocho to the leader's right, particularly after the cross, it is perfectly simple for the leader to gancho the follower's forward right leg with his own right leg.

There are two keys to the success and safety of this manoeuvre. One is that the leader's weight is fully committed and balanced forward on his left foot. The other is the leader's ability to dissociate so that, as he leads the forward ocho by a right upper body rotation, he ensures that his pelvis stays facing the front at the very least. It is better still if it faces a little away from her. Turning your backside to your follower may

152

not seem polite but does allow you to make contact between the back of your right thigh and that of the follower's right thigh and bend your right leg backwards to wrap it up. Even on the move, if you are in thigh-to-thigh contact and the leader's foot movement is at right angles to the space between the follower's feet, the chances of damage are small. This gancho resolves simply by the leader replacing his foot. It is neither elegant nor necessary for the leader to lift his leg out with his knee up to his chin, as is sometimes seen.

Ganchos are great fun but can be dangerous to ourselves and other couples around us, so they have a minor role in social dancing. It would be nice to occasionally see a gancho that fitted the music and was not just being done for the sake of it. However...we only dance for fun don't we? – and I am beginning to sound too serious already. Besides, I am as guilty as anyone I know of the irrelevant gancho.

I suppose we ought to think for a moment about what we are going to do after the gancho. Because it is such a fun thing to do, I notice a tendency in me to concentrate very much on the lead-up to the gancho, and then inspiration fails me. It's almost as if I want a few moments to sit back, watch an action replay and break for adverts. It is very tempting to be like this because, at the moment of the gancho, our senses are heightened to the present and not thinking forward at all. We can actually allow the momentum of the gancho to solve the problem. I mean, if you walk into a door we all know which direction you will take just after impact; the opposite one – right? But for the gancho that we have deliberately led we should not be suffering the same dazed surprise. We knew the door was there, we shut it and we had our hand on the handle. Surely we have the power to open it too? One teacher of mine teases with ganchos, and I like to do it too, but I'm not sure that I am at all elegant when I do. He leads the gancho and intrudes the limb, but a fraction of a second before impact takes it out again to allow the giro to continue as before. It looks great and, when I pull it off, it seems to cause some mirth at the very least.

Finally, after years of leading ganchos that were not accepted, being kicked by followers who chose to attempt a gancho when one was not offered, I come to something of a sad conclusion. Perhaps ganchos share a similarity with some universal but unattractive personal habits that I am too much of a gentleman to mention. Could it be be that they are suitable only for consenting adults in private?

The parada

The parada is a stop, or is sometimes called a 'catch'. The leader arrests the current action of the follower by a sudden and clear signal of deceleration. This is, as you might expect, indicated from the torso, but it is also usually accompanied by a touch of the leader's foot against his follower's, lending the illusion that the woman's foot has been 'caught' by the man's. This is an area of considerable misunderstanding in social dancing; in fact it seems to me that, if I really want to throw a follower into a 'wobbly', this is the way to do it. I suspect it may be for two reasons. The first is that it seems not to be widely taught at all. Secondly, and much more importantly, many followers do not appear to grasp that the lead will always come from the chest and that they should not concern themselves at all with the actions of my feet.

The stop is not indicated by the foot touch, as so many people seem to believe. The stop would and should have happened anyway because of the lead for a stop from my chest. I stopped moving my chest and, by stopping it moving, I had hoped to stop my partner moving too. The foot touch serves to signal that something new might happen next. Therefore, I can use a parada as a tease in its own right, but often I like to use it as a prelude to a movement that requires a particular body position and the follower's complete attention. In my experience it is a piece of the tango language that is often poorly understood by followers, and I think that this is because many followers fail to recognise that it means only that they should be alert to developments. Some have been so used to sequencing that they make the assumption that any foot stop manoeuvre is the first element of a particular figure. By now, I hope you have realised that this is much too simplistic a view for the 'real' tango.

If you have followed my thoughts as far as this section you may have grasped that I disapprove of sequencing, but at least the follower who expects the next move to be the 'usual' one has received the message that something is going to happen. With luck, from here onwards she can be surprised enough in the dance to stop making assumptions. A much more disturbing thing for a leader is when he has well placed a parada, only to find that the inexperienced follower takes her foot away. This has happened to me frequently and it never fails to throw me. One day I will work out some sort of strategy for progressing that makes the assumption that this negative response to my invitation is bound to happen. On the other hand, the fact that the follower is in a position to remove her foot means that either she is not respecting the lead or that I have allowed her to transfer her weight too much onto the other foot.

It may also be that the foot touch has distracted her from the chest lead and I may have moved too soon to touch or touched too forcefully. The follower who prefers to dance at arm's length and does not understand the maintenance of the frame and floats in and out seems much more likely to take her foot away than the closer, well-connected follower.

The problem may be that we often place a parada at the moment when we know that the follower is fully committed onto one foot, and we hope to stop the other one moving by giving it a signal to stay put. The inexperienced follower can easily remove the foot because it bears no weight and wrongly reads the parada as a sacada. Reasonably, then, she removes the foot. The bigger problem is that the leader becomes focused on what he wants to do with his foot, forgets to lead with his chest and alters the balance of his own axis in an attempt to place a foot where it has no place to be. The signals to a follower must then be a mass of confusion.

So, the big message for one and all is that the parada is a full stop, led from the chest. And that's it; nothing more and nothing less. The foot

Corrientes   _Photo   DM_

touch is at least an embellishment, a tease, and might lead on to something else, but it is not the way to stop a follower. It is, however, an excellent way to trip a follower up, particularly if she does not have relaxed ankles!

There is a useful form of parada that is not capable of being misinterpreted, and I shall describe it now. It is a very useful tool for lots of reasons.

The leader leads a simple step to his left, but instead of closing his right foot to his left he places it forward, beside the follower's right foot, so that as she brings up her left foot to close she meets it. This is a 'follower sandwich' position. This intrusion of the leader's right foot is felt as a strong and surprising signal and usually stops the follower in her tracks, as desired. The still body posture of the leader also reinforces the signal that the follower is to stop where she is. From this position, all sorts of possibilities open. For example, it lends itself to a very reliable 'foot lead' that I was taught by Alex Krebs, who pointed out to me that, if from this position I merely rotated my chest to the left, my partner would perform a pivot in anticipation of a backward step around me to my left. The subtle movement of my foot induces the opposite pivot. It has never failed me yet.

If the leader twists his right foot to his right, he is giving a signal to the follower for a rotation of her body to her right, and from this he may lead a forward ocho to his left. If you remember the 'rule' about pigeon toeing you will realise that, if you had wanted to lead an ocho to your right from this sort of parada, the parada foot would generally have to be your left one. I find that this 'foot lead' is particularly useful in close embrace, where I find that the usual signals for leading an ocho are that much more difficult – I suspect that some would say impossible. This variation on the forward left ocho is all the more elegant because the follower is obliged to lift her foot over the leader's foot and ankle to manage the ocho, and this is a flattering move for the follower. However much this is true, followers should not get into the habit of picking their feet up to perform ochos where no relevant obstruction exists, because without needing to lift the foot to step over an obstruction this foot lift looks 'cheesy'.

The leader may simply use this parada to effect a pause for whatever reason and may release it by leading a step back in the direction they came from. If he does so and it is to his right he must be absolutely sure he has space to do that. Frequently on a crowded dance floor, if a couple take a sidestep in towards the middle of the floor and pause long enough, the space they have just vacated will be soon filled. Remember too that any step back is towards the 'blind' side; the closed side of the embrace. He might also do so by taking the parada foot out and stepping back on it, obliging the follower to step towards him on her left foot, assuming that he has not asked her to ground it already. If, however, the couple are in the general line of dance and have just paused, the chance that any back step a leader might take would cause a collision is great.

Many of us use the parada extensively for its ability to lead a change of direction or mood and as a precursor for the sandwich and all of its variations. Perhaps, however, the next most useful application of the parada (for me, personally) is as the fun entrance to the 'barrida', or sweep.

The barrida

The Spanish verb 'barrer' means to sweep, and the action of the barrida is to sweep the follower's foot from one place to another. The most important, if rather obvious, thing for us leaders to realise is that, for the follower's foot to be swept anywhere at all, it must be bearing absolutely no weight whatever.

The barrida can be another tango illusion, giving the impression that the leader has swept the follower's foot to one side. The reality is that the follower has moved her foot in response to a specific body lead by the leader, but the leader has kept his foot touching hers. The illusion is even more impressive when the leader's foot appears to draw the follower's foot behind it, as if by 'magnetic' forces. There is a classic move in which the leader does indeed heave the follower's foot around, called the 'arrastre'. The word means a drag. I think it is less elegant and depends more on a knowing co-operation between partners. The barrida as taught to me is based elegantly on simple tango logic and works well anywhere as long as we understand how it works. For me, a sweep is more delightful and seductive than a drag, any day.

To enable you to visualise this, let us consider a simple form of barrida, which starts from the easy parada of the right foot insertion. I will remind you that the leader has stepped to his left and now stands, weight on left foot, right foot between the feet of the follower, whose weight is on her right foot. The leader now leads a full step back to his right but with a little right rotation of his chest, so that the follower steps with her left foot in a slight curve around the leader. He, for his part, keeps his weight on his left foot and moves his right foot so that it stays in contact with the inside of the follower's left. The effect is that it appears that the leader has swept the follower's left foot in a small arc around him. The reality is that, after indicating the step, all the leader did was time his right foot movement to keep it where it was in relationship to the follower's left foot.

For a long time I found this quite tricky to do without pressing her foot too much or, on the other hand, being left behind. The reason for this was all to do with my own poor balance skill. I had two faults. One was looking down at the feet. Where did I think they would be, anyway? Thankfully, I learned to visualise where the feet were by looking to see where my follower's shoulders were. What a delight to discover that the feet were not enjoying a life of their own but were attached to my follower and – until she fell over – generally obliged to carry her weight! I know it sounds silly and obvious, but you'd be surprised to discover how long it took me to work that out. The other big breakthrough for me was Stephanie's mantra. "I concentrate on my standing leg." No more falling over, cracking heads together and other forms of non-tango foolishness. After all, if I can stand on my own without a partner, balance on one foot and place the free foot anywhere it will reach, why can't I do that in the arms of a woman?

Once I have swept the follower's foot, what do I do now? Well, if I can make this work one way, surely I can lead the reverse? "What could be easier?" you might think. Actually, maintaining contact with the follower's foot when mine is behind it is a lot easier because I can adjust the pressure to keep up with her. When we make the return trip, remember, my foot travels ahead of hers. It is so easy for me to move my foot too quickly and our two feet become disconnected. Again, I am so often tempted to try to judge the movement by looking at the feet, and that becomes a self-fulfilling prophecy. I worry that I will lose touch; I look down, so I lose my balance and – for sure – we lose touch. How much better to time my foot to travel under her shoulder and keep my head up. The illusion is all the better for it, too. The follower does not sweep the leader's foot back, though she can help a bit with the illusion.

Fig. 1 James enjoys foot play. Here he has led Isabelle into the back step of a giro to his left. At the same time, he has placed his free right foot beside her right before asking her to take a step to her right and around his axis. He knows that the effect of his giro lead is that Isabelle's right foot will now travel from his right side to his left.

Fig. 2 As Isabelle steps right, honouring the giro lead, James pivots on his left foot, allowing his right foot to travel with Isabelle's. It has not pushed it; this is another of those tango illusions we so love. The primary concern is the giro lead, not the foot play. Given the lead from James's chest, Isabelle would have taken that step whether his foot accompanied or not.

Sometimes, however, I find it nicer not to lead the return journey but to close left to right foot as a resolution, and use this movement for a quarter turn to the right. I depend, of course, on my follower doing the decent thing and closing her right foot to her left and resuming the parada position in any case, unless I rotate back to the left.

As ever, almost anything that can be done in tango to the right side can be done to the left. What follows is one of the exceptions as far as I am concerned, because, the embrace being asymmetrical, it feels very odd to me.

From my experience, this next example is a much more interesting barrida, which can be done from the same parada position between the feet. The leader indicates a strong left rotation so that both partners pivot on their weight-bearing feet to the left, ending right hip to right hip. The follower feels the need to step back on her left foot because the leader keeps turning, and she does so. Their hips should be in line but, just to make it plain, the leader's feet and pelvis face one way and the follower's the exact opposite. The feet are not in line. The result of the pivot means that, while the couple's left feet are facing squarely in the opposite direction, the parada foot of the leader has been left behind his centre of gravity. This foot is still hooked round the right foot of his follower, which is stretched in front of her centre of gravity.

The leader's right foot is now in a position to sweep the follower's right foot. This is forward for him but, of course, backwards for her. I like to think of their 'joined' feet as the swing and their left legs as the support for the swing. Having swept the follower's foot, the leader has a choice. He can swing it back, looking as if he has drawn it back by 'animal magnetism', and from there he can take a back step into the follower's active sandwich position and let her choose how she plays with that. Alternatively, from this same position the leader can lead a forward ocho to his left very easily. He may, however, choose to step up to the sandwich position himself after one forward sweep. Choices, choices; what a great fun dance this is!

An elegant barrida is also possible from the sandwich position. The follower has her weight fully on her back foot and is capable of pivoting on it in either direction, leaving the other foot stretched out in front of her. Therefore, from the sandwich, the leader may step in either direction with one foot, using the other to sweep the follower's free foot. This is a good juncture to re-emphasise that the barrida is an illusion. The leader does not move the follower's foot with his. The leader induces a foot movement by the follower and allows his foot to accompany it. Forcefully scooping the follower's foot from place to place is

Practica   *Photo DCT* usually a recipe for disaster, though I have been taught to do so in a class given by a teacher of sequences and it worked well enough when it was all expected and rehearsed. I have never managed it successfully in social dancing, whereas the illusion method is very reliable.

Since the follower's free foot would describe a circle if the leader went all the way round and she rotated on her weight-bearing leg, the leader needs to step and sweep along the circumference of that circle. I think it would be rather boring for the follower if you swept round much more than a short section.

Imagine, then, that the follower has her weight well back over her left foot and her right foot is sandwiched. The leader may step to his left and slightly around to the right side of the follower, then, once his weight is fully on his left foot and he is well balanced, he can sweep the follower's right foot to her right with his right foot in a quarter circle.

My friend Al has perfected a lovely little barrida that he often uses when simply walking forward. He makes it look so easy. Walking simply to begin with in parallel, he changes into cross system and uses his free foot to trap and deflect the nearest follower's foot to himself, moving it across the mid-line. The deflection is minimal and it puts the lady into the cross (cruzada) position on whichever side he elects. I'm sure I have seen well-known football stars doing the same thing, but from behind and just outside the box, of course. I mention this just to remind us all that if we scoop our follower's foot in front of the other and just keep on walking we may both end up with a penalty, and the leader may well find himself sent off!

Now, here is another type of barrida that I really enjoy. If I lead a conventional giro to my left I know that at some point my follower will be pivoting and taking a back step. As she pivots, her right foot will be near to me and fairly static for a while before it sets off to sidestep across me. If I have my weight on my left foot as I pivot round to accompany the giro I can allow my right foot to trail somewhat lazily and in a relaxed fashion, and it quite naturally comes up to hook round the follower's weight-bearing foot. Then, as she takes her normal sidestep, I make sure my right foot stays with her right foot. She actually does nothing more than the giro that was led. It all sounds so simple, but there are often problems in practice. What I frequently find is that the very touch of the foot unsettles an inexperienced follower, who commonly fails to continue the giro and the whole idea has to be abandoned. It feels really good when it works, however.

I wish I could tell you that I could manage this to the left side of me as well as to the right, but I simply can't. I am sure I am not alone in

161

this. All manoeuvres in the giro to the closed side of the embrace feel much more awkward, and, human nature being what it is, most of us take the line of least resistance. I will make it look and feel easier in the end if I work on it enough. It's just that, at present, I am having so much fun doing it the easy way!

I am sure that, once they understand the principles involved, any couple could invent all sorts of amusing variations around these three elements of the tango language. They share several things in common. They test the couple's relationship and connection and they can produce uncomfortable experiences for the dancers and those dancing around them. Perhaps I am being over-critical but, while they have their place in terms of improvisation and interpretation, I have yet to see many couples fit them into the music really well.

CHAPTER 10

Sacadas

The Spanish word 'sacar' means to take out, or to extract, and when a sacada is performed it looks as if one dancer has 'taken out' the other's leg, as if with a kick or a nudge. Like many things in tango, this is, to some extent, an illusion; there has often been minimal contact between the legs of the dancers. There must be some contact though, however slight and brushing, for the sacada to work. If we can agree that tango is a conversation in body language between two people, a sacada is an interruption. In purely mechanical terms, one dancer interrupts the movement intention of the other, during a step, by intruding a leg into the line that was to have been taken

Kenny and Natalie   *Photo DM*

by his or her partner's free leg. The leg that receives the sacada is obliged to take a detour, at least even if only a small one, in an attempt to arrive at its original destination.

Another way of thinking about this is to imagine that, in the sacada, the one dancer places his or her leg in a position that will cut the line between the other partner's legs. When I first tried to effect a sacada, I was taught that the important feature was the placing of my foot for the interruption. I was told that my intruding foot should be placed as near as possible to the foot of my partner that was about to depart for a new position. Finally, I was taught that I had to take my weight forward onto the intruding leg. I could understand the logic of this approach but it produced several distinct problems for me that, for years, made sacadas become movements that I only managed in class and never in social dancing. Fixating on the placing of my foot led me into bad habits of looking downwards and made me anxious about treading on my partner. Looking downwards ruined my balance and the anxiety about foot placing stopped me thinking about the real issues for the sacada, which are simply these: where is the leg we are intending to sacada moving from; and where is it moving to? Failing to perform a sacada became a self-fulfilling prophecy. The more anxious I became that I would hurt my partner the more likely it was that I would do so. The outcome was that I simply shied away from even trying.

In classes and even in social dancing I have watched others effect sacadas by grotesque heaving movements of their legs. So keen were they to produce a displacement that they treated their follower's leg as if it were a weight to be shifted over with a mighty thrust. I feel sure I have done the same thing at times. The reason is that we just have failed to understand these simple mechanics of the movement. If the follower tries to step and her leg encounters an intrusion to one side of it, the leg will be unable to change its position in a straight line and will have to arrive by a curved route. As a leader all I need to do is be able to intrude a leg enough, in the right place and at the correct time, and the follower's action should be inevitable and natural. Well, that is true if my follower has learned to receive a sacada by being well balanced on her weight-bearing leg and permitting her free leg full freedom of movement. It's a tall order. It is a wonderful example of the eternal paradox within tango. Movements that look simple can be surprisingly difficult to learn to do well.

I have lost count of the times that, in a class, a mystified student has asked the teacher to explain the difference between the lead for a gancho and a sacada. The confusion is understandable because, of course, both these manoeuvres are interruptions of the follower's leg movement. Similarly, I have frequently danced with women who read any interruption as a gancho whether there was space for one or not, and cheerfully kicked me. This is one painful reason why I wish to take a little time to explain how both interruptions work. Sadly, many who teach seem to believe that the main difference is the spot in which the leader places his foot for the intrusion. Thus I have been told many times that, for the gancho, the foot is placed near to the follower's weight-bearing leg and, for the sacada, to the non-weight-bearing leg. While these statements can both be true, up to a point, these foot positions are not enough to ensure that the gancho or the sacada actually happen. It is a bit like telling a learner driver that when the red traffic light turns to green the car goes forward. The two things are connected, but not by direct cause and effect. There are issues that relate to gear levers and throttle and clutch that actually get the job done.

The biggest breakthrough for me was to finally understand

the timing of the interaction between the two legs: the intruder and the interrupted leg. Let me use the model of tango as a language again. If we are chatting and I want to interrupt you in a sentence I must do it after you have started and before you have stopped. I have a range of choices of timing my interruption from during the first word to within the last one. My success of getting a word in edgeways will depend on my timing. So it is with the successful sacada.

As my follower steps, she creates a space between her feet that starts small, widens to about 50 cm (more or less), then closes as she collects her legs. This is the gap into which I must intrude my leg. In the journey her leg will take, I want it to encounter my leg softly and be deflected, maybe not much, but enough to feel different to her and look different to an observer. This means that my leg must be in place before her 'receiving' leg gets to the midway stage, as a rule. I must intrude, therefore, in the early phase of her step. Just think of the implication this has for the timing of my movement. If she is stepping crisply on the beat, she will have collected her legs and feet on the beat. If I think I can place my foot on the same beat it will always be too soon or too late. It simply will not matter which of her feet I want to place mine next to.

Just imagine what a breakthrough this revelation was to me. All those years of thinking that I had to step on the beat and shove a foot somewhere and always discovering there was no 'somewhere' left.

If all I need to do is ensure that I oblige the moving leg to deviate, I want a follower who steps evenly and predictably and, because I can sense where her upper body is, I know where the gap should be. If she steps on the beat, I know *when* the gap is available. Now I need to learn how to feel the beat, not from my own steps but from hers, so that I can move exactly when I need to. If I insist on timing my step to the identical moment she times hers, there is no gap and we collide. I should point out here that I am referring to the sort of sacada in which the leader places his intruding leg 'on the wing', so to speak, as he too is moving. A much simpler set of sacadas is possible when the follower is induced to step around a leader leg that is already in place and waiting.

Another difference between the gancho and the sacada also crops up in lessons almost every time. This is the business of the leader's weight. It is undoubtedly true that, for the gancho, the intruded leg should not bear weight. This is a great deal safer because, when the intruded leg is relaxed into an 'S' shape, it is less likely to be injured than a stiff leg. Moreover, when the leader intrudes his free leg he is able to raise its heel, which allows this thigh to adopt a position that is a little nearer to the horizontal, allowing a more successful gancho. In comparison, the intruding leg for the sacada can bear weight. It is not essential that it does and, indeed, the very simplest and safest sacadas I have been taught are with the intrusion of a free leg. It is an obstruction, but this time not for wrapping around. The obstructing leg for a sacada needs to be rather more vertical than for the gancho. Unless the leader continues to lead a step, the follower will stop and her moving leg will not come up to the obstruction at all. The movement of the axis, however, can be rotational. It is just that we leaders must lead a step across our bodies so that we have a line to cut in the first place.

The point of contact with a sacada is usually lower down the leg than for the gancho – even as low as the ankle. I would suggest, however, that for the most comfortable and successful sacadas the impact between the legs occurs at mid-shin level, where there is softer flesh for the meeting.

If the foot of the intruding leg is placed too soon, or nearer the follower's new weight-bearing foot, both dancers will be attempting to occupy the same space if this intruding foot of the leader is soon to bear weight too. The timing of the placement of the intruding foot is critical. If the intrusion takes place before the axis of the follower has passed the mid-point between the start and finish of her step there is the potential for impact between the dancers' bodies.

You are already familiar with the concept of the axis: that imaginary rod that runs vertically down through the top of the dancer's head to the ground and about which the body may be spun smoothly. Remember that when we take a step we shift the whole axis from one balanced position to the next. Much of what we learn to do in simple walking and connection is to avoid embarrassing the axis of our partner. In a sacada one dancer deliberately attempts to interrupt the step during the shift of axis by invading the space of the other. This could result in the invaded dancer losing balance but, when we learn about the sacada, we learn to respond to that invasion by a change of direction and posture, which preserves the axis. The sacada, therefore, is a method by which a leader induces a natural, even instinctual, balance-preserving movement in the follower.

Well, that is one philosophy, and in a perfect world it might work well enough. The reality is that just as a leader needs to learn how to place a sacada, a follower needs to be taught how to receive one. You will not be surprised to discover that the basic necessities for leader and follower alike are sound balance on the supporting leg and relaxation of the free leg.

I am sure that a couple, just left to their own devices, could imagine many different ways this might be achieved. Just think of all the ways a partner might be induced to step; think about the gap between the feet you are left with; and think of all the possible ways you might insert your lower leg into the gap. Indeed, if you can think of a way that a dancer might insert one or other foot between the widely spaced feet of his or her partner, you may guarantee that it will have been done in tango.

To make this clearer, I will describe the simplest form of sacada I know; the one I had least difficulty with, even when I was in my most frustrated/demoralised state about all this. The leader indicates a reasonably wide sidestep to his left but keeps his own weight on his right

James has set up for a sacada. He is leading Isabelle to take a side step to her right as part of a giro to his left. By intruding his lower right leg next to her left leg he makes it impossible for her to collect her feet together directly. Her left leg will be obliged to make a small semi-circular detour around the obstruction so that she will be able to continue the giro.

foot to keep his left foot free. Because we need to keep close for this to work this sidestep is a curved one, and my biggest problem here is always remembering to allow my left hand to go back as I lead the step. If I cramp my follower's right hand she is likely to step away from me, and if she does so the only way I can intrude a leg is to lunge it forward, ruin my balance and perhaps give a lead towards her that I had not intended. As the follower steps to her right, and as she is beginning to transfer weight onto her right foot, the leader places his left leg straight forward to come to a position centrally between her legs; or, if to one side at all, it's better to be just inside the follower's left leg, with the foot – if anything – a little past it. We are going to interrupt the line that the follower's left leg will make as it tries to collect to the right, so I find it helpful to ask myself if my action really will interrupt that line. Remember that I suggested the leader should indicate a good-sized step. You really do want the follower to commit herself to a generous step here, both to give you a good space to aim for without looking down at your feet and for the momentum this manoeuvre needs to succeed.

If I stay still, our legs make contact and a small, stress-free sacada results. I can now enhance the drama of the moment and the size of the sacada by moving my weight onto the intruding leg. I transfer my weight forward onto my left foot while at the same time continuing to lead the giro to the left. This is where a simple movement has the potential to become a complete mess; and I am the man to do it. To avoid disaster I have to time this forward movement and rotation to enable me to occupy the airspace my follower has just vacated. I have stepped directly forward and pivoted to my left to stay connected to my follower. The timing is critical. The rotation is essential not just to maintain the frame, as usual, but also to provide the impetus for the sacada. This impetus means that my follower's left leg quite naturally swings out, away from my leg, almost as if it has been kicked away. The follower's left leg should swing away from the hip and the movement of the whole leg should feel quite natural. This movement of the leg may be sufficiently flamboyant to look at and feel different, but, of course, not enough to kick somebody or lose balance.

At the end of the movement the leader closes right foot to left and has taken an (approximately) 90-degree left turn. The follower's left leg may also return to close to the right, but it looks much more elegant, to my eye, if it continues its natural swing to come to rest with the left ankle just behind the right, without bearing weight. You will not be surprised to hear that this can be done on the opposite side too, and that couples will discover that they find it easier to do one way or another.

I want to be very clear about this. The sacada will not happen unless the leader's intruding leg cuts the line that the follower's free leg would take to allow her to collect her legs together. It is also likely to be a failure if the follower is one who does not collect properly anyway. The added force of the more flamboyant sacada is merely because the leader moves his body weight forward onto the intruding foot. This action is potentially much more destabilising to the follower, who is obliged to take a bigger action to restore her equilibrium. Her leg may swing much more widely, if not wildly, as she is obliged to pivot. For this reason, I am strongly of the belief that, for beginners, it is better to learn to invite the

Fig. 1 As Annette has stepped backwards, Sam has pivoted on her right foot to free her left leg for a backward sacada entrance, close to Annette's departing foot. Notice the extreme level of dissociation that Sam achieves to maintain full connection with Annette while, at the same time, keep the original leading intention along the line of dance.

Fig.2 Annette attempts to collect her left leg to her right but Sam's intruding soft calf prevents that. Annette chooses to lift her leg out to detour the obstruction. Notice how Sam's upper body control prevents Annette from pivoting to her left but keeps her firmly aligned. Sam may indeed lead the pivot here but it will be her choice and not enforced upon her by poor technique

follower to step around a static, non-weight-bearing intruded leg for a gentle, pleasant sacada before progressing to a manoeuvre that has such potential for imbalance and traumatising the local population on the dance floor.

From my experience, a more difficult form of sacada is executed when the leader places his foot backwards – that is, heel first – between the follower's feet. This variation of intrusion is the one I love to see most; it looks so much more aggressive and gives a greater impression that the leader has kicked the follower's leg away. It is so much more flamboyant, partly because of the determined way a leader is obliged to place his body to prepare for the intrusion. Think of the backhand, in tennis, in comparison to the forehand; much more dramatic. This movement has to be done with a great deal of care, but the sacada I shall describe is relatively easy to do because it begins from a relatively static and controlled position. It fits in nicely after the follower has been led towards a left backward ocho and is positioned with her weight on her left foot, which is behind her.

The leader 'paradas' the follower's forward right foot as if he is about to complete a sandwich, and steps forward onto the parada left foot and rotates towards the left to confront the follower squarely. It looks as if he is to finish the sandwich, but instead of doing so he steps over his left foot well towards the follower's right. He has therefore crossed his right thigh over his left and so needs to rotate his upper body well to the right to maintain the frame. The idea is to step forward and across so deeply that there will be space behind him. The leader must dissociate very considerably, so that his toes are pointing one way and his upper body almost exactly the opposite way. Now, I know you are thinking this is anatomically impossible and, of course, you are right.

What I want to convey is that the leader makes sure his undercarriage is backed up to his follower while maintaining somehow the *presence* of his upper body in the opposite direction. I twist as much as I can and cheat a bit to make up for the fact that I am not an eel. I find that if I move my left hand forward to restrict my follower's desire to move, and also turn my head to my right too, I get the desired effect. After all, if my follower has received a signal from my chest to come round to my left, she will do it before I place the intrusion and the sacada will fail. With my weight now well forward on my right foot, I can release my left foot and place it behind my follower's right foot. The trick to prevent injury to the follower is to let the free hip open, allowing the foot to rotate so that it advances towards the danger zone with heel and toe close to the floor. If I have dissociated well, I will be placing my foot straight backwards, not crossing my legs at all.

Another vital ingredient, before any leader moves a hard heel backwards towards his partner's ankles, is to collect his legs neatly together, heels touching. This ensures that the intruding foot begins its perilous path from 'neutral', directly under the leader's axis. If he has positioned himself correctly with lots of dissociation, a straight backwards movement of the foot should find the gap between her feet. If you want to thread a needle, you line up first, not as you advance the thread.

This piece of advice is all the more important when attempting the sort of flashy backward sacada that follows a wide planeo or lapiz. The free leg has left the 'safety zone' of neutral to take a wide detour. That certainly helps the dissociation. The problems arise when the anxious leader tries the backward sacada using a flailing leg that, naturally, approaches the gap at an angle. It is a bit like attempting to convert a try from the touchline.

170

How much safer it is smack in front of the posts? The massage is simply this. Learn to finish planeos and lapiz collected, in neutral, with knee and ankles together, just like every other step.

Once the intruding lower leg is in place, safely between the follower's legs, the sacada happens as the follower attempts to collect her legs as she continues the giro. Soft calf should meet soft calf. The well-placed static leg is intrusion enough, but we can make it more dramatic. As before, if the leader moves his axis backwards something more powerful happens. The leader, sure he has found a safe place for his foot, can lower his heel and move his axis backwards onto his left forefoot. He does not step backwards onto his heel. As he steps back, he leads the same leftward rotation that actually makes the follower move and causes the sacada to happen. When you have been in a state of extreme dissociation, this is no hardship! The effect of this is to gently nudge the follower's right leg outwards with the soft back of the right thigh, although the real impetus for what happens next is induced by the follower's attempt to stay connected and pivot to her left to enable her to move right. The follower, feeling this lead, swings the right leg up and outwards to perform a boleo as flamboyantly as she likes. (For an explanation of this in greater depth you might turn to chapter 12.)

Another interesting form of sacada is possible in straight walking but it requires that the leader convert at some stage to the cross system. The easiest way to be in the correct position is to be walk in parallel and direct the follower over to walking to the leader's right side by dissociation. If you remember, this means that the leader continues to walk straight along the line of dance but rotates his upper body to the right so that the two dancers are making 'four tracks in the snow', not two. The leader takes a conventional right step but, in half a beat, brings his left foot up behind the right and immediately steps again with his right. This time, instead of continuing along the line of dance, the leader steps in line with the way his chest faces, directly at the follower at about 45 degrees to the line of dance. The timing of these three steps is slow-quick-slow. The follower does not double step because it has not been led; if she did it would be a disaster. The leader's change of weight occurs when his follower has already committed to her normal back step, in any case. The leader needs to be sure that his second, right step will land in the gap between the follower's feet, just behind her left foot, and slightly before it leaves to go backwards. To avoid leading this as a double step, the leader must avoid at all costs any shoulder 'rock and roll' that might convey the impression of a double step. He might consider leaving the quick left foot to the last moment and concentrating on keeping his chest advancing at the same rate towards the follower. If the left foot steps forward too soon, or is accompanied by a sudden deceleration of his upper body, some well-tuned followers will skip a beat to try to stay in parallel. After all, we do lead double steps often enough. Incidentally, the simplest way to change weight as a leader without being followed by your partner is to do so when her feet are apart. When she is collected, she too can change weight – which is just as well when you want her to.

Let us assume that we have effected the weight change as planned and proceed to the sacada. If the intrusion of the leader's leg has been successful, as the follower attempts to step back on her left foot her calf softly meets the back of the leader's right calf. At the same time the follower has become aware that there has been a 45-degree shift in direction. The follower, therefore, allows her relaxed left leg to swing out left slightly to negotiate around the leader's right leg and describe a small arc to arrive at its weight-bearing point. I mean a small arc; not a wild swing. The leader must not think he is forcing the follower's leg out with his right knee. He steps forward naturally onto his right foot as if the follower was not there; he has merely performed a 'lock step' in double time and a 45-degree change of direction to his right. The effect of the sacada is incidental and caused by the accurate placing of his right leg.

While I have referred so far to the leader leading a sacada, this is because it is a more common situation at the basic levels of tango, but there is no reason why a follower could not perform a sacada on a leader. It is my belief that the sacada is one of those dance movements that looks deceptively easy but which is actually difficult to master. Not only does it need the intruder to grasp how it works to be able to deliver it, but it really also needs a partner to know how to receive the sacada. If we see the sacada as a movement inevitably initiated by a leader and received by a follower, we halve the fun. This is another good reason why it makes so much sense for us all to learn to be both leader and follower when we learn to tango.

Here is another difference I find between the sacada and the gancho. I find that the gancho is an essentially stable manoeuvre that depends above all else on a well-balanced, competent leader, but it can work well enough

172

with an inexperienced follower, even if it feels rough. If I successfully interrupt the leg movement of an inexperienced follower with a sacada, she can easily become anxious. It seems to me that the key to receiving the sacada is the relaxed leg of the follower and the moderate, but positive, response. Most leg intrusions are actually minimal but positive and ask for a fairly small deviation of the sacada-ed leg from its first intent. Huge flailing legs look unseemly and are inevitably followed by loss of balance. When followers react excessively to the sacada followed by a giro, they commonly take the back step over the mid-line. They have failed to grasp that, although the sacadaed leg is to deviate from a straight course to a curved one, it should ground on exactly the same spot it would have done had the sacada not occurred. Any further swing of the leg results in crossed legs, which inevitably interfere with balance and block the follower's hips from a full range of subsequent movements. In effect, the follower has taken a change of direction without her leader.

Finally, I have suggested that the sacada is performed by the leader intruding his leg into the line that the follower was going to take. There are other possibilities. For example, if the leader induces the follower to step over his already outstretched leg in a giro and continue in the same direction, her trailing leg will come up against his and be deflected. This will happen naturally, particularly if he has held his forward leg extended but not bearing weight and then transfers his weight onto it. He has effected a sacada 'in advance', so to speak, and is then able by means of reversing the lead of the giro and advancing his forward leg to sacada *both* of the follower's legs, one after the other. To manage this properly, the leader must realise that, as she progresses around him, the follower's axis shifts and he must extend the forward foot and move his mass onto it for the second sacada by aiming for the centre of his follower's axis. This is a tricky manoeuvre but feels and looks wonderful when it comes off. I find that it really only works for me in close embrace.

Follower Sacadas

I have already said that there is no reason why a follower should not perform a sacada on a leader but it is interesting to discover how difficult that appears to be for many followers. I think that there are two distinct problems that mean that, for all intents and purposes, the follower sacada is likely to be one of those moves that depends on regular partners working on a routine. The reasons are these. The sacada usually needs to be planned fractionally in advance. The leader who offers a sacada will have led towards the situation where he knows that the opportunity will present itself and is confident that it will be received. Many followers find taking the lead a hard thing to do at the best of times. We often play role reversal in class, obliging followers to lead and leaders to follow for the entire evening. It takes ages for followers to switch from feeling to planning and all sorts of crashes occur. I'm not saying that the leaders find it any easier to be followers; they don't. Some of them prove to be a nightmare faced with a small woman telling them what to do for a change. You would not have imagined that, would you?

It takes quite a sharp mind in an experienced follower to sense, in a moment, that they have been offered the chance of a sacada. Once they have entered fully into following and expecting 'la marca' for almost every move, they reach another plane. Leaving it is hard.

The other problem is that it becomes counter-intuitive for a follower to step actively into what is bound to feel like a dangerous position, close to the axis line of the leader. Followers get used to walking backwards, away from the chest of their leader and rarely find themselves taking more than a step or so towards him. This is simply because of the need for their leader to see where the couple are heading.

There are several nice opportunities for a follower to perform a sacada, most easily offered by the leader if he takes a forward step across the face of his follower, leaving his trailing leg, temptingly behind. He needs to lead the movement, however, by opening the frame to make her feel she wants to step towards him and this sometimes requires a good deal of dissociation on his part.

I have described a few examples of sacadas merely to illustrate the principle. The number of permutations that are possible is huge. The adolescent in me once cherished an ambition to manage a series of sacadas I once saw performed. It involved a sacada for each and every consecutive step of a giro with forward and backward intrusions. It looked amazing but of course was on stage and must have been rehearsed for hours and hours.

..

CHAPTER 11

The sandwich and the planeo

The sandwich

On the face of it there may be something faintly ridiculous about the name of this move, when all the other names sound so glamorous in Spanish to the English-speaking ear! The plain fact is that the Spanish word for that indispensable item of food, invented by the Earl of Sandwich so that he did not need to interrupt a card game, is 'el sanwich'. For some reason the 'd' is often left out. Now, here is a thought that tickles my funny bone. I have long realised that we English seem to see glamour in almost anything 'foreign'. We borrow words from other languages to dress up the reality a little. Underwear becomes 'lingerie', the best-quality goods are usually 'de luxe', and nowadays I am more impressed if my

Joanne and Dario *Photo DM*

gravy is a 'jus'. I feel confident that we prefer to think that a 'gancho' is so much nicer than a boring, mundane old 'hook'. Is this only an English idiosyncrasy? I doubt it. Could it be then that, to the Spanish-speaking ear, the only truly glamorous word in tango is 'sandwich'? There is another term for this manoeuvre – 'el mordida', coming from the Spanish verb 'morder': to bite – and I have read some quite ridiculous alternative reasons why it was called this, including one about a tanguero having a bite out of a sandwich while dancing. What a needless complication of a simple concept!

The sandwich position is one in which one of the dancers traps one foot of the other partner between both feet. One partner provides the bread and the other the filling. It doesn't matter who provides what too much. Commonly, the leader performs a sandwich on the follower, at least to begin with. The roles may then reverse as a sequence of foot play.

Indeed, it is a really good exercise in inventiveness for a couple to spend a few minutes developing different ways of reacting to the sandwich. I shall describe this in greater detail later on in this chapter.

I like to think of the sandwich as a form of 'playing footsie', as you might with the object of your affection under a dining table at a dinner party. I have always fantasised that the original purpose of this gesture was to test out the response of the lady in your arms while in the thicket of the dance floor. The benefit would have been that, if she was under the critical scrutiny of her chaperone (perhaps a beefy brother), he would not be able to see that you were being suggestive. She for her part would have the freedom to respond in kind if she fancied you and, on the other hand, ignore it if she did not.

There are lots of ways of leading a sandwich but the classic and easy way to do so would be from any form of parada. Perhaps the easiest of these is achieved at the back step of a backward ocho. I still remember where I was first taught the sandwich from this position. The reason I remember it so vividly is that the experience was such a culture shock that it ranks in my mind with remembering where I was when JFK was assassinated or on 9/11. Judith and I had been taught the basic eight fairly well but not even the backward ocho by that time. We were both terribly keen and went to any class we could. All tango teaching we were exposed to in those days was very similar to countless ballroom classes we had attended; lots of 'men do this, now ladies do that, and bolt-it-together' style lessons. At this particular time we had been encouraged by our teacher to join a class in a village hall, several miles away from our base, and which had a very pronounced sequence base to the teaching. Coming from a distance to an unfamiliar venue we arrived slightly late, so we felt flustered. A frosty welcome did not bode well for the evening. For a moment it looked as though we were not going to be allowed to join the class at all but the power of money and grovelling won in the end. Somehow or other, we stumbled through the class. We had only missed the warm-up in any case.

I remember being told to find the back ocho position without having a clue what the teacher meant, but watched and copied those around me. It was not so much tango but Ikea assembly. At least I had gathered that I should stop my follower's body at a point where her feet were apart but her weight was mostly on one leg and her non-weight-bearing foot was

Exchange of sandwiches (and related vulgarity)

Fig. 1 David sandwiches Judith's left foot. He holds all the power in this position. He could step back again or continue forward or even make a rotating chest lead. Judith will just have to wait and see.

Fig. 2 David steps back and Judith follows accepting the offer to place her foot so as to sandwich his foot, left as an invitation. Now she has more power. If he leads a forward step to his right, how will she respond?

Fig. 3 The shoeshine. I often think that this is quite a provocative, even vulgar gesture from a woman to a man and the higher the foot goes up your leg the more that is being suggested to you. Either that or she needed to clean her shoes.

Fig. 4 Once she has satisfied her desire to inflame him, Judith continues her step forward. The lead has not changed; it was always for her to step over the obstruction to his right. She simply did it her way. Quite right too!

forward. We were then told to parada the forward foot. Unfortunately, that particular teacher suggested that the foot touch was the reason my follower would stop where she was. Little wonder so many people believe that. I then found it quite easy, most of the time, to place one of my feet against the side of that forward foot, although we were very unstable as a couple by this time. Where it became more difficult was to step up with my other foot and place it to lightly trap my follower's foot on the opposite side without holding onto her for balance. At this time, of course, I had little idea where my feet or my partners' were and felt the need to look at them much of the time, as if they might actually leave of their own accord. This had a terrible effect on my own balance. Worse still, my partner's forward foot rarely ended up in the same place; sometimes I had to stretch out to connect with it. The wobble factor was maximal, most of the time. I look back on that lesson and so many others like it and it makes me even more determined to promote the Aguerrodi system of helping pupils understand the basic principles of movements and their consequences. The teaching of steps and figures by the 'because I say so' system may work for some dances, but not for tango.

Years later, thanks to el Chino, I came to understand so much better the reasons why some leads have the desired effect. I now know that, when I parada, I have arrested the follower's motion by stopping my chest lead and not by any action of my foot. I have learned to be able to stop my partner in a wide range of positions, including the one needed for the sandwich; with her weight mostly committed to one foot but before she feels able to collect her legs. Thanks to grasping the concept of upper body connection between partners, I am now able to sense where my partner's feet are from her upper body position so that my own balance is not ruined by looking at the ground. My follower has learned to follow and to step so that the frame is maintained and I can now lead her to take her back step in such a way that she is near me. I now move to be stable and balanced on one leg while the other is free for any action. The result? The effort of the parada is now minimal. Stepping in to the sandwich is always comfortable. In reality, these are such simple movements, but heavily dependent on very basic skills. If only more teachers would explain the logic of the body mechanics that allow a lead to produce the desired body positions of the follower, our understanding of the dance would be greater and our path to success smoother.

After years of social dancing I can now see clearly the obvious problem with this manoeuvre: it is that it is essentially static. On a busy flowing dance floor it would be a nuisance for following dancers for any couple to simply stop and occupy the next few minutes of music playing footsie. One reason I am not a devotee of the sequence system of learning tango is that, when I visit milongas where this is taught, there appears to be very little progression around the floor. Leaders in these venues see no reason why they should not stop and play, in the line of flow. It is plain why this should be so. Many of the other dancers are doing the same thing. They have, after all, devoted a good deal of time learning a 'figure' and want to do it as often as they can. I have watched a pair of dancers in a milonga perform the most involved set of sequences in the normal line of dance as if they were performing on a tiny stage. I will admit it was fun to watch, but less so for those in the mêlée behind them.

There is a right place for everything. This is where the 'snake pit' known as the centre of the dance hall could be used. Another place that lends itself nicely to such goings-on is the corner of the room, where it is useful to be able to use a move such as the sandwich to effect a turn, taking a reasonable amount of time doing so without impeding other dancers.

The beauty of the sandwich, however, is that it can be just another tango moment or it can occupy the entire song. The position can be held very briefly; perhaps for one beat only. A very useful exercise is that which is taught on the Daniel Trenner and Rebecca Shulman video on the subject of 'Exchange of Lead and Follow'. They set up a sandwich and then each take a turn to invent something new before stepping back and allowing the other to adopt the lead position. At all times they leave one foot touching one of their partner's. They incorporate shoeshines, ganchos, barridas and all sorts of adornments. They begin in a very useful way. After one dancer has performed a movement, the other copies it exactly. One invents, then the other copies. Eventually they tease and flirt and attempt to outdo each other. As you watch them play it seems clear that it is a fun exercise to do and extremely useful for exploring all the possibilities of the sandwich.

I have described the sandwich in the simple position of squeezing the partner's foot between the insides of our own feet, but this is just the easiest possibility. Suppose I have effected a parada with the *outside* of my right foot against the outside of my follower's right foot. What then? As Daniel Trenner shows us, it is completely possible for me to cross one of my legs behind the other and sandwich my partner's foot with both outsides of my feet. This is sometimes referred to as a 'reverse' sandwich. It feels quite awkward to begin with and I must admit I rarely use it. Try it out, and discover for yourself all the possible permutations that you might achieve.

Another very useful exercise relating to the sandwich position, which Mike Rose taught me some years ago, is this. He asked us to imagine that we were dancing tango but that one of the partners had one foot nailed to the floor. That foot was allowed to swivel but not move from its place. Once you have recovered from the 'ouch' factor the very thought of this produces, you will discover a whole new field of inventiveness, which you might then apply to the dance you do. When you think you have exhausted the possibilities of one dancer of the couple pinned by one foot, change the foot; and it goes without saying that both partners should try it. Sequences can never achieve such a level of freedom as this. I want readers to see the sandwich as a doorway to another roomful of possibilities and not as a figure that becomes yet another cliché.

Planeos

The Spanish verb 'planear' has two common meanings. One is to plan, and although you do need to plan quite carefully before you lead a planeo in social dancing this is not the meaning intended. 'Planear' in the context of tango is to glide. The movement referred to is a pivot with balance fully on one leg, whilst the other leg is held away from the body. The supporting leg can be bent to allow this to happen while maintaining an erect upper body. The further we wish to extend the free leg, the more the supporting leg must bend. I think that the free leg looks more elegant if there is a little external rotation at the hip, the knee is locked straight and the toe is pointed slightly outwards. For balance, I find that the body weight should be well forward on the supporting foot, which is the usual case if we want an easy pivot with minimal friction.

The degree to which the free leg is allowed outwards depends entirely on the space available on the dance floor. Quite a nice, but minimalist, planeo can be achieved within the normal space around a couple even on the busiest of evenings.

Planeos can be for leaders and followers, and the key to considering them is to think of the possibilities for circular movement.

A follower planeo

Fig. 1 Tony first leads David to make an intention movement of his left leg. Looking at this shot with a critical eye, this is a pretty pathetic, half-hearted intention movement. A really good follower would reach further with a much straighter and more elegantly extended leg and the heel would be much lower.

Fig. 2 Tony lowers his left hand thus indicating to David to lower his body. Just close your eyes and imagine that you are seeing an elegant woman's left leg being extended and the pain will soon go, I assure you.

Men dancing with men

The images on this page are different in many respects from all the others and serve to remind us of some other important facets of tango.

Clearly we see two men dancing together. It may seem unusual but, in fact, there is a long and honourable tradition in tango of men helping each other to perfect their tango skills. Originally because of a severe shortage of women in Argentina at the time tango was born, it has become second nature to many who care enough about tango to learn both skills of leading and following and to practise them with anyone. Therefore, it seemed appropriate to have at least a few images to reflect the reality, not only of the original tango scene but even of how many of us learn tango today..

Fig. 3 Tony steps around David, making the axis from David's right foot up through his head the centre of the circle. As long as Tony keeps the frame intact David will stay on that pivot. Pity he can't extend his left foot elegantly!

181

In any circular movement involving two people in a continuous embrace we need to think about where the centre of rotation will be. Will the axis pass through the head and spine of the leader or that of the follower, or will it be halfway between the two of them? As we saw when dealing with the grapevine manoeuvre in the giro, for a couple to stay together and preserve the space between their bodies it is a good idea if we learn two things. One is that the follower must be able to perform the grapevine evenly, so that she describes a track about the leader that is as near to a perfect circle as she can. The other vital piece of the jigsaw is that the leader must be able to pivot with his weight on one foot so that the axis stays on the same spot. Like so many leaders, I used to shift my feet about in the pivot and move my axis excessively. It is hard enough for a follower to perfect a sweet grapevine step around a fixed point, but to be forced to continuously adjust for a wobbly leader is worse. That's not conversation within connection; that's bickering in the language of tango!

Before we can consider the planeo, therefore, we need to be very well able to pivot, fully balanced, on one foot.

Planeo for the leader

The following description is just one form of leader planeo that I like to do and I offer it merely for example. I find it fits into the giro to the left comfortably for me, but I must make sure I do not allow this to become repetitive. I lead the left giro and at the moment my follower pivots prior to her back step I take a small step right and pivot a little on that right leg. It is a very small step and a little forward, if anything, but its main function is to allow transfer of weight to free my left leg. This allows my left foot to arrive, poised, across the right ankle. You might think of it as a leader in the cruzada position, if you like. As my follower takes her back step, I extend my free left leg with toe pointed straight forward and I continue the leftward giro lead by pivoting my entire body on my right foot. The extended left leg begins a leftward arc as my whole body pivots, but then I take it to a position directly to my left but not backwards. Finally I bring it in to collect at the side of my right foot, but I do not put weight on it. This left leg is now free to step forward out of the giro once my follower has arrived with her weight fully on her left leg, having completed the pivot after her forward step but *before* she takes her next sidestep. This is just one resolution of this movement. I could equally easily accompany her sidestep, to break out of circular into linear movement, or I might take any of the opportunities always offered to me in a giro when I have a free left foot.

An elegant termination of this sort of planeo is some sort of foot intrusion. This is because, for me, the feeling of the planeo seems to call for the next movement of my left foot to be in a forward direction rather than letting the momentum just die away. It so happens that the collection of my left foot to the right coincides with my follower's forward step, and two clear possibilities present themselves for a leader's left foot in this situation. One is to sacada the gap by placing the left foot straight forward. If we as a couple have successfully maintained the frame, my follower will be stepping across the front of me and the gap is just perfect.

Alternatively, if I place my left foot slightly to the left and arrest my upper torso rotation, I might be able to stop my follower at the point of her stride and parada her left foot. I may then lead a forward ocho return towards my right and oblige the follower to lift her right foot over my left shin. She might choose to 'shoeshine' her instep up my shin on the way through, too. How suggestive is that? What fun!

In this planeo, the axis is through the centre of the leader. When we move the axis to the follower we can perform a follower planeo.

The follower planeo.

Again, the basic presumption is that the follower has all her weight balanced on one leg while the other leg is allowed to extend backwards or sideways. In this position, the follower pivots on the weight-bearing leg and the free foot glides in an elegant arc. The arc may be tiny in its radius if space is restricted, or, by bending the knee of the weight-bearing leg, quite a wide arc is possible. It is vital, both from a 'health and safety' point of view and for the sake of elegance, that the follower's back is upright, and the movement requires considerable balance and stability if the planeo is flamboyantly wide. As with a good deal of tango moves to be seen in stage shows, this particular move is best if kept slightly understated, on the social dance floor, in my opinion.

The lead for the planeo can be extremely simple but it relies to a great extent on being recognised for what it is by the follower. Some leads we offer are self-evident to even the least experienced follower, but this is a little different. First, the leader arranges the weight change he needs. This might then be simply followed by the minimal indication of a backward step for the follower, who initiates her leg extension in anticipation of a simple step. (I have referred in chapter 4 to this anticipation of movement, which is sometimes called 'intention'.) I have been taught that a leader can indicate that the follower should lower her body and extend her leg further by lowering his left hand. I have to confess that this 'hand lead' really has an effect solely on those followers who have been taught it, and for me, so far, these are restricted to those followers who were on the same course on planeos! I suspect it might work better if I lowered the entire embrace slightly by lowering both arms together. The leader does not lower his own body in general, although, in passing, I should add that there is no reason why he should not do so if he wants to. He might, for example wish to perform a mirror image planeo at the same time. Tango lets you do whatever you like, as I hope you will already have realised.

For the sake of this example, however, let us allow the poor leader to stay upright, balanced and in full control. In my experience he will need all this, since the lowering movement is commonly the time that the follower loses her balance, at least to begin with. Once the follower is in the lowered position with the free leg extended elegantly backwards, and – for me – ideally with her toe pointed and her ankle slightly externally rotated, there are some choices. The leader may simply indicate a return to the normal upright position by raising his left hand. I think that, if he did, his partner might suspect he had tendencies towards being a control freak. Most of us leaders, once we have placed our followers in this quite vulnerable position, would, at the very least, bring in a rotational movement. This might be minimal; sometimes a small rotation of the follower, first one way then the other. We might walk round the follower in either direction, making very sure we understand where her axis is so that we do not pull or push her off balance. I hardly need to point out that a full circle of a follower in her most lowered extended position will occupy an immense amount of space on a dance floor, and the likelihood that she will overbalance is considerable. A short, modest arc followed by recovery and stepping back with the free leg, as had seemed originally planned by the intention lead at the start of this, would be quite adequate for most of us. It could be a fun way to complete a 90-degree turn in a corner where interfering with other dancers would be less likely.

When a leader steps round a follower, he could, of course, use her classic grapevine steps, but in this situation such a leader would need to be very skilled at the backward step and its preceding pivot. I suspect it is best to forget the feet and shuffle round as elegantly as possible, merely concentrating on the follower's balance. I find that, if I move round to her right, I walk forward, and stepping backwards feels more comfortable if I rotate her to her left. It's that asymmetrical embrace thing again.

The follower also has some choices here. She may decide how far she extends her leg and whether she maintains the same posture all the time or alters the relationship of her outstretched leg to her body. She may advance her foot round the circle more quickly than the leader is moving, or more slowly, or advance and retard it, rhythmically.

Like a lot of these more advanced movements, although they can be a lot of fun between those consenting and highly trained adults – our regular partners – I find that they generally produce bewilderment within the context of social dancing when the lead is as subtle as the slight lowering of the embrace. If we want to spin our follower on one foot we have no difficulty inducing her to transfer her weight. The problem arises when we attempt to move around her axis because we need to ensure that she realises what we intend and does not thwart our purpose by changing weight back or stepping somewhere. I have discovered that the easiest way by far to secure the situation is to rotate around the side of my follower's weight-bearing leg. Imagine that she has stepped to her left and her right foot has collected but not taken weight. If I try to rotate her to her right, unless I crowd her by stepping close in towards her right side she may well misinterpret my intention and step right or backwards. It will be a great deal easier if I start the rotation to her left because her choices are so limited in that direction. I am not saying that you can't rotate to the right, but that it is easier to go round to the left. If I want to rotate to the left, I place her weight on her right foot.

It may be worth reminding ourselves at this point that the cross position (la cruzada) is another excellent place to start a circular movement about the follower's axis because, to some extent, the crossing of her legs blocks her choices. It is in this position that I sometimes like to spring the 'surpresa' or surprise on my follower. Such surprises can only be pleasurable if they work out as planned. It is a simple thing really but very effective. Once my follower has completed the cross and fully transferred her weight onto her left foot, if I lift her right hand above her head and 'stir the pot' anti-clockwise, she spins to her left. I can twizzle her right round through 360 degrees so that she comes to face me again or I can take hold of her left hand as it leaves my shoulder, in my right hand, and only allow her to pivot 180 degrees so that we come to the cuddle hold or 'sweetheart' position, facing the same way, her left side cuddled into my right. From then on, anything goes. It is a good move when things are getting a bit too serious and as long as the leader waits to be sure that his follower has truly arrived on that left foot and then is decisive, it works beautifully.

While once again considering the issue of one dancer acting as the hub of a horizontal wheel and the other as the rim, I want to remind you that the most serious consideration seems to be realising where the absolute centre of the circle is. The central partner tries to maintain a well-balanced pivot so that the central 'axle' stays in one spot. The partner who is moving around the circle attempts to maintain an unchanging distance from that 'axle'. If the 'axle' waves about, the rotating partner simply cannot cope from step to step with the need to readjust all the time. It is just the same principle that we have to bear in mind when either partner performs the giro as we need to consider here with the planeo. It is all about staying close and evenly spaced from each other throughout the manoeuvre. This is not something that feels very easy when we start dancing tango. It is one of the things worth practising, over and over, until it is second nature.

CHAPTER 12

The boleo

When I begin to consider writing about the boleo it feels as if I am entering a danger zone. Of all the movements in tango, this is the one most likely to cause a crisis on the dance floor because somebody has been kicked. They are fun to do but, my goodness, are they trouble on a stick? Now, here is a very interesting thing. Up to now I have been able to explain quite well how the name for a tango move has been derived, mainly from the Spanish language. All over the world, it seems, those of us who dance tango have chosen to continue to refer to the movements in their original language rather than translate them into our own tongue. Why not? It adds colour, after

Kate and Herney   *Photo DM*

all, and any name will do as long as it does not interfere with our ability to learn the dance. In addition, there seems more glamour in the word 'giro' than the word 'turn', and everyone likes a bit of glamour in their lives. When we come to boleos, however, I find I have a problem. The exact word does not appear in my everyday Spanish dictionary. So, what has happened here?

Well, some people write the word as 'voleo', with a 'v'. Is this the same word with a different spelling? Can both spellings be correct? Could both words really refer to the same movement? I've been studying Spanish for some years now, and even today I get quite confused by the way a Spaniard pronounces his 'v'. It sounds so similar to a 'b'. I, for one, have some difficulty telling the difference. Actually, the sound the Spanish make for both letters seems to be a soft compromise between the two sounds that native English-speakers make so distinct. We need to if we are to be sure we mean 'best' and not 'vest'. I hate to 'bicker' with the 'vicar'; don't you? If you hear a Spaniard order a glass of wine when you are on holiday in Spain, it sounds more like "Un basso de bino" than "Un vaso de vino", which is how he would write it. So, do we have a possible clue here that maybe the word is indeed 'voleo' with a 'v'? After all, the Spanish verb 'volar' means to fly, and as you will soon grasp you can certainly let fly some types of voleo/boleo. Great! Another small problem solved! That is, until you realise that, in Argentina, they *do* pronounce their 'v' as a 'v', not as a 'b'. Drat! One of the endearing things about some of the Argentinians I have met is their ability to be maverick when they feel like it. I am reminded of the caterpillar in *Alice in Wonderland* saying: "When I use a word, it means precisely what I choose it to mean." I believe that this quality is part of the fabric of tango and why it is so different from other dances.

Full of confusion, I sent off a salvo of emails to Argentina to hunt for the authentic derivation of the word. You would have thought I would have known better, wouldn't you? A dear friend pointed me in the direction of a tome called the *Real Academia Española*. It has numerous references to both words, 'boleo' and 'voleo'. And – wouldn't you know it? – they both have some validity. All we have to do is decide which we like better. 'Voleo' appears to have a strong claim. Of its four possible meanings, at least one is "a rapid movement of a Spanish dance"; but then it rather spoils it for me by adding that this movement "consists of lifting the foot up as high as possible". Not quite the thing, in fact.

With 'boleo', we have much richer ground. 'Bolear' is a verb from Argentina or Uruguay, the first of 12 references tells me. It means to throw 'boleodoras' at an animal. Even when I was a boy, I knew from comic books that gauchos whirled paired, weighted balls on strings around their heads and flung them to wrap themselves around the legs of cattle, to bring them down. They were usually referred to as 'bolas', but I suppose we 'gringos' would have had trouble with 'boleodoras'. This meaning makes a lot of sense to me. It has an Argentinian origin and the link with a circular, flying motion seems to work too. I can see some slight validity for 'voleo', so it seems it becomes a matter of personal preference. Who knows for certain how the name arose? Does it matter? Not really; but it may be relevant that this is also one of the tango moves that I find most difficult to describe in words.

Basically, the common characteristic of the basic boleo is a flying follower foot, but the movement is not linear, like a kick, but circular. The follower is led to pivot in one direction but before she is allowed to

The Boleo

Fig. 1 Sam leads an intention movement to free Annette's left leg and, as it begins to come out from Annette's axis, also firmly leads a pivot, as if setting up for a backward ocho to her left.

Fig. 2 Sam has led Annettte to pivot during the intention but at this very point she reverses the rotational lead abruptly, as if she has changed her mind. Notice Sam's left hand

Fig. 3 As Annette returns her pelvis to face Sam, notice how Annette controls her movement and the elegance of the boleo by keeping her knees together. Boudicca's scythe - her lower leg - is about horizontal.

Fig. 4 Sam has led the momentum of the pivot to continue, thus allowing the backward boleo to run into a forward boleo. My favourite follower tends to 'steal' one of these, led or not, because she likes it that way!

resolve her movement by grounding the free foot she is led to pivot in the reverse direction. The reversal of the pivot lead is normally sufficiently powerful that the follower's free leg lags behind the follower's upper body rotation. The effect of this is similar to what we see when we crack a whip. Naturally, the whiplash effect on the leg is proportional to the speed, magnitude and timing of the lead and may vary from a very small movement to quite a large and dramatic one. I have made this sound rather physical, so I need to make it clear at this point that the lead is a set of pivot leads from the chest, not a wrestling match from the arms.

I was being led by Mike Rose one night. We were working on the illustrations for this book and he was showing me some gancho variations. Without warning, he led a boleo with some force. It was an amazing and slightly shocking experience, but it worked. The reason it did so was partly because he is such a great leader and I was feeling confident. I am sure that this meant that I was relaxed and balanced, so that, as he arrested my body movement and reversed the lead, my free leg was able to swing naturally. I had little sense, however, that I had contributed much to the movement. It had happened not because I did something in particular but more because I allowed it to happen. If I had stiffened my free leg it could not have flown at all unless it had been subjected to extreme force. As I write this, it occurs to me that if had Mike said to me: "Hey, let's try a boleo!" it might well not have worked as well as it did, because I would have felt the need to do something different.

This idea of combining control with relaxation never came easily to me. If I concentrate on control, I tense up. At the other end of the scale, when I focus on relaxation I am quite liable to imitate a jelly. The best way I can envisage the feel of the boleo as an individual is not so much in my legs as in my arms. If I let my arms hang loosely by my sides then, by rotating about my axis, move my chest from side to side, I can see that my arms swing away from my body and tend to move rather behind the action; they move a little later than my body. If I make my body movements bigger and the change of direction more forceful, my arms fly out further away from me and arrive even later. If I want to I can enhance the action by the timing of my change of direction. If I change as the arms are at their greatest point of swing the resultant force seems to be bigger. I can, of course, increase the tension in my arms to control the amount of swing up to the point that I am so stiff that body and arms rotate as one.

I have used this model of the arms because it really does show us what the dynamic logic behind the boleo is. We are using the energy inherent in centrifugal force to produce a limb movement by reversing the direction of energy flow in the body. It's the same reason that, whenever I sneeze, my hat flies off! Now we need to transfer the idea to the legs. We need to remember that the power, mass and length of the legs are greater than the arms, and therefore the potential force is that much greater. We dancers must realise the possibility that the force in question could hurt someone. Thankfully, as we have found with our arms, the whole thing can be subject to control and we know what those variables are.

The arm exercise demonstrates to me that the variables in a boleo that will produce a wide range of results are these. The leader may lead a variety of speeds of rotation of his chest and arms and he may time the change of direction to maximise the reaction it causes. In addition, I find as a leader that I can accelerate through the rotation to change the feel throughout it. What I mean is that I can lead as if for a soft conventional pivot at the beginning of the movement but I can then steadily exaggerate the movement to a point that the boleo is almost inevitable. In this case it is not so much the velocity of my body rotation as the acceleration of it. My follower may, of course, resist or permit a wide range of reactions, as she feels appropriate.

What I propose to do is describe some of the boleos I know about and enjoy leading regularly. For convenience of description, I like to think of boleos as front and back, further divided into high, medium and low. I shall start with the most common ones that I lead, which are the medium back ones. Here is the situation. I am dancing in a thicket of other couples with very little room to manoeuvre for fun footwork. Our path is blocked. What can we do? I transfer my follower's weight onto one leg and stop her there. I might lead some sort of intention because, although we are unable to progress round the dance floor, the music is still playing with us; we don't stop dancing and behave as if in a bus queue. I lead one or two chest rotations as the music moves me and I can sense my follower's free foot describing a series of curves behind her standing leg as if searching for something. I like to feel it because it is tangible evidence that we are still a connected couple. It's a form of whispering to each other; our secret. With the right partner it's amazing how long we can play this way if we want to.

This sort of boleo is safe, looks elegant and feels lovely. If my follower wishes, and she feels she is being offered the chance, she may bring her free foot in front of her standing foot and enjoy a front boleo too. If she does so, I must be able to sense this and not lead off forward, like a bull at a gate. I must consider that, when her free foot is in front of her standing ankle, she is at a disadvantage and needs a little extra time to carry on walking backwards. It would be most unfair of me to ask my follower to offer her free leg, relaxed enough to boleo on one side of her standing leg, then without notice expect the same leg to take weight in the opposite direction. There are potential problems for the leader with this variation of boleo, because it is an intrusion of the follower's leg towards the leader. When I've led it, I expect to allow for it. If a follower just takes the boleo, unled, it may end in more than a bruised ego!

The boleo that excites most of the interest and attention and probably causes the most tears is the high back one. I mean this in both the senses of the word 'tears'! Here the follower lifts her foot so that her lower leg is horizontal, or higher at the moment of reversal of the body movement. Her knees stay together. Only her lower leg rises to be horizontal, so that as she pivots the foot describes a curve around her axis. When the rotation comes to its finish the foot drops down to the point of collection. You can see at once where the problems are likely to arise. If I am thoughtless about those in the immediate space behind my follower, I have just entered the world of Transformers. I have transformed my beautiful, elegant and sweet-natured partner into Boadicea's chariot, complete with scythes on the wheels.

Commonly when I lead such a boleo I find I need to power it up by beginning the movement with at least 45 degrees of chest rotation from one side or the other, but I feel sure that it is my inexperience that obliges me to need all that. In addition, I like to continue the rotation after the back boleo has occurred, which has the effect that my follower's leg continues to want to fly round forward and ends up in front of her. Her knee is up and her lower leg has been so full of momentum it has crossed in front of her standing leg. This then has begun as a backward boleo and finished as a front boleo. My particular weakness is to lead a small, low backward boleo and crescendo the lead until it finishes in a high forward one. This is not just my weakness. Judith is so fond of this movement she performs it whether I lead it or not! And, while I am talking about weaknesses, I must point out that this composite boleo is for an open embrace where there is plenty of room for my follower to pivot towards me with her knee raised. This manoeuvre would be quite out of the question in close embrace. Besides, I do not wish to qualify for the Gelding's Plate.

The low boleo incorporates an extended follower's leg. As I lead the step that will free the boleo leg I bend the weight-bearing knee so that we both drop down a little. I think it is most elegant if the leader does not seek to collect as he sidesteps but leaves his trailing free leg extended straight to the side. This lowering of our bodies has the effect that the follower can now take her free leg further back away from her body, and as the boleo happens the foot of her extended leg 'scythes' the floor behind her. Naturally this needs lots of room, but at least the moving foot is close to the ground. I particularly like the look of the low to high front combination. Picture a boleo that begins with this low boleo and gradually straightens up to finish with a high front boleo. Wonderful!

Here is another example of a very safe, high front boleo that seems to work easily for me. I lead as for a backward ocho up to the point of the pivot. So I have led my follower's back step, but just at the point that I would normally begin to encourage her return by reversing my chest lead I do something different. I accelerate the lead in the same direction and transfer my weight onto my other leg. The effect is that my follower's chest over-rotates, away from me, and her free leg (the one nearer to me) swings outwards and upwards. I have taken the energy that was about to enable her to pivot had she simply completed a backward ocho, and released it through a leg swing.

I have talked a lot about the lead for the boleo but I would not wish you to get the impression that the follower is passive. Sure, the lead should be firm enough to set up the impetus required, and the relaxed nature of the follower's free leg is a most vital element, but that does not mean that the leader is flailing the follower's leg about. There is much more to it than that. Alex Krebs, so frequently able to spot a practical way forward, helped us iron out our problems with the boleo. He noticed that I was attempting to reverse my follower's momentum with merely a tiny reversal of the rotational lead. "All well and good, if it works," he said, "and, lots of people do it that way. It's just not working for you, that's all.". He showed me how much more clear the lead was if I planted my feet a little apart and changed weight from side to side at the critical moment. If I turned my chest around my follower- just as we do when we accompany a backward ocho- I could help her to stay on her pivot point. In addition, the lead of a reverse movement was so much stronger. When we tried it, the boleo was so much better, we almost laughed.

The follower has a range of responses to the offer of the boleo. She may manage it minimally or make the most of it if that is how she feels. She can add her own energy to enhance the movement. She may also stylise it in her own way. I have seen so many different responses to the same lead, which no doubt reflect the confidence, skill and – to a great extent – the agility of the particular follower. I have a particular fondness for the follower who allows her free leg to swing up to the horizontal while almost straight, then allows it to bend at the knee and slides her shoe down her lower leg slowly to the ground. The other salient point for the follower is this: the momentum for the boleo comes from the waist and all the movement must be from the waist down. This means that to set up the tension that powers the boleo, the follower must beep her upper body facing the leader. If she turns her whole body, it feels to the leader as if he is stirring treacle with a rubber spoon.

The linear boleo

Although I have suggested that the boleo is a rotational movement, there is a form of boleo that is actually linear. This is the boleo that is done straight backwards, or even forward. The lead is that of slightly more than intention, so that the follower takes her leg backwards, but then the lead is abruptly stopped. The effect is that the follower checks the backward movement of her body but her committed leg continues to fly. It looks absolutely wonderful, but is, of course, the most dangerous leg movement on the dance floor and therefore needs to be well planned so that no one gets a kicking. I used to have a serious problem with this form of boleo, and it was this. The only feature that links it to the circular type of boleo is that it demands an extremely relaxed free leg of my follower. Other than that, in essence it looks like a kick backwards. The reason it rarely happened in my earlier days when I led it was that it appeared to need a follower who recognised the lead for what it was. I came to believe that this form of boleo was a seriously advanced matter and I simply stopped trying to lead it. I mentioned this to a teacher, who said: "How odd! I guarantee you I could make anyone in this room do a linear boleo, however experienced they are." I said: "You are *on*," and was then totally amazed to see what he could achieve. What he did was three things I had left out of the

194

The linear boleo

Fig. 1 Lachlan leads Claire to step back and when - and only when- she has fully arrived on her right foot he gives her the intention for another step but with some momentum.

Fig. 2 Lachlan increases the momentum but also allows the frame to open. He does not push Claire away but rather eases his arms to allow her to progress backwards while he decelerates and stays very grounded.

Fig. 3 Now Lachlan starts to apply the brakes. Claire feels her committed left leg swing as her body is decelerated. She realises what is being led so does not tense up and resist but goes with the flow and.......

Fig. 4 BOLEO! This picture demonstrates so well that the boleo is led from the chest. Lachlan is barely touching Claire's back, not pulling her to him. Claire is totally balanced, her leg freely swinging from the hip. This is not a kick.

195

dynamics up to that time. Firstly, he decided which of his follower's legs was to fly, well in advance. Then his forward step was more positive to provide the level of impetus needed. Finally, he accentuated the backward momentum by expanding the frame. I use this terminology for a reason. He did not push the follower backwards with his arms; he simply allowed her to take a bigger backward step. Make no mistake: there is a considerable difference between these two things. Pushing with the arms would only interfere with the follower's balance. Expanding the frame looks similar but all the effort is on the follower's side; she is merely enabled to make that effort as we had planned.

After this momentum has been created, all the leader has to do is put the brakes on his forward movement and – boleo!

This type of boleo is actually another one of those tango illusions. I say this because, in truth, though it may seem that the follower is being used as a rag doll, she is actually putting in a good deal of effort to swing her leg. The skill is in the timing of the leader, who needs to judge precisely when the follower is fully arrived on the leg that is to bear the weight. Indeed, timing is the key to all types of boleo, because if the lead is at exactly the right moment the follower feels the power of the impetus and is then able to augment it. She takes the beginning of the movement that is offered to her and completes it as she feels she wants to. In a sense, that is true of the whole of tango. The model is not one of power steering in a car where the driver puts in minimal effort and the engine responds proportionately and predictably. In tango, the secret of leading and following, not only in the boleo, is that the leader offers the idea and makes it feasible but the follower performs the action to her own pattern of desire. This pattern is a function of her ability, her mood and her connection to her partner. Perhaps, more than most tango moves, the boleo needs it all to come together to work as it should.

It is probable that the boleo is the most anti-social move in a Milonga environment and you might make a strong case that it is better left out. So why describe it? Well, it is easier to describe such a movement in its most flamboyant form. The advanced, more technically skilled tangueros are so deeply and finely connected, they can lead and follow subtle, minimal but still very delightful boleos. No vulgarity and no injury. It's that whispered conversation between a man and a woman again, isn't it?

CHAPTER 13
Concepts of linear and circular movements

Tango as a language

It seems to me that one possible reason why tango often looks complicated to the newcomer is because it is improvised. The very nature of improvisation means that an observer may be unable to see the patterns that we dancers all use for our convenience. It is hard to see where one movement ends and another begins. I have already written about the notion that tango is a 'conversation' in body language between two people, and I believe that the analogy is very strong. Tango is a non-verbal communication of ideas and feelings, backwards and forward between the two dancers. When you hear a couple conversing in a language of which you know a little, it sounds like a continuous string of sound, and individual, familiar

Wayne and Victoria   *Photo DM*

words that you listen out for seem to get lost, unless the speakers take care to speak slowly and space out the words. We speak of being 'fluent' in a language, and this means flowing; a veritable stream of words. The same is true of the conversation that is tango. What is so noticeable about good tango dancers is that their movements are flowing.

Just as a language has a vocabulary, so does tango. When we talk we can use stock phrases and even complete sentences 'off the peg', for our convenience. We use clichés from time to time because we feel lazy or we want to free our minds for more interesting things to come. These common patterns of language permit us to speak about one thing while actually thinking ahead and planning the next topic. So it is with tango. If we continue this analogy, we can think of ochos, sacadas and ganchos as phrases, even as clichés. We might consider a complete giro as a sentence. So, what are the most basic building blocks, the words? However complex tango looks, most of what we do breaks down into two hugely significant 'words'. They are the step and the pivot.

The step is a way to move the body mass from place to place without necessarily changing the way we face.

The pivot is a change of directional facing without any shift of mass away from the point of balance. The mass is rotated. Almost everything we do in tango is a planned mixture of steps and pivots to attempt to travel around a dance floor in a way that entertains us while staying connected, chest to chest, with each other.

The step

If, as we stand and think about our own individual bodies, our feet are parallel to each other and our pelvis is facing the same way, we there are just three simple steps we can make: forward, sideways and backwards. These steps are straight and uncomplicated and we can take them without losing balance. We are able to shift our body mass from one stable resting place to another, and in tango terms we think of this as shifting our axis, that imaginary rod that runs from the top of our heads vertically to the ground. As dancers it is important to consider this because this is the force line that gravity takes and we are at our most stable when this line passes down through our straight, upright bodies. When we stand still we have no problem, even in an embrace. When we begin to dance we risk losing the control of our own axis, and when we do so in the arms of another we spoil their balance too.

Because tango is all about improvised interaction between two 'wilful' beings, some rules are required for harmony. In many other dances those rules can be simplified. In tango, because there is no limit to the numbers of variables we may play with, it seems to work best if we step back a little to think of the basic principles of movement, both of individuals and the couple as an entity in its own right. I refer to the four-legged animal two people need to become when they seek the 'oneness' that is the magic of tango.

It always surprises newcomers when they discover how hard it is to begin with to merely take those three basic steps – forward, backwards and to the side – in the arms of a stranger. At first glance it would seem to be such a simple thing to do, yet we all find we need to experience it for hours in beginners' classes before it feels comfortable to us. Once we have managed that simple walk, the really hard part arrives. We cannot be content with shifting the axis merely in a linear fashion. We want more. Now we need to be able to rotate the axis at will to gain an infinite range of new possibilities. To do so we need to learn to pivot.

The pivot

To be able to pivot is to be able to turn your axis on one spot rather than perform a 'deboule', a ballet movement where the axis changes during the step. In tango we need to be skilled at stepping from one balanced position to another, collecting at each spot and pivoting on that very spot *before* moving the axis again. The step must be completed before the pivot and the pivot must have finished before the next step. In general, the pivot happens when the body, legs and axis are all on one spot, but there are exceptions at the higher levels of tango expertise that need not trouble us at this moment.

Pivots are rotations of pelvic alignment with respect to the compass, and they are needed to allow us to continue to make those stable and safe simple steps in more directions. Pivots also permit changes between those simple steps; for example, a side step can follow a back step, as we move our axis in the same direction.

For stability in the whole dance we need to learn to combine the inherent stability of the simple steps with two other discrete entities: balanced collection and balanced pivoting. More importantly, we need to clearly distinguish between these three elements (step, balanced connection and pivot) and avoid movements that are hybrids of them. The line from a song comes to mind: "Don't mess with Mr In-between".

The consequence of being able to add pivots to our simple steps is that we can now manage both linear and circular movements.

So, as much as it is vital to learn to walk in a smooth, balanced way, it is also crucial to be able to pivot well.

It is, to begin with at least, a useful basic tenet of tango that the steps we take are directly forward, back ward and sideways, and that our feet maintain the usual relationship to our pelvis all the time, more or less. By this I mean that the toes point forward and that we avoid crossing our legs and walking diagonally. Actually, there *are* exceptions to this, but for the time being sound balance is best achieved by this simple method of walking.

The feet point in the direction the pelvis is facing and, from the belt downwards, the whole undercarriage operates as one unit. So far so good, but if that was all there was it would be ridiculously restrictive of choice. If we want to have total freedom of movement then we need to rotate the pelvis to face the way we want. So we pivot. We move the feet to point the way required. We could just shuffle round, but it would hardly be elegant. The well-effected pivot is exceedingly so.

At this point I want to make something very clear. A pivot may involve a change of facing for the whole body but it need not do so. This has a special added significance for those of us who lead. We need to remember that the upper body gives the lead. If, by pivoting, I rotate my upper body, I must realise that I am giving a lead. If I intended to give that signal, all well and good. As leaders, we need to be able to make the choice. We should not allow our lead to be dictated by our feet any more than is absolutely necessary. I mean to say, there are limits to anyone's ability to dissociate at the waist, and I have yet to find a leader who can walk forward with his chest facing backwards.

As a follower, it is my duty to concentrate on the lead coming, primarily, from the upper half of my leader's body. I should never be concerned with the direction in which his feet point. When I am a leader, my job is to be able to dissociate so well that I give one clear signal to my follower irrespective of the alignment of my 'undercarriage'.

To best effect a pivot it is necessary for the weight to be well forward, and I have always found it easier to pivot with my weight on one foot. It does not matter which foot we use and we ought to become adept at pivoting in either direction on either foot at will, because we can then free up whichever foot we need for more interesting movements, such as sacadas, barridas, adornments and so on. It makes some sense, to begin with, for the leader to get into the habit of pivoting for a giro on the same foot each time. This is because the virtue of the pivot in this situation is that the leader's axis is the centre of the circle around which the follower steps, and it really matters to the connection of the couple that the centre of that circle stays on the same spot. If the leader can pivot well and keep his axis steady and the follower can grapevine well, then the couple will stay connected and not spoil each other's balance. I don't mean to suggest that there is only room for a perfectly circular giro. Any rule in tango is there only to be interfered with in the name of enjoying oneself. It's an option to have an elliptical giro, but only because you intend it to be so; not because you are incapable of pivoting on one foot and keeping your axis in one place.

As a beginner, I had a great deal of trouble with pivots. The first problem was keeping my axis still so that the rotation could be a pure movement without loss of balance. My other problem was finding the power source to effect the pivot. I was perfectly able to step and swivel round in one direction or another but I needed to swivel on the foot that suited that one side only. I mean that I could swivel to the left so long as my weight was on the left foot. I needed the step forward to give me the momentum to get round. If I tried to do this from a standing start, I could do so only by flailing my arms about, and always ended up with a serious session of rock and roll. In doing so I was committing myself to a wild movement, which started off with high energy and then tailed off. The whole thing had to be done 'in flight'. The result was a nightmare for any partner because I had to fling myself into the pivot. It made the principle of step, collect and then pivot impossible; but I had never heard of those ideas at that time.

I watched teachers and experienced dancers pivot effortlessly in either direction. They could do it on either foot, either way. They appeared to do it at a constant velocity, too. It looked like perpetual motion, or something you would expect only Michael Jackson or a street magician to manage. I assumed that I would be able to do as they did if I spent more time doing what I did. I could not have been more wrong, and it was a great day for me when I found out how to pivot from a stationary position.

This is how it was explained to me, and I offer it to you as one way to understand it. I suspect what follows is a gross oversimplification but I think it might help some to escape the trap in which I found myself for so long.

I was shown, at the extremes of dissociation with the upper part of my body rotated on the hips as far as it could go, how much tension I had built up in the middle of my body. When I restored my chest to its normal position it was so comfortable again. After a long absence, I had reintroduced myself to my abdominal muscles. "Hello; I had no idea you were still there," I said. "Ouch!" they said. It was then pointed out to me that I could have released the tension in those muscles another way. I could have kept my chest at the point of dissociation and allowed my feet to come round to realign to my chest. In short, I could have pivoted. Controlling the speed of the pivot is a matter of putting more or less energy into the pivot. Just as you can move one arm at a variety of speeds and forces, we can train the muscles of our waist, back and buttocks to operate at our command.

I find that it is a great deal easier for me to pivot when I am well balanced and when my weight is well forward and my knees are relaxed but not actually bent. Having the weight on one foot and forward means that friction is kept at a manageable level. Friction is a function of the surface area, and the smaller the better. Of course, we could also reduce friction and make pivoting a good deal easier if we wear shiny soled shoes and sprinkle a good deal of talc or French chalk on the floor; but skating is not part of tango. I attempted to suggest to one teacher that I was having trouble with my pivoting technique because the floor was sticky. He put me in my place very firmly by telling me that, in Buenos Aires, folk are used to pivoting in crêpe soles and hobnailed boots on cobbles. In reality there is no finer way to trash your knee joints than to attempt pivots under such adverse conditions. As it happens, the old orillero and canyengue styles of dancing in the old days largely dispensed with pivots just for this reason. The floors on which people danced when tango was young were brick, cobble and gravel. Smart dance floors were a later luxury.

In the beginning I had a tendency to rush the pivot and begin it too soon. This produced the pendulum effect, with the feet and legs attempting the pivot before the upper body had arrived and before the entire axis had been shifted.

My next major problem was that of inadequate dissociation, accompanied by allowing my pelvis to lead the pivot. I would be so concerned about getting my legs round that I would hotch my hips about. This was cured for me by pointing out that I could conserve all the power I would need in my body if I left my hips behind until the last moment and allowed them to catch up with the shoulders slowly. It was brought home to me best when I held a broomstick at arm's length to stabilise the upper

202

half of my body, enabling me to focus my attention on forbidding my hips to move first. This worked a treat. Later, the stick could be brought closer to the body and eventually discarded. It is very poor show to take one on a dance floor. I joke.

The pivot is the single most likely manoeuvre to lead to loss of balance, so it is well worth practising solo for considerable periods of time.

To begin with it is tempting to use the arms to pull oneself round but this would be dreadful for the partner. The arms are needed for a nice, calm, alive and secure embrace.

It is also common to see people using impetus from a step to create the force for rotation – as I used to. What happens when we try to take a force and try to reverse it? Overshooting, swaying, and writhing about; that's what. I insist that we understand that the pivot is performed at rest, after completion of a step. If we use momentum to achieve it we then have the problem of somehow killing the residue of the momentum, and that means creating an equal and opposite force to that. If, as in the ocho, we couple a step with a pivot, we must ensure that the step has been fully completed before we pivot. The full mass has been transferred, and the axis has fully arrived on the new spot, so that the pivot may happen with no further shift of the axis. More shifting of the axis during the pivot is the reason for rock and roll at this manoeuvre. So, despite the temptation to force the pivot by using the momentum of the preceding step, we should resist it. There is no harm in beginning to dissociate and start the process of winding the spring as we step, but we must not allow the hips to start to change direction until we have fully arrived at the pivot spot.

In 2003, el Chino introduced me to a skill that was to further refine my ability to pivot. By this time, I had become able to dissociate at the waist to a degree that I had never believed possible. Truthfully, I doubt whether I used these levels of dissociation in social dancing - which continued to be very safely within my limits of technique - but when I wanted to dissociate to an extreme, I could do so. My waist had become very flexible, my waist muscles did more than just restrain my paunch and I believed that I could pivot really well. Nonetheless, there were times when I would assist matters with a bit of total body hotching, semi crouching and other less attractive postures. Worst of all, my beloved began to nag me about lifting my right shoulder up and eventually, Chino pointed the same thing out to me. I was using inappropriate upper body techniques to achieve the pivot and these adjustments were interfering with my balance and with connection.

The blessed Chino had already taught me that for stability and elegance, it is best that the effort for the pivot be only just as much as is needed so that, at the end of the pivot, there is no need to suppress the momentum by an extra equal and opposite force. I wonder if Newton would have enjoyed tango? Now here was the new concept: the other major component was that the effort to create the pivot should be applied as low down as possible. The pivot should begin at the ground and come upwards. How on earth can this be achieved, I thought? I soon found out and it was to be one of those 'no pain, no gain' situations we often meet in life.

It turns out that it is quite possible to manage a pivot, using the muscles of the ankle joints and calf. If we stand with our weight forward on our toes and our heels free, we are quite able to shift our heels to one side or another by about 45 degrees, without moving the alignment of the pelvis. It's not a bottom waggling effort; we are not doing the Twist, although this effort at the ankle does add to the total displacement we achieve in the Twist.

What this means is that if we practice, we can strengthen and educate those muscles at the very bottom of our legs to rotate the whole body a little without changing our posture, alignment or balance. Like any new skill, it takes a while to perfect and those muscles around the ankle complain a bit. As with all bodily things, it appears to be a great deal easier in one direction so we need to practice it both to left and right. Many of us will have the memory of an hour's torture under Chino's whip, twisting away first to the left, then to the right for all the world like a drunken chain gang punished by Chubby Checker.

There is much more point to learning this skill than just to perfect the pivot, though that would be enough in itself. Think about this if you are a leader. Imagine that you are fully dissociated to your right, and when I say fully, I mean that you are capable of no more. Suppose you then want to lead a giro to your left, without losing the dissociated position. How could you do that without unwinding at the waist? The answer is at the ankle.

Why should you want to do this? Well, suppose you intend to perform a really safe leader gancho as your follower takes a back step around to your left. You want your bottom to be facing towards her but that means considerable dissociation from you to stay connected, doesn't it? The ideal position to be in is very close at the hip with good contact between your right thigh and hers. If, as you lead the continuation of her giro, you do so by losing the dissociation, your pelvic alignment will be wrong for a backwards movement of your right leg through the gap. The truth is, for this intrusion to be safe and successful, your whole body must rotate to lead the essential step of her giro that makes the gap. The ankle muscles can do that; not a lot, admittedly, but enough to lead the movement.

Actually, although each individual effort at the ankle produces a small rotation, once I had grasped the concept and mastered the technique it became slightly addictive. Sainsburys saw a lot of it at one stage. Now I can do it repeatedly without much thought in either direction. If I keep my upper body really still, I fancy I am creating an illusion worthy of David Blaine. Perhaps not.

With practice, both leaders and followers can become so competent at pivots that they can turn in either direction and remain balanced perfectly on either foot in both directions. For the follower it is obvious that well-balanced, controlled giros and ochos demand good pivoting ability. It may seem to some leaders, therefore, that the pivot is a 'follower thing'. Not so. While it is possible for a leader who is lucky enough to partner a well-balanced follower to survive without good pivot skills, most leaders discover that, as their pivot competence increases, so does their enjoyment of the dance. When you have conquered the skill of balancing on one leg and turning your body without falling over, the range of possibilities for the free leg becomes enormous.

Linear and circular movements

It's quite useful to break down the sorts of movements that a couple can make on the dance floor into *linear* movements and *circular* movements.

In linear movements both dancers in the couple move together from one point to another. In circular movements one member of the couple is moving more than the other, who is usually (but not always) still.

In linear movements the couple will travel together along the same line, which will often be the line of dance.

The line of dance will usually be anticlockwise around the edge of the dance hall. The most obvious linear movement is simple parallel walking – leader facing the line of dance, follower stepping backwards – but I want you to consider that even a sidestep together is a linear movement.

Now consider the ocho. Let us take, for example, the familiar backward ocho to the leader's left side. Both dancers often take a sidestep to begin with, which serves the function of placing the follower's weight on her right foot. The leader leads the pivot with a chest rotation to put his follower's hips at 90 degrees to their original alignment. The follower then steps back with her left foot into the first element of the ocho, along the same line that the initial sidestep was taken. The leader, for his part, transfers weight onto his right foot to be able to take one sidestep to the left, accompanying the follower to his left. He has changed into the cross system. The first and second steps for each dancer are both linear steps. If the leader has pivoted to his left, he could accompany his follower, not with a sidestep but a forward step. In effect he would be performing the first part of a forward ocho to his left as she was taking the first part of her backward ocho to her right. The dissociation at the waist needed for this is so that the leader can continue to indicate a linear movement to his left. Whatever his legs do, his chest always faces the same way, so that the couple's line of movement – the direction in which they travel as a unit – remains a straight line.

If, however, the leader were to allow his chest to continue to rotate to his left, he would now be indicating a *circular* movement, such as a giro. Having taken a left step backwards as for an ocho, in order to stay facing the leader, the follower is now obliged to make her next step a sidestep on her right foot around the left side of the leader.

There is a very important reason why the leader at least should be capable of separating in his mind the concepts of linear and circular motion, and it is simply this. Whenever we lead a giro, we have to realise that we are obliged to stop it sooner or later. We can reverse it, of course, but the giro is essentially a static manoeuvre on the dance floor, and the nature of a throng of dancers is that they expect to progress around the dance floor in an anticlockwise direction. Dance moves such as giros lend themselves well to corners when a change of direction is needed and for those moments when the couples in front of you halt, briefly. Unless you are dancing in the centre of the room – and that is where the snake lives, if you remember – a prolonged giro is plainly antisocial. The solution for the leader is to convert any step his follower takes into a linear movement by performing an equally linear step to allow him to convert to a linear lead. The decision has to be taken at or before the pivot, and the lead has to be confirmed by the leader's own linear movement. The timing for this is crucial.

I rather like this image, offered to me by Stephanie Gögelein. The follower is on a boat that is moving along a quayside. The leader wants to step into the boat with such precision that he doesn't rock it. He plans his step and times it precisely. Don't rock the boat by being too early, and certainly don't miss it by being too late.

Similarly, one method of avoiding a collision with another couple on the dance floor is to convert a linear movement into a giro. Any sidestep is an element of the giro, but before it is completed the leader must begin to signal that he expects the next step to be in the circular series.

If we think simply about the transfer of our body masses in linear and circular movement, we are taking a further step away from sequencing and a step nearer to improvisation. We can free ourselves from the tyranny of choreography if we concern ourselves with issues such as the space we have available and the way the music moves us. Our concern should be to stay together as a couple, and that happens at the torso end – not at our feet. Because, you see, if as leaders we are considering accompanying our followers out of a circular movement into a linear, we can do so in such a variety of ways. Each choice we make will lead to a different set of possibilities. We can take a simple sidestep or we can learn to pivot and take either back step or forward step. By doing a pivot we have borrowed a piece of the follower's tango vocabulary and performed the first element of a backward or forward ocho. If we have learned to dissociate our upper body from the lower the follower gets the same indication, and we stay connected without distorting the airspace between us too much. Where we end up in terms of possibilities for the next step has been trebled, however.

If we dance alone, the permutations and possibilities are

considerable, using just steps and pivots. As soon as we enter into the tango embrace the possibilities at each moment for us as individuals are no different, in reality, but to begin with we come to believe they have been reduced. At first we are inhibited by the close proximity of the other body. The process of learning tango, as long as our lessons focus on our connection skills and our individual balance skills, allows us to overcome that inhibition, however. Learning to lead and follow well restores our confidence in our range of possible movements. We can learn to be even more creative than one individual with but two legs when we learn to move as a unit with four.

In the past there have been many attempts to analyse, classify and notate tango permutations. So, what is the purpose of such analysis? I think that taking a moment or two away from the dance floor to break down what we are doing into simple ideas can help us to break free from some preconceived notions of how to dance. These fixed ideas are often embedded in the minds of learners of tango because of the progressive – dare I say? – stepwise way we have to learn anything. Because, you see, if we understand how both dancers of the couple have the freedom to stand still or take any of the steps described above, we can work out our own permutations. After we have been dancing tango for a while, most of us come to be quite familiar with the notion that the leader is the centre of the universe and the follower moves around him like a planet round the sun. We become addicted to it, in fact, and really cannot progress until we have learned to abandon such an oversimplified view of tango.

This is where the concept of the dissociation of the top half of the body from the bottom is essential. As a couple, we must dance together, maintaining the same upper body relationship to each other as much as possible, particularly in closer embrace. This is easy to do if we both simply walk in a straight line, and easy, too, if we take simple sidesteps. We tolerate a little distortion of the frame as the follower goes round the leader in a giro, and the better she is able to dissociate at the waist the less distortion there will be. Up to now, the level of distortion of the frame has been minimised by the leader, who has, for example, taken accompanying sidesteps for a backward ocho with a small curving step to stay in full touch at the chest. More commonly, the leader has kept things as simple as possible by standing still and simply pivoting to stay with his follower. Suppose now we throw away the rule book and think about all the possible ways both dancers can move, simultaneously in relation to each other. If we assume that they are both capable of full dissociation at the waist, so many new possibilities open up. Think about them in the following list, first with the follower performing the first named step, then the leader, and you will see what I mean.

> Sidestep with sidestep.
> Sidestep with forward step
> Sidestep with backward step
> Forward step with backward step
> Forward step with forward step
> Backward step with backward step

I don't propose to go through the different ochos and giros here to show what I mean, but you might think about it one dull wet afternoon and come up with something quite new to you. One thing I will point out that arises from this sort of analysis. The backward ocho is not simply a reversal of the forward ocho. You might never have thought it was, but many do. The forward ocho is usually a circular movement, whereas the backward ocho is a linear one. It is quite easy to lead a forward ocho around one static leader axis, but most uncomfortable for a follower to try a backward ocho if the leader does not step to accompany her.

Now, if you think again, you might realise that there is another element that further increases the possibilities. I mean, which foot does the stepping? Let us consider how this changes one of the combinations, and the one I shall use is forward with forward, simply because I love doing this one in the dance. If the leader indicates a forward ocho, the follower is about to take a forward step. As we know, the follower is using this step to attempt to stay in front of the leader, who has rotated his chest to one side or the other. At this point, I need perhaps to be a little more precise about what I mean by 'rotation' in this context. When a leader wants to draw his follower to a circular movement around him, the movement of his chest is not just a rotation about a central axis passing down through the centre of his skull. For sure, when he has completed the movement of his upper body it will be facing several degrees to right or left from its original position, but this is not quite enough. Imagine that we are trying to produce a space for the follower to step into. We are not going to push or pull her around us with our arms. We are going to produce a sort of 'vacuum', which sucks her into the space. It is important to see this distinction between a mere swivelling movement and one that is almost impossible not to respond to if you are a follower.

Imagine that the leader's upper body is a door with the hinge at one shoulder. If he wants to entice his follower through the doorway he does this best by pushing the door open away from her. So, if he wants his follower to perform a forward step to his left, he 'opens the door' by taking his left shoulder backwards away from her but keeping his right shoulder – the hinge – where it is. He may find that he balances best if he pivots to his left with his weight on his right foot, which may allow the feeling of the 'hinge' to run down to the floor. He may allow completion of the ocho and return his chest to its original position, or he may continue the rotation, whereupon the forward ocho becomes the first part of a giro. During all this he has taken no step to shift his axis; but you might now think of ways in which he could do so. As the follower takes her forward step, the leader may accompany her in the same direction with a forward step of his own. He would need to be well dissociated and stay in the parallel system because the dancers would then be stepping hip to hip on opposite legs. He could, however, choose to perform a forward step himself, on the other leg, but he would not be able to accompany his follower by doing so. Using this leg, the forward step is taken in the opposite direction to that which the follower is going, and it is a movement in the cross system. This means that the leader would have needed to change weight to free up the same leg as that used by the follower: left with left, or right with right. The effect of this movement is to produce a complete change of orientation of the couple as a whole, known as a 'change of front', because – as the step completes – it is necessary for both partners to pivot towards their joint centre axis to maintain their frame.

If you have followed me so far, I am sure you will now be able to work out all the other combinations using either leg, to achieve a wide variety of movements for both the individuals and the couple as a unit around the dance floor. What is the point of this? Well, in social dancing, there is often little scope for the flashy things of tango such as ganchos, and we want to have as much fun as possible. Maths may not be my strongest point, but, as I compute it, the sum of the three different movements for two dancers each with two legs to choose from comes to…comes to…well, hundreds of choices; that's what it comes to. No room for boredom within a three-minute dance there, I would suggest!

CHAPTER 14

The Axis

I hope by now you understand roughly what I mean by the axis, but to make it clear again, imagine a rod passing down through your body to the ground, absolutely vertically. It is this imaginary line that we can use to represent the completely balanced body. If you were standing on one leg that line would pass through the ball of the big toe. If we stand with our weight evenly balanced on both legs, the line would touch the ground between our feet. Why bother to think of it? Well, in tango, perhaps even more than other partner dances, I found that my technical progress seemed to stem from the "Aah! I see...." moment that arrived once this was explained to me.

Zero Hour   *Photo DM*

Nowadays, for me, and many other leaders our perception of the precise stae of our follower's axis has become the very essence of tango. Playing with our partner's axis by minute leads is where we get our kicks. From a leader's point of view, if you find yourself in the arms of a really good follower, it can be tango heaven.

New leaders have a lot of concepts to grasp. For example, the whole new idea of 'forgetting' one's own body in favour of tuning into your dance partner's body is quite a culture shock for some of us. I know many people who tango that never get it and one or two who deliberately reject all advice to dance in any other way than to place their feet, both in time and space, irrespective of unity with a partner. I am fascinated on one level to watch some couples who come to practicas, performing weird and wonderful gyrations that only they can possibly understand by rigid adherence to choreography. There is so little understanding of lead, follow and connection that they might as well be line dancing. Actually, what they do more resembles ballet than any social dance. Don't misunderstand me here. I am not saying this is wrong. They clearly enjoy themselves this way and you can't get much better than that. I just feel that what makes tango unique and is the point of it for me- and many others - is the business of improvisation and serendipity. I mean, how would it be if we met at a cocktail party, only to speak lines written in advance by a playwright? Would we enjoy each other's conversation, having to remember them, and their cues, and not really finding out about each other? I doubt it. Actors call that work.

In order to be more likely to stay fully connected, it helps if both leader and follower sense the axis management of their partner. By this I mean three things that really matter when dancing a fully improvised dance socially.

1. Where is your partner's axis?
2. Have they fully arrived, totally balanced at their new point of axis?
3. Is there any sense that they have already committed themselves to a next move?

From a follower's point of view, there are few worse things than being manhandled onwards before you have completed the last step. The leader's version of misery involves partners who don't follow and who never stop still for a second. All leaders can do under these conditions is predict what their follower will do and dance around them as best they can.

Over the years I have attended many classes and have registered the frustration of some pupils who came to learn some new trick and found themselves being asked to practise slow axis control exercises over and over again. I have even seen two couples walk out of such a class. From what I saw in the warm-up dancing, they really needed these skills. They had learned enough 'choreographed flash' to last a lifetime but they didn't look good doing it. I have come to the conclusion that most tango dancers, myself included, would be better occupied on a weekend, practising at home stepping backwards onto one foot than attending some workshops for which they have paid considerable amounts of money.

Many dancers have the most fun in classes when learning new tricks. Teachers know that and, besides, they have a living to make. Many teachers would be very poor if they kept pointing out, class after class, how terrible our balance was. Many of them have survived hours of brutal repetition in dance classes themselves. All but a few know that we ordinary folk are motivated differently.

So many tangueros I meet appear to be looking for ' the secret' to tango. I have come to be very sceptical about this, which is one reason I wrote this book. Those poor souls try teacher after teacher in the hope of finding this 'secret', the hope of which is dangled in front of them by some teachers. Some of those teachers are stars of stage and screen and come at a high price because of that. They must know that, whichever famous name taught them, there is no 'secret'. They did not become fantastic dancers by one pearl of wisdom from an ancient tango teacher but by hours and hours of gruelling, dull, physical practice. I was recently criticised for failing to jump on the bandwagon of ' the greatest tango dancer in the world'. It was said that there had been an outlay of £10,000 to bring him to the UK. The thought was that, to miss such a great dancer's input was to be completely out of the picture. The man who had put up the money told me this with great passion, God Bless him. I'm sorry to say that my immediate reaction was simple. If this famous teacher really does hold a 'secret' to successful tango, if he sells it a few times, surely the cat is already out of the bag? In my view, those who search for a short cut by buying into such workshops are deluding themselves. When will they realise that last year it was some other teacher and that didn't work either. The sad truth is that we all need to work harder than we like to, perfecting our most basic skills; those of balance and elegance under slow moving conditions.

Another sad truth is that it is a great deal easier to dance fast without axis control. When you are always on the way to somewhere you can exist in a permanent state of 'intelligent toppling' as one teacher calls it. Just as long as you both topple the same way, there is some chance of connection. Just don't attempt to reverse direction though.

Ask the average person to stand on one leg without rock and roll and they find it extremely difficult. Try to do the same with your eyes closed and few of us manage to balance more than a few seconds without a great deal of practice. If you become self-conscious about it or look downwards, it becomes worse. When you consider that upper body flailing about in terms of its implications to the partnership it makes sense to reduce it. After all, who wants a partner who needs propping up? Who wants a leader whose chest can never be still or quiet? Following such a person is like trying to understand someone speaking with a background hum all the while.

Consider this. If the leader's chest is always moving, which is the movement that is a lead? It must be the bigger movement. When tango can be a whispered intimate conversation between lovers, this man is shouting his head off to try to be understood. How delightful!

Dancing slowly is very hard in comparison and shows up all the areas of poor leading and following. Dancing with constant momentum is a lot easier but is like skating on thin ice; as it cracks you move onto a fresh bit. You never find out how thin it is. If you scamper about the dance floor, you may develop a sense of competence that is entirely bogus; I certainly have.

It seems to me that the whole point of tango is connection; the relationship between the two people. At its most mechanically simple, we attempt to maintain the same distance between us while facing each other. In close embrace, we have no choice. The further apart we dance the more likely it is that we become separated. The whisper is more likely to become megaphone diplomacy. Dancing in close embrace is delightful but actually, dancing a little further apart can be more fun, simply because it takes different, perhaps even greater skill and things happen that we have to sort out. Little moments of lapsed concentration, missed signals, misunderstandings, teasing and downright, deliberate naughtiness are all part of the excitement.

What makes it possible is an understanding on the part of both dancers of the axis relationship. We try to manage the relationship of those axes. When I was a beginner, the most I could grasp was to try to keep the distance between the axes the same. As with most things we learn, it helps to over-simplify until you have achieved a certain standard. Later, I learned that we can play about with varying the distance but always because we want to, never because we can't control it. I still become quite frustrated by followers who appear not to have grasped the concept of connection and who dance in and out of my arms without any notion of the effect it is having on me and the dance we are trying to share. It freaks the neighbours too if they have made the assumption that we are a neat campervan and discover that we are effectively a car and caravan with an elastic tow-hitch. For me it feels as if my lady is actually dancing solo.

The main skill to learn is for the individual to be able to transfer the axis in all possible directions from point A to point B, neatly without rock and roll and with the newly freed leg ready for any direction we choose. This is for both leader and follower and when you try it out you soon discover that side to side is easy enough. The problems increase when we step forward and are even worse when stepping backwards. This is particularly so if we desire to maintain the weight on the front of the foot. A small step back is not so bad but a really long one is a different matter. This is when the leader begins to realise how much he is asking of his follower when he takes a beefy, confident step towards her. The following, really excellent exercise taught to me by Rodolfo helped me with this control and I still feel I need to do it whenever I get a moment, as in a post office queue.

Rodolfo taught us to keep the body still, balance fully with the weight forward on one foot and then stick the free foot out to the side. He then got us to press down increasingly on that big toe and finally, in one movement, transfer the total body weight onto that toe and the ball of the foot. Once we were fully balanced on the new foot - and not before - he allowed us to collect but not change weight. The process was repeated, almost to exhaustion, in each direction. It sounds simple enough but you would be surprised to find out how few people manage it to begin with. The issue about breaking down the step into 3 elements

1. Stick out one foot without any axis shift whatever.
2. Full shift of axis
3. Collection

Put another way

1. Leg no body
2. Body, no leg
3. Leg no body

I have used this in my classes at all levels of competence. What interests me is that, whatever their level of tango skill, so many people have great difficulty in controlling the axis and committing the weight definitively to one foot or another. When they stick a foot out, their axis begins to shift. They prefer to use both feet to balance on even if it is for psychological support only. It is hard to understand how years of natural

215

balance skills fail us when we start to think it is a dance. What this exercise does for me is teach me to separate out the axis transfer from everything else. I can then deal with the axis transfer in isolation and get it right. The business of pressing the toe down grounds me and allows the axis transfer to be smooth and slow and feel secure. It prevents me transferring my axis by a jump. I think this exercise has been the most valuable I have ever used.

As we develop a true sense of control over where we place our own axis we also need to consider the axis of our partner. A good leader is able to sense the moment when his follower has fully arrived on her axis point and is ready for whatever comes next be it another step or, perhaps even more vitally, a pivot. Pivoting on a totally balanced axis is both easy and enjoyable. If you want to see ungainly dancing, watch a follower who has been asked for a reversal of motion before she has arrived on a good pivot point. The 'pendulum' ocho is the obvious example, leading to flailing feet and arching of the back. You cannot be neat and elegant and off-balance at the same time. For me, an elegant, collected forward ocho is a thing of beauty. Wide flailing legs are not.

Pivoting and the axis

There is no doubt in my mind that second to transferring the axis effectively and completely, the next great skill to be learned in tango is to pivot well. By this, I mean pivoting elegantly without jeopardising the axis stability. The pivot is a rotation of the body around the axis and in general needs to be without transfer of energy away from the central point of the body. This is most easily done with the weight forward on the front of one foot after the axis has been stabilised on it. As I have suggested in earlier chapters, pivoting with momentum to be killed at the end of it is the sure recipe for discomfort in the partnership. The ideal pivot is achieved by setting up a tension at the waist by dissociation during the preceding step and then resolving the tension by pivoting. If we do it this way, at the completion of the pivot, our bodies are more likely to be balanced and ready for anything new.

I was in a class where a pupil asked, "Is it not possible to pivot on the heels?" and I am afraid to say that the teacher was completely thrown by this question and burbled away for ages without shedding a glimmer of light. I wish they'd had the courage to say they didn't know. A moment's thought tells us that of course it is possible to pivot on the heels and we all do it in ballroom dancing. The woman does it in a heel turn and a man in a spin turn. In tango, we do it in giros where we hang outwards. You know, like kids in a playground holding hands and going round and round with feet in and bodies out. As long as the axis is stable, heel or toe, the pivot will work but it will look and feel different depending on whichever you choose.

As a beginner, it was good to concentrate on one way to pivot. It helped me to transfer my axis and become fully stable before managing to pivot. After a great deal of practice I discovered the joy of this new basic skill, pivoting on the axis. Achieving this basic skill is worth every bit of time and effort and I cannot recommend working on this too highly. Only after pivoting on my axis had become second nature to me was I able to take on board the notion of pivoting *off* the axis. Why would you want to? Well, there are times when you want to pivot on a particular foot but the ideal place is the one currently occupied by your partner's body. You could wait until your partner has vacated the spot but by then they are in a different place and on a different foot. Besides, you have done that combination of conditions many times and want something fresh. For a new situation you are obliged to 'borrow' the pivot place for a brief moment. It is not necessary to transfer your weight onto that place to do this. Think of the film, 'Singing in the Rain'. When Donald O'Connor runs up the wall he can hardly shift his axis onto the wall. His body mass stays in the same relationship to the wall as it would if he were standing next to it. Because of his momentum towards the wall his feet 'stick' to it but he only has until that momentum is used up to effect the trick. If he stopped halfway for a chat, he would fall.

A wall is a very useful prop to use when practising pivoting off the axis point. If you stand about half a metre from a wall and place one foot on the floor with your toe to the wall and try to shift your axis onto that toe you will discover that it is impossible. With some momentum your body can stay touching the wall for a moment but soon falls back towards the foot that can support the axis. You are merely borrowing the vantage point for a brief moment but cannot occupy it. If you keep the one foot, toe against the wall, and stand with your front facing the wall too you can launch yourself at the wall and at the same time pivot backwards so that in the end, you have your back facing the wall. You have just pivoted *off* the axis with the help of centripetal force. It takes a bit of doing. I was in a class that spent a good thirty minutes getting their heads round this, and half of them had PhDs.

So when could we use this new skill? I used to use it a lot in my quickstepping days when I did spin turns. They feel lovely because of the impetus they produce. The logic was that I would invite my partner to side-step across me to my right, stick out my right foot between her legs and pivot anticlockwise, to my right. A little like a sacada. Indeed this is one place where you can use it in tango. The usual ploy with the simple sacada to the right is to wait until your follower has vacated the spot you want to step into. This has the benefit that you can be sure you are taking out her non weight-bearing leg. Of course if you leave the axis transfer too late, she has gone and no sacada happens. Try the manoeuvre pivoting off the axis and now you introduce another element altogether. More rotational whoosh, and therefore, in my view, more fun. It can be dangerous on a crowded floor so like most dramatic movements, it needs to be carefully positioned.

One place I like to use it is when I have asked my follower to continue to walk backwards but I have quickly changed weight and stepped round her left side to put us into an 'L' shape. My right flank is against her left and I have allowed my right arm to move further round her back towards her right armpit. My left arm moves forward which prevents her turning to face me but also ensures that she takes her right foot backwards to take weight. This frees her left foot that is still forward. At this point I can pivot backwards *off* the axis. I'm pivoting on my right foot, which is placed very near to her right foot. I can't transfer my axis there. She is occupying the space and I want her to stay there but pivot to her left still keeping her left foot free for the next step. This is a lovely movement because there is little potential for the follower, even a relatively inexperienced one, to fail to come for the ride. It is a safe change of direction because in this 'L' position, I am able to cuddle my follower into pivoting to her left and then stepping around me to my left. It is the first and easiest part of a movement called 'la cadena' or 'the chain'.

The cadena is one of those new skills I have acquired since the first edition of this book. Actually, to refer to this one sequence as 'the' chain is to over-simplify it. In fact there are a number of chain movements which progress down the line of dance by a series of giros. Usually these giros involve the centre of the circle being alternatively the leader and the follower. They can be tricky and rely heavily on the leader being able to take on board two concepts. One is keeping his follower on her spot while he nips round her and the other is the leader staying on one spot allowing the follower to grapevine about him. Most of us come to grief as the axis that represents the centre of the circle passes from one dancer to their partner.

Ruth Zimmerman once ran a tango taster show that she toured around the country from time to time. One of the first things she teaches total novices is an exercise she refers to as 'leaves in the stream'. Couples hold both hands, face to face and move round in the line of dance, rotating as they go, in both directions. Think of it as a loose giro, if you will. Part of the idea is to get people to feel the general movement of a crowded dance floor and stay with the stream. However, there is also the issue of who controls the rotation and the lead is formally take and passes by both dancers at will. What looks like a silly childish game also breaks the ice and gets the class away from the notion that tango is about steps and into grasping the concepts of relationship with partners and other dancers.

A rather more serious extension of this game is a really useful exercise I found for an 'all leaders' course. I call it the 'Now' game. Take two men, get them to hold both hands whilst facing each other. Now that takes a bit of doing for a start but it is easier to ask your the average Anglo male to hold hands with another than to get them dancing in tango embrace. Funny thing that. One of the guys begins as the designated leader and leads his partner to perform a giro with really good pivoting and frame control. The giro can stop start and reverse. At a moment the leader chooses, he says 'now' and passes the lead. The other man then starts to lead a similar giro. Of course, once this has been successful the word, 'now' is dropped and the lead is given up solely by body language. Later we can play with 'stealing' the lead. Again, this helps develop the understanding of your own axis control but in addition it teaches you to read and manage your partner's axis.

It is interesting to realise that leaders progress faster when leading each other than when leading followers already familiar with that role. What powerful psychology is at work here? We remember of course that in the history of tango and to this day, men practised with men and not women. My impression is that we don't do enough of that here in the UK.

The sloping axis and the window of opportunity.

In 2005 I was lucky enough to take a series of lessons from el Chino who helped me understand over 15 hours or more a new way of looking at axis management. He pointed out that we had hitherto concentrated on waiting for our follower to arrive fully balanced on her axis point before asking her for another movement. This, he assured us had been fine up to our present level of competence, but had drawbacks. The problem of waiting so long was of missing opportunities to influence our follower on the way to full balance.

He showed us how to step backwards, first creating a sloping, straight line from mid ribs to the ball of the big toe. This involved stretching out the flank muscles and opening the hip of the advancing leg before transferring our weight backwards. We could then envisage that new, sloping but still straight line becoming one and the same with the axis line we already understood, on fully collected arrival. He had us posing for a moment on a forward slope before falling forward again onto the briefly free foot. In a sense, we were borrowing a vantage point just as we had when pivoting off the axis but this time the movement was linear. In one brief moment we were poised with our bodies straight at 45 degree to the horizontal. He wanted us to grasp the idea that this point in a back step was a 'safety point', a threshold from which the leader would be able to lead an extra movement. There was obviously both time and space for more lead to happen after this solid, safety point in a backward walk. Clearly changes of direction were impossible but rotational movements about the follower's axis were not only possible, but desirable.

It was from this point to the full axis arrival point that Chino taught us to lead boleos, using simple well-timed rotations of our own axis. It worked like a charm. The follower was already in the momentum of moving towards her final resting point. We simply re-directed that same momentum to create the necessary logic for the boleo. If we had waited until she arrived fully upright, we would then have needed the hoicking and arm pulling leads we so often see. No more " Oh, was that a boleo?" It just happens.

CHAPTER 15

Vals and milonga

If you go to any tango venue in the world you will become aware that, while most of what you see is clearly, recognisably tango, other dances are also being enjoyed. At a milonga that uses the 'tanda' system you might notice that, every now and then, a group of dances are played which will be other Latin dances: salsa, cha-cha, rumba and samba, for example. I have even danced a quickstep tanda in Barcelona, and friends report some appearances of rock and roll at some venues. Why not? What fun! After all, most people who are interested in dance have learned several others, and we are only there for fun. Dancers love to dance. Just because we have found

Milonga at the London Welsh   *Photo DM*

tango does not mean we dance nothing else, although I am bound to admit that tango satisfies me the way no other dance ever has. Even within the canon of tango alone, however, there are two other significant dances (at least), and these are vals and milonga. This use of the word 'milonga' often brings momentary confusion, because we also use it to refer to the dance event. It is just one of the quirks of tango, and I have yet to hear a plausible explanation for it.

Vals

Waltz was the dance before tango to shock the easily offended, and it found itself banned as being louche when it was first seen. That may be slightly difficult to understand in these liberal, vulgar days but every society has its own limits of morality. By the time Argentina was absorbing displaced Europeans waltz would have become very fashionable, particularly at the tempo of the Viennese waltz. Germans and Austrians pronounce the 'w' as a 'v', and the Spanish-speaking world has few words beginning in 'w', so the dance became 'vals'. It wasn't just a name change, though. Tango vals is a dance in its own right.

At its most basic level, the way I came to understand vals was to think of tango danced on the first beat of the bar only. Waltz time, as we know, has three beats to the bar, and even in the basic pattern of waltz the forward step is placed on the first beat. In addition, this first step tends to be of a good length and the next two beats are used to take a more modest sidestep. What follows is that we then close the feet together and change weight on the third beat, ready to repeat the same pattern on the other leg. I always think of the movement of the knight on a chessboard. At the pace of the Viennese waltz, this becomes pretty energetic. Tango vals, on the other hand, may be quite relaxed for the same tempo, since we move on the first beat and it is still a walk. Unlike waltz, there is no rise on the toes followed by a fall. This all means that you frequently see tangueros dancing basic tango to the vals tunes as if there has been no change of genre at all. If they are happy with that, it's fine by me; but why stop there?

I don't wish to sound critical but it seems to me that vals offers so much more. To begin with, vals has a different feel about it. Gone is the 'chippy' staccato beat, and gone with it is the anguish, longing and hard passion of some tangos. Here with vals we have an entirely different feeling. In vals there is more softness and more joy. It is almost as if the look back to the European mainstream conjures up images of happiness, of love and youthful exuberance, which we associate with the swirling waltzes of Johann Strauss. Just listen to 'Desde el Alma' and, however wistful it becomes at times, it has an air of joyous optimism to the last note. So we should dance vals as the music dictates: lovingly, sensuously and with an up-tempo approach. We can take good, crisp steps to the first beat, being positive and optimistic. Our relationship with our partners can be more daring and playful and, perhaps, more teasing. If we listen to the music carefully, the clues are all there. As with most tangos, the phrases of music are usually in eight bars. The first beat of the first bar is very positive, and of the fifth bar slightly less so. There is a 'hanging' quality about bar four. At bar six there is a feeling of tension, resolved by bars seven and eight. These feelings will alter the way we move if we allow ourselves to tune in.

We don't just step on bars one and five, however, although (as I have said) some people do dance like that. In vals we can also take two steps in the bar; but where does the second one go? The beats go one-two-three, and the second step is taken very quickly and positively on the second beat.

A very useful way to feel your way into this is by trying this exercise, which was taught to me by Stephanie Gögelein in Cambridge some years ago. To a vals tune she got us stepping forward and back on the first beat of each bar; forward on one bar and back on the next. Both steps needed to be on the first beat and to be taken generously. Stephanie asked us to imagine that we were kids on a swing and to consider our bodies as pendulums, allowing our legs to go, leaving our heads behind a little. If you try this and find it difficult you might help with this feeling by bringing both arms forward as you step forward, and back as you go back. Then, once you are comfortable with this, collect and change weight. If you started with the right leg going forward first, now it will be the left. I am always amazed how hard it is for me when I try this, and it seems to me that the reason is that I have built up a pattern of leading the movement on one leg and my brain wants to make my body return to it. The collection of the feet and changing of weight can be done on the forward step or the back step, or – of course – on both. That really does feel like rubbing your belly and patting your head at the same time! I recommend this exercise because it certainly did help me feel the timing of extra steps within the vals beat. It is quite hard but well worth the effort.

Because I have absorbed the special feeling that is inherent in tango vals I probably enjoy tango vals the most of all the three dances we do. It is more romantic and easy going and uplifting. More importantly, I get the distinct feeling that the women I dance with would agree with me.

To begin with, most of us will manage to enjoy vals in social dancing by listening to the music and using all the usual tango elements that fit into the character of the tune. Some things fit in better than others. I find that the more 'spiky' things we do in tango don't work for me; nor do those elements that tend to be essentially static, such as manoeuvres that involve the sandwich or paradas. I think this is because the tendency is for the music to power us forward in a flowing style. If most couples feel they want to go with the flow, other couples coming to a halt for some play somehow doesn't seem to work too well, unless they are in one corner of the room. It seems to me that when a vals such as 'Desde el Alma' is played the flow around the dance floor becomes easier. It is as if the music moves us all so similarly that, as a room full of moving people, we gel as a group, much as a shoal of fish or a flock of birds do. As we dance, it is not as if we are marching to the same tune. Perhaps it is that the music is freer? Or could it be that the insistence of the rhythm obliges us all to dance similarly? Whichever it is, it seems to me that, in tango vals, we all allow each other more freedom. More than in tango, for me, I feel that the music 'plays us' as much as we play the music.

This is not, however, true of milonga.

Milonga

There seems to be some dispute about the dance we do today and call milonga, because, although it was very popular in the 1920s, it fell resoundingly out of fashion and it was necessary to resurrect it in the 1980s. The problem seems to be that this resurrection occurred without too much factual input. I do not feel that arguments about authenticity help anyone. All I know is that the milonga known to me is a fun dance now and a refreshing change from tango and vals through the evening.

The feeling I get from milonga is one of cheekiness. As the background to the tune, the beat is characteristically dum-dee-dum-dum; a series of strong beats alternating with weaker ones. I find it helpful when practising Milonga to say to myself the words 'FranCISco *SAN'* to help me feel the different accents we should hone in on when we dance Milonga. I am sure that it was an American teacher that pointed this out to me, but can't think just who it was. I am grateful nonetheless.

The lyrics of the songs are often amusing, to match the fun spirit, and were – apparently – even vulgar and suggestive in the old days. There is not a lot of wistful angst in milonga and the dance can be free and easy. Some people I watch dance it with a lot of bounce, but this is not to my taste. One thing stands out when the subject of milonga comes up, or when the DJ plays a sequence of them. Evidently, for one reason or another, many people seem to dislike milonga. Quite a number of people I know stop dancing and leave the floor when the familiar rhythm strikes up. Some women partners have said to me, in as many words, "I don't dance milonga." When I enquire why I discover that some of those people dislike it because they have come to believe that it is just like tango but too fast for their comfort.

I find this very sad, because it is a gross misunderstanding of the dance I have come to love. I have come to the conclusion that it is best if milonga is seen as an entirely different dance, which needs to be learned for its own sake. Like any new or different dance, milonga demands some new skills, which merit practising like any others. Not only that; milonga need not be a fast dance at all. While the underlying rhythms are always in the milonga character, the tempo ranges widely from really quite sedate to bubbling over with exuberance.

It is true that many milonga tracks played can be faster than dances we are used to. How can we cope with that? The answer is to take smaller steps. When I see people coming unstuck when dancing milonga it is because they have plainly failed to grasp the different way of moving from tango, and find themselves running around the dance floor like bulls in a china shop. No wonder they find it stressful and abandon it altogether. It looks to me as if some people view milonga as a form of aerobics. I once watched an English couple flailing about in a tango bar in the Café de Las Artes, Barcelona. They were a menace to shipping; feet and elbows everywhere. The music sang "miloooon-ga" and they danced *"bullfight!"*

For me, the main purpose of any dance is that two people connect with each other. This is no less true of milonga than it is of tango or vals, or any other dance. Anything that interferes with that connection spoils the

Nushka and Marco   *Photo DM*

dance and defeats the entire purpose of being together. This is particularly true for couples who have differing levels of expertise and who, in any case, are moved differently by the music. Speaking purely as a leader, under these circumstances, if I am more experienced than my follower, I concentrate maximally on the connection with her. It works best if I do not concern myself with fancy items of the dance vocabulary that are hard for her, or for me. We will have a good time together with simple bonding to the music. Apologising to each other when advanced movements don't work is no substitute for true connection at a more basic level. The reason that I raise this here is that many of us who have learned milonga as a different dance have been taught some specific and sometimes subtle differences in the character of the dance, including the walk. In addition we may have been taught milonga con traspie, which needs a considerable amount of practice to perfect, in my experience. This means that, while it may be reasonably easy to tango with a new partner, some of us find it harder to milonga with one. If one of us has learned milonga from scratch and the other thinks that milonga is just faster tango with more bounce, connection is bound to suffer.

Here we come up against the problem of definition that seems to dog the subject of milonga since its 'rebirth'. I mean, what exactly is the 'correct' way to dance milonga? When you watch people dancing to a milonga tune you might be forgiven for thinking you were seeing several different dances; and to some extent you would be right. For example, we have the 'bouncers' and the 'non-bouncers'. Which are representing the authentic style of milonga? In the context of enjoying ourselves, what has 'authentic' got to do with anything anyway? Does it matter?

I suspect that this whole issue may well have its origin in the variety of styles of dance you would have seen in different provincial towns in Argentina, and even across the city of Buenos Aires. So, what I believe is that it probably matters very little so long as it works for you. It probably all boils down to a matter of taste. I personally do not like to see tangueros dancing milonga with great amounts of upper body movement and pumping elbows, and I don't like to dance it that way myself. I'm not saying my way is right, but that it suits me and, more vitally, I think it makes connection with my partner easier.

There is a school of thought that appears to feel that, if you dance conventional, sequenced tango figures but in a milonga 'accent', this is fair enough. It is a nod towards the traditional flavour of milonga. I suspect this idea has arisen, in part, from a well-known instructional video that appears to teach just that. The teachers demonstrate a different walking style, then show a series of sequences that you can bolt together. It is all based on the basic eight, then removing step 1 (the leader's back step) to produce a classic movement, which is called 'la baldosa', or the floor tile. This set piece is quite useful for those circumstances when space is limited. The sequences taught in the video would work quite nicely for a regular couple on an empty dance floor, but like all sequenced dance teaching they are neither tailored to the conditions we find ourselves in on a Saturday night, nor to being in the arms of a new and unfamiliar partner.

This was my first experience of milonga. Judith and I studied the video and tried it out on a dance floor. It was a nightmare for me, and probably for the other dancers too. At brisk milonga speed I could never remember the sequences, and other dancers kept getting in the way. We charged around taking huge steps and were totally foxed when we came upon a 'logjam' on the floor. It was a revelation to us when we were taught to express the feelings suggested by the music more simply and minimally, concentrating on connection.

I know some would disagree with me about this but I prefer to think of milonga as something very special and different from tango, and part of the characteristic difference is a very different flavour to the walk. The style of walk that I have been taught and which I believe suits the music best is one in which bounce is kept to the minimum. Since I have come to enjoy milonga all the more in close embrace, bounce could be inappropriate anyway, and using smaller steps is helpful too. It seems that, when we consider the special characteristics of the milonga walk, many teachers have told me that I should be thinking 'bajo y seco', or 'down and dry'. The word 'down' refers to taking on board a concept of thinking about the body weight being lower, with relaxed but not bent knees. The modern English equivalent of this feeling might be 'grounded', or even 'rooted', though that sounds too static to me. The opposite of this would be the elevated, floaty-looking position you would expect to see in ballroom waltz, or in a racehorse up on its toes in the parade ring before a race. 'Dry' refers to stillness in the upper body and a total lack of any other movement. In particular, there is no hip sway. The opposite of 'dry' would be salsa or merengue. In musical terms, 'dry' for me means a pure note from, say, a flute without echo or vibrato.

227

I was first taught this particular way of moving by Alex Krebs, who, characteristically, introduced an image for us to focus on. It was that, as we stepped, we should imagine that we were briskly but quietly crushing cockroaches on each step! Unpleasant, but surprisingly effective for me. While many good followers will pick up on this style and fall into it to stay connected, you can see how a 'cockroach crusher', in the arms of a 'bouncer', might have problems.

As I have indicated, for me the most enjoyable way to dance is close, and this brings extra rewards in terms of connection, which becomes much easier. It also means that my partner and I have to learn how to take faster movements without losing the connection and achieving only nipple rash. It seems to have taken me years as a tall man to realise that, just because I have long legs, it does not follow that I have to take big steps. I have simply had to learn to take tiny steps that suited my smaller partners well and allowed faster movements. Milonga can be such fun for so little movement. How it took me so long to work that out is a mystery to me.

So, the case I am making is that, if you add the various factors all together (the speed of the dance, the need to maintain connection, the cheeky flavour of the tunes, the desire to be able to dance an even faster tempo dance in close embrace), you may end up discovering – as I have – that the most satisfactory way to dance milonga is as milonga con traspie.

Traspie (pronounced tras-pee-ay) means a trip, as in "trip over the dog"; not the other meaning of an outing or journey. It is a double time movement on the weak beat in the milonga rhythm. If we think of the rhythm as being 'one-ah-two', the traspie – if single – is on the 'ah'. Actually, it is possible to put more than one traspie in this gap, but for the sake of description here let's just think of one. Speaking for myself, that's all I can cope with in the dance anyway.

I have heard the story that the 'trip' was first seen on the dance floors when an old milonguero with a gammy leg took to the floor. Sometimes the story is that he had a wooden leg. Don't you just love the idea of it? Apparently he was mimicked and the traspie took off as a fashionable way to dance. Well, perhaps so, but if it is true why don't we only trip on one leg when we do the traspie? Or did he have two wooden legs?! What is certainly true is that the traspie is taught in many differing ways by different teachers. I, for one, have been taught it by two distinct methods.

I think this is because it can be quite a hard concept for beginners to grasp quickly. I shall try to describe it in the way that I came to understand it best.

The 'trip', for a leader, is represented by a quick weight change backwards onto the foot we have just transferred it from, but without any tendency for the axis to go back again. To see how this works you might try this. Stand with one foot forward and transfer most of your body weight forward over this foot. Now, very quickly and without moving your upper body backwards even a fraction, attempt to lift your front foot to crush a cockroach just in front of your toe. In order to manage this you need to replace your pressure onto the back foot for a brief moment. You simply allow the back foot to take the whole of your weight for a second. I find it easier to do if I allow this back foot to move backwards on the ground and to take the weight in a slightly different place. There is no need to rock backwards to do so. If you have followed me, you will have managed the very simplest forward traspie on one foot. Obviously, this is repeated on the opposite foot, with the outcome that, given that we have a never-ending queue of waiting cockroaches in a line in front of us, we progress in really tiny increments around the room. The follower does the same thing but in a backward step, briefly replacing her weight onto her forward foot.

Clive and Jean at Belvoir Castle

The steps are easiest if we keep them tiny, and part of the discipline for me was to only take a step that was half the length of my own foot each time. By doing so I allowed myself time for greater speed and better balance, and avoided most of the tendency to rock backwards and forward in the movement. I love to dance the traspie, but I still find it exhausting and tend to drop in and out of it throughout the song. The music often suggests a change anyway, and I'm usually quite ready for it.

In the dance, if you were to allow your upper body to rock backwards it would spoil the connection, and before I grasped the vital point of making this movement in the leg and keeping the upper body in the same place my partner and I suffered a good deal of chest bumping. Minimising upper body movements is the simplest way for me to maintain the connection.

All the usual 'vocabulary' of tango is possible in milonga con traspie – the ochos and giros, for example – but it needs refinement because of the speed and the embrace. I have discovered that closer embrace demands better leading from me. My lead must be positive but sensitive and I must be very capable of dissociation at the waist and secure in my personal balance. In a sense, the follower's task is easier because the lead can be more obvious and her response more inevitable. Once I discovered milonga con traspie, with all its numerous variations and possibilities, I entered a new high of dancing to this special rhythm. What was even better was that I realised that many of the skills I had been taught could translate back to tango, enhancing my repertoire of possibilities further still. I do so wish that those who are negative about milonga would take the time to learn milonga con traspie and join in the fun.

CHAPTER 16

The music

Tango for me has been a sort of journey. Even in the time it has taken me to write this book, I have moved on. Here I am, as late as Chapter 16, dealing with the music when you could make a very strong case for starting the book with this chapter. That's because, in a very real sense, the music is the most important thing. And yet, years ago, I would not have agreed. When I first met tango, my preoccupation was with the dance. I'm not sure that the music that I was then exposed to had such a great effect on me at all. Now, for me, it is the very soul and I doubt if I could happily live without it. I feel sure that, unable to dance, restricted to a wheelchair in my dotage, I shall still treasure tango.

Rich and Dorit   *Photo DM*

When I first met tango, the music I was introduced to was from a compilation of modern versions of famous tunes. La cumparsita, El choclo, Don Juan, A Media Luz, Adios Muchachos. Nice crisp modern recordings and quite vibrant in their own way. The beat was obvious and the music digestible and quite interesting. We danced to the same CD over and over. After all, nowhere in our corner of the UK could we find any authentic tango music. I think the CD was entitled 'Buenos Aires by Night'. I came to believe that this compilation was the essence of tango because I knew no better. It took years for me to realise that this was a modernised, shallow production, not designed for the dancer and totally lacking in the soul of the real thing.

You can see what happened to Tango music over the years if you listen to the recordings made by Juan D'Arienzo well into the 1960's and compare those to the classic tracks he laid down in the 1930's. Thicker string sections that take liberties with the tempo replace the rhythm and discipline of the bandoneons. I can imagine that those violinists were much happier to play long lilting but sludgy passages than the scores they were offered in earlier recordings. In those earlier tracks we can hear fantastic sections of repetitive pizzicato and spiccato to create the driving attack. It must have been hellishly exhausting for those fiddlers but it is, all these years later, still wonderful for us.

In addition, let us spare a moment of sympathy for those bandoneon players freaking out in the last few bars of instrumental tangos. They give dancers the clue that the tango is drawing to a close. You don't have to see them attacking their instruments to realise that, playing like that must lead to a finish pretty soon or the bandoneon will catch fire. As a fellow bandoneon struggler I have often felt for those players. I suppose a string player of today might feel for the violinists, chipping away in the middle sections as the bandoneons sing the tune. The sheer physicality of the demands on the players in those days was tremendous.

Because of the similar line-ups of many bands of the Golden Era, incorporating several bandoneons, two or three violins, piano and double bass, newcomers to tango can be forgiven for not distinguishing between the styles of each band and another. Of course the primitive recording technology of that time also adds a false impression of uniformity. The more you listen and collect CDs the more you realise that they are as different as were the Beatles and the Rolling Stones.

Perhaps the greatest numbers of recordings still available were made by Juan D'Arienzo, known as the 'King of the beat'. He is credited with the responsibility for filling dance halls wherever he went because his music was so easy and inviting to dance to. Those of us who have been soaking in the music for many years still have immense respect for the vast bulk of D'Arienzo's output but less so for the tracks laid down after about 1955.

D'Arienzo's pianist during the most successful years was Rodolfo Biagi whose playing contributed a driving rhythm. Later Biagi was to break away to start his own band, which had its own distinctive sound, even with a similar line-up of instruments. Many of the well-know tracks by Biagi bring something rather fresh to tango that gives us dancers something more to play with; the off-beat. If you listen to, for example, 'Racing Club' or 'Zaraza', you find the usual tempo with one powerful beat alternating with a secondary pulse but, from time to time, there is a difference. The accent is not on the first beat of the bar but the second. It doesn't go on for the entire song but just now and then. This entices us to leave the mesmeric plodding that is so tempting in the canyengue style of tango and step in a more syncopated way. The lovely thing about that is that, once you have tried it, like many novelties, it can become addictive. I can find myself doing it to any bandleader's music. Of course, you wouldn't want to step off the beat all the way through a tango. The impression that would give would be that you knew no better and it would drive a musical, follower totally crackers. No, the way to introduce it is when Biagi puts us up to it. Try it then and you find it is most entertaining.

From the 1950's, tango, as a dance form became less popular. After all, even in Argentina, the younger generation was more into Rock 'n' Roll. As tango became less of a dance phenomenon and more of an attraction for a devoted (but seated) audience, the nature of the recordings changed. I'm not saying you can't dance to the later tracks. It's just that the intricacies and musical cues that are present in the Golden Era music have been left out because they were no longer needed. They also required longer practice, more forethought and greater band cohesion. Tango is not jazz and never has been. Those great bandmasters wrote down every note. The music was not improvised and woe betide the musician who deviated from the written score if they played for Canaro, D'Arienzo or Troilo.

Working as a bandoneonist under that sort of rigorous regime no doubt formed the creative drive of Astor Piazzolla who was fired more than once by Troilo for playing pranks and taking liberties with the music. Admittedly, Troilo always quickly relented, presumably acknowledging Piazzolla's undoubted skills as a bandoneon player and reinstated him. Eventually, Piazzolla quit the band explaining later that he ' wanted to be me'. It seems that he despised the classic but restrictive style of Francisco Canaro, a martinet of the old school. The feeling was mutual. Canaro had no liking for the 'New Wave'. It is said that the name 'Di Sarli' had the same effect on Piazzolla as the title 'Macbeth' has to actors.

Contrary to the tight discipline of earlier bandleaders, it was Piazzolla's habit to give out the written parts to his musicians but, at the same time, encourage them to improvise. The problem about improvisation, however, is that there is little room for all members of an ensemble to improvise simultaneously. Jazz musicians learn when to take a turn. While they have their moment in the sun, the rest of the band keeps the basic rhythm and key going as a solid background. For a dancer to be free to improvise, the entire band has to toe the line. Most importantly, it seems clear that Piazzolla never had any time for the needs of dancers whose demands cramped his style. Despite that, it is interesting to see how many modern tango dancers prefer his music to that of the Golden Era. Perhaps he would turn in his grave if he knew that his music lived on in the dance halls but less so in the concert halls. It may be that many modern tango dancers simply do not know the deeper significance to the dance of the intricacies of the music created to power it.

Tango, as danced originally, evolved at the very same time as the music was being created. This explains why, even today, the old styles of dancing are suited to the music, even in a packed Milonga. The present younger generation has been raised on music with a harder, drum and bass based rhythmic insistence. They are not offended by a mesmeric, repetitive throbbing beat. They evidently enjoy discos where the volume is above the health and safety level, all night long. In comparison, the early, pioneering tango bands were not amplified and, of course, drums have never been a traditional feature of tango. The 'chan-chan' of the bandoneon and the spiccato of the strings supply the rhythm of tango. This is often augmented by a single piano and double bass or strumming of purely acoustic guitars. There is a vital social benefit of a purely acoustic ensemble without a drummer. The non-amplified sound level of an 'Orchesta Tipica' is loud enough to be heard all over the dance floor but low enough to permit conversation off the floor without shouting.

The old bands were about subtlety, not vulgarity. The arrangements were angled towards giving the dancers fresh enough variations to which they could improvise without abandoning tango altogether. As with life itself, progress towards perfection is usually by evolution, not revolution.

Tango Nuevo

If you are a child of the 1980s those old recordings may sound very alien to newcomers to tango who probably listen to them with small enthusiasm. Tango Nuevo, on the other hand, is entirely familiar territory. If you attend a live concert by the Gotan Project – and only suffered one once- you will find it ear shattering and 'enhanced' by strobe lights. Such experiences were portrayed in the film 'The Ipcress File' as torture and I see no reason to declassify them as anything else. When they toured the UK with La Revancha de Tango, I first left my expensive seat for the safety of the foyer and at the interval, left the building altogether. The band could still be heard in the next county.

One other major feature of Tango Nuevo music bears consideration. Each track of a modern band usually well exceeds 4 minutes in comparison to the two to three minute's maximum of the Golden Era. This means that a tanda of Nuevo tracks lasts forever, or at least seems to. Within the two and a half minutes of a track by Di Sarli, two or three major tunes will be offered up in a variety of different ways. In comparison, we can hear everything there is in a Gotan track within 30 seconds. All you get thereafter is repetition. What it lacks in subtlety it makes up for in sheer insistence. Interestingly, the less the band has to offer, the longer they thrust it into our ears.

As an aside, I offer a simple solution for DJs who try to incorporate some Nuevo music into their Milongas. As a DJ myself, always under pressure to serve up Nuevo material at Milongas, I have taken the trouble to cut two minutes out of the middle of Gotan tracks and splice together seamlessly. Five and a half minutes of self indulgent, monotonous stuff is reduced to a bearable and danceable three and a half. Nobody ever notices. Why would they?

Why bother with the tanda system?

I sometimes attend milongas where guest DJs are being proudly presented. What normally transpires is an eclectic selection of old and new tracks to dance to but rarely is there any sense of purpose or cohesion. The DJ sits at a console, staring fixedly at a computer screen and seems never to take much heed of the floor. Sometimes the music is appealing. Frequently it is not. There seems to be an idea that the good DJ brings novelty and has scoured the world seeking new ways to feed the needs of the dance floor. At the end there will be a call for applause for the DJ who acknowledges this with evident pride. I often feel the desire to boo. Why is this? What on earth is this nonsense about the cult of the DJ personality? Why should a mere DJ take the plaudits that ought to be reserved for those long deceased master bandleaders? Why shouldn't the DJ be the servant of the dancers, rather than their master?

The more I dance and the more I study tango music, the more I understand how the tanda system came into being and the more I approve of it. Not only that, the more frustrated I am as a dancer that so few DJs use it. I believe they don't understand its strengths and few are willing to do the work required to compile, well in advance, a working set that will offer a wide range of dancers exactly what they need for fully improvised tango.

I suspect that some of the DJs I have observed make two major errors in selecting tracks. One is that they want the tracks to be a reflection of their own narcissistic personality. The tracks have to please them, whatever the audience thinks. Secondly, they seem to want to keep the dance floor packed throughout the evening. Why is that such a bad idea? Simply because when the whole world is dancing, nobody is free enough to express themselves fully. There is just not enough room. The floor must be managed to have frenetic times and quieter ones.

I, and others who have spent a great deal of time with this music, like to know, when we ask somebody to dance with us, what sort of musical challenges and opportunities will be on offer for the next 10 to 12 minutes. We want four tracks of the same genre, the same tempo and rhythm, more or less, to allow us a voyage of discovery with at least some hope of success. The first track of the tanda is for quiet exploration of the feel, the rhythmicity, the musicality and the technical skills of the new partner. How do they react to the openings offered? How well do we gel? The first track must give us an insight so that we can use the second to become a little more adventurous. By the third track, we have made some mistakes, recovered and are starting to play, tease, exchange body language signals that reinforce that we both feel at home. Finally, the fourth track brings it all together and we can fly.

At the end of the tanda of four the cortina allows us to leave the floor with honour and no sense of rejection on either part. We concentrated deeply on each other and on the music for a full 12 minutes and, to be frank, we are spent. Indeed, speaking personally, had I the energy for more and more, the only implication is that I simply had not fully committed myself. I must have been barely concentrating. I was only going through the motions or that last dance would have drained me of all my energy - for a while, mind you. All I need is a small rest and I can do the same thing all over again with a new partner. Can you think of any other area of life that compares to this? I can but I am too much of a gentleman to spell it out.

Am I alone when I remember finding myself rising to the very heights in four tracks, only to find the thoughtless, ignorant DJ has pushed us onto a fifth and a sixth. I may have coped with number five but by six I was past my sell-by date and now I'm dancing like a donkey. Perhaps even worse than that, he changed the format of the dance so we began with a canyengue style Carabelli number like Alma and we now have Gotan's Lunatico, then a track of milonga.

I know I am not alone when I recall asking a perfectly lovely woman to dance and discover within half a track that she is lumpy and unmusical or frenetic and inappropriate. As a gentleman, I will do my best to make her enjoy my company for the entire tanda, whatever it takes. She probably hates every minute of my company too but it is for her to quit not me. I once had a partner invent a bleeding foot to get away from me at a Milonga so I do not delude myself that if I am having a bad time the feeling is likely to be one-sided. This whole issue is about sensitivity to one's partner. After all, even totally competent, lovely people can fail to hit it off.

The cortina allows honour to be satisfied all round. If we have enjoyed each other's company that much we can always stay for the next one, once we hear what the DJ has on offer. Best of all, we can choose to ask somebody to dance towards the end of a tanda, in case we are not confident how well we will dance together.

If the DJ starts a tanda of milonga, I want to know within a moment what its general speed is going to be. I am not happy to begin with Canaro's 'Milonga Sentimental' at 54 beats per minute and end up with Sosa's version of 'Taquito Militar' at about double that and, to boot, probably un-danceable for us as a new 'team'. No, I am not calling for 'samo-samo' but thoughtful and appropriate. It is nice to plan a tanda on a rising plane of speed, particularly milonga and, from my point of view, also of Vals. I love a Vals tanda that invites me onto the floor with a modest but toe-tappingly lyrical rhythm and then gradually steps the pressure up over the four tracks, little by little. Now we really do fly.

When I refer to 'flying', I do not want you to imagine the sort of dancing that resembles flying a helicopter through the pista. That's not the flying I admire. I want to make a clear distinction between dancing, feeling as if you are a foot off the ground, in the moment and as together as a couple can be without the removal of clothing, and the sort of dancing that is the equivalent of football hooliganism. It only takes one couple 'showboating' on the floor to spoil it for us all. I am strongly of the belief that the type of music that we dance to - and even the type we learn to - can have a profound effect on our behaviour on the dance floor.

The people who ruin any pleasure I might have in a Milonga are easily recognisable. They dance in open and infinitely variable embrace. This means that, even static, they occupy the maximum amount of floor space two people are capable of. As they move, they double the space. She kicks in all directions and, not to be outdone, so does he. They love the deep, wide planeo and that 360-degree giro where he uses her body like a scythe behind him. Whatever the song being played, their style is just the same. It is also unpredictable since they are following a floor plan of their own, not any musical clue. They are having a whale of a time and, in a cruel and ironic pastiche of the deep connection we so admire, are in a world of their own. They have spent a fortune and aeons of time learning fancy moves in sequences and they are determined to enjoy themselves.

I think the worst sin I used to commit was to cut across the corners in the inside lane when confronted by what I saw as a log jam. There may actually have been one, or it may simply be that the more experienced and socialised dancers in front of me were responding to a musical pause. How could I tell? In my callow youth I was less connected to the music anyway. I had never really listened attentively to it and was not then able to distinguish one band from another. So, seeing a gap, I would nip across. Now, where is the problem with that? If I had stayed in the inner lane, there wouldn't be a problem.

It's just like the traffic flow on the motorway. If we all stayed in lane at the speed limit, the flow of traffic would never clog as has been readily demonstrated on the M25 section by Heathrow with its averaging speed camera system. It's as sweet as you like. If a nippy couple cuts across and stays on the inside track, there would be no problem, but often they don't. They squeeze back into the outer lane, and guess what? The five couples behind them grind to a halt. Maybe now we know why there was a log jam to begin with.

I realise that this is beginning to make me sound like a grumpy old man. Well, I may be, but when I think that the antisocial culture of some of the European Milongas is risking the future of tango I become cross.

The problem seems to stem from the way the tango culture has been grafted onto ours. Europe is seething with tango teachers who have found a ready market for show tango. Show tango is a great deal easier to teach to gringos than the tango that is deep in the culture and history of Buenos Aires. The economic situation in Argentina is dire and you cannot blame young dancers finding whatever way they can to escape their poverty and sometimes-risky lives. There are not enough mature, deep-thinking, socialised, fuddy-duddy people like me around, wanting the real thing, to pay the rent. On the other hand, there are a vast number of energetic, striving, keen youngsters, tearing up the ladder of life. Some of these did start life in the punk era but I am sad to say, some of them are now grandparents enjoying a second adolescence. Let us not forget that ours is a culture of 'I want it, and I want it now' and besides, 'You're worth it'! Yob culture is commonplace, so why would you not find it at a Milonga?

If I had not experienced the real thing, I too would know no better. Visiting Buenos Aires was a mixed blessing, to say the least, but it did show me how a Milonga can be at its very best. I am not talking about show dancing, which is ballet by another name (and I have little enthusiasm for it). I am talking about being at a Milonga, surrounded by people who live inside the music and whose technical skills far outweigh what they actually get to do when they dance socially. They could do all the fun things that suit a stage performance but they are happy to get their delights from subtlety, precision and finesse. Most importantly, those Argentinians have experienced tango music, if not the dance, from their infancy. They are so familiar with the pauses, the nuances, the fleeting cues from the tracks they dance to that it would go against the grain to dance in any other way. Besides, tango in Buenos Aires, away from the tourist traps, is a social function, not an antisocial one.

I'm amused by the saying, 'The definition of a gentleman is one who knows how to play the pipes, but doesn't!' The definition for me of a real tanguero is similar. It is a man who can lead any movement but elects to use his skills to maintain his integrity and that of the woman in his arms in a Milonga. In many Milongas in the UK, I often feel like somebody

239

who has seen a wonderful inspiring landscape spoiled by the detritus of a thousand picnics. It's like seeing Buckingham Palace 'improved' by Banksy.

I suppose we shouldn't be surprised about this when we look at the world in general. Here we are, the affluent people, consuming as if there was no future in a self-fulfilling prophecy, making it very likely there won't be one for our descendants. While we struggle with the 'problems' of obesity and overspending, across the world there are still people starving to death. The selfish and basically incompetent behaviour of a few couples in Milongas not only spoils any evening for the dancers around them but also tarnishes the name of tango and makes more generous and gentler folk come to hate Milongas. The worse it gets, the worse it will become.

So how does this fit in with consideration of the music? I believe it goes hand in hand. The music of the 1920s, '30's and '40's was the music of a more socially elegant era where good manners were a vital ingredient. Men raised themselves up from the gutters by learning to dress behave and dance elegantly. Manners were the hallmark of the gentleman. His status in his local society was hard won. You showed off your tango skills to your rivals, but not at the expense of the community or, perish the thought, the precious woman in your arms.

The music held within it, enough subtle messages for any competent tanguero to make so rich a pattern of dance moves within those two or three minutes that the woman in his arms would be entertained, impressed but as safe as houses. Modern music has few of these attributes. The best it can hope to achieve is a driving raucous message of crude display, endlessly repeated. Little wonder that the dancers that love such music dance the way they do. 'Winner takes all' music for 'winner takes all' dancers. It's not tango and I just hope that as some of our younger dancers grow older, they see something wonderful in those values that brought tango into life all those years ago.

Tango Nuevo, as a brief novelty interlude, is fun. When it becomes the default, it can have as much appeal as the drunken mooning in the street to a CCTV camera.

It appears to me that there is a significant factor that makes tango stand out from any other dance. It is the way the different pieces of music

240

change the way we dance. You would think that, as with waltz or samba, the beat would be all you would need and that although you might prefer one song to another, the dance would be stay the same. I'm sure that this is not so. For a long while I simply couldn't grasp why, at times, on the same night I could fly while at others I felt I danced like a brick. I was aware, because I had avidly read interviews, that some older tangueros would say "You can't dance to Gardel" or "I love to dance to Pugliese", or some such, but I never gave these stories much credit. To tell the truth, I thought it was snobbery and posing, and, I must admit with some sadness, there is a little bit of that in tango. I have, however, learned better as I found myself becoming sufficiently competent to stop thinking about technique and relax into the music. It just hits you after a while. The music is different and it makes you feel different things, so you try to dance to suit. When you first start being moved by the music, certain tunes stand out as old friends. They appear to resonate with your particular mood, and maybe that of your partner. Just one dance can be bliss; not just fun, not just good enough, but sheer bliss. At the end of the dance you seem to take a breath and laugh as if you had been teetering over some giant chasm and reached the other side.

Gradually, the truth dawns: you have been 'played' by the orchestra. Now let us take a moment to look back to the origins of tango and see how this could happen. However sophisticated the musicians were in the 'golden era' of tango, the first musicians would have been amateurs, who may have never been able to read a note of music. There was no set group of instruments, either. People got together and played the instrument they had brought with them. The first bands were combinations of guitars, flutes, fiddles, harmonicas and even comb and paper. They played from the soul, by ear, and busked and jammed along as best they could. It was all live and vibrant and, as they played, they no doubt induced people to dance. Because the musicians were making it up as they went along and not slavishly following notes on a score they were able to get feedback by watching the dancers, and so, just as the music formed the dance, the dance also formed the music. The musicians would have been able to 'play' their dancers, just as a good DJ in a night-club feels as the evening progresses what sort of people are on the dance floor and changes his set to match.

Because we are so heavily into recordings nowadays we rarely get to imagine what it must be like to dance to a live band. When we do, there is another dimension altogether. If we set up a tango evening with prerecorded tandas it works extremely well, but when somebody manages the PA system, watches the dance floor and gets the feel of what seems to be moving the dancers it has a different feel altogether.

There is another thing to consider when we try to dance to older recordings of tango. While a band quite enjoys playing to move an 'audience' of dancers, what they really love best of all is when we all stop whatever we are doing, watch them with 100% attention and applaud. Otherwise, it has been suggested to me that some musicians begin to feel like wallpaper and they either become sour about audiences or start playing only to please themselves. In either case, the music suffers and so does the dancing. It is just human nature to want attention and reward over and above your pay. So, some of the tunes composed for tango were really not for dancing to but for listening to. Some of the tunes have little jokes in them to wake up the dancers; little changes of rhythm, breaks, silences and odd harmonies. Much would have been improvised, and some changes and novelties would have been lucky mistakes on the night and written in because they worked.

Although we closely associate the bandoneon with tango, its appearance on the scene was fairly late; somewhere between 1900 and 1920. It brought a new flavour, that of poignancy, to the tango, and although it can flesh out the basic rhythm well enough it speaks more volumes in melody. As an instrument, it has great flexibility both as a soloist and an accompanist, and unlike the guitar it is hard to drown out.

The different bandleaders had their own funny little ways and competed for their niche in the market, it seems, often with gimmicks. Each of the famous bandleaders and composers of tangos that we know so well came to their positions of power and influence from an amazingly wide range of backgrounds. Some were classically trained as pianists or violinists. Some, like Anibal Troilo. Had always been bandoneonists. Many served their apprenticeships in other bands before being able to set up on their own and make their own mark on the tango genre. This means that, while there is the constant thread of similarity that all tangos share, the range of feelings explored by the composers over the years is vast.

It is sobering to remember that our thoughts about an 'authentic' tango sound are only possible because of the survival of some recordings, and – of course – these do not go as far back as the very origins of tango, because recording was not possible then. Not only that; many recordings from the earliest days were of poor quality and, tragically, many were destroyed by recording companies RCA being perhaps the most notorious offender. By the time that we begin to hear good-quality, mass-produced recordings, tango as music had moved away from the simple need to accompany dancers. By this era, the bands were gaining a big following and their conductors and singers were acquiring superstar status. Tango had become big business and needed to appeal to a wider audience, way beyond Argentina. Though there were bandleaders who attempted to hold onto traditions and turn out fresh but danceable tunes, many believed in evolution. They felt it was more than reasonable to introduce novelty to the scene; and it was, clearly, financially rewarding. Besides, bandleaders are often egotists. They probably need to be.

Here is the point where there develops a tension between those who want tango to be as it always was and those who are happy for it to move onwards and stay alive. It seems odd to me that any tango should be described as un-danceable, but Piazzolla's music is often considered so by some. I must admit that the older I get the more it bores me. There are those who have said that, in their opinion, Piazzolla's music "is not tango". To be truthful, when you start to feel able to release yourself into the music it is easier to do that for the two and a half minutes of Di Sarli's 'Don Juan' than some of Piazzolla's long tracks. Incidentally, Carlos Di Sarli was a really talented pianist who created a band with a recognisable style that suits dancers well because it is extremely rhythmic and steady. As you listen more to Di Sarli you hear more internal nuances to play with in your dancing. Indeed, for me Di Sarli represents the most tasteful, refined feel of tango. He is great to start off a Milonga and good at the end of the evening to steady down with. For the beginner wanting to practise at home and perfect the technique of shifting axis from one full balanced spot to another, Di Sarli lends the perfect music. Later, though, Piazzolla offers up a different challenge. We can all dance to him; it just needs a developed skill, or perhaps merely a desire to allow his music to move us in its own way in the dance. If only his music was less repetitive and more brief.

At another end of the scale, Mariano Mores was a showman whose music has been described by some in interviews I have read as being "not for dancing", and yet, in collaboration with Discepolo he wrote 'Uno', 'Gricel', 'Cafetin de Buenos Aires' and 'Adios, Pampa Mia' – all lovely to dance to.

Each of the bands you will hear playing the tangos of the 'golden era' have their own feel and flavour, and because all dancers are different you will discover which you prefer. The longer you dance tango the more eclectic your taste will become, and – in my judgement – the more fun you will have, because of that.

It seems to me that, if it is the case that the tracks of Carlos Di Sarli are easiest for beginners to tango to get their heads round because his style is classic, then as you become more skilled you might well prefer Osvaldo Pugliese, who – being more inventive – is also more exciting to dance to because he lets you be more ambitious, more daring. It's all tango, but if tango is about anything it is about improvising as the music moves you. If the music leaves you cold, and much of Tango Nuevo does me, then you are not moved at all. Many find the music of D'Arienzo a fine compromise; still classic but with a lighter touch. Others prefer the passion of Tanturi, the expansive grandeur of Troilo or the elegant rhythmicity of Miguel Caló.

I have pointed out that the addition of a singer to the orchestra changed the flavour of tango and suggested that the superstar status of singers – and, indeed, soloists – deflected the musicians from their original task of providing music for dancers. Some bandleaders, such as Juan D'Arienzo, attempted to ensure that, even if they did use a singer, the voice

Steve and Nicole   *Photo DM*

stayed as just another instrument. There is quite a different feeling to be had when dancing to the same tune played by different orchestras, to be sure, but even more so when dancing to the same tune as an instrumental number or with a vocalist. The vocalist plays with the rhythm and milks the emotion in a way that a bandoneon or violin manages only from time to time. Here is another strange thing. Whereas most tango singers were men, there were, and still are, some wonderful women singers. The tradition in Argentina is, to this day, not to dance to them. As it was explained to me, this was all about wanting to listen to the words and the female singers' voices rather than actually wanting not to dance; but I find that rather odd.

Here is one final thing on the subject of the connection with the music that may be worth considering. There is a type of leader – no, I will be clearer about this: a type of male leader – who has the notion that the woman in his arms is another instrument in the orchestra they are dancing to. He has very strict and simplistic responses to the tunes and wants his follower to skip to the rhythm as if she were his drum to beat. He allows her no space, nor time to interpret her own feelings, and when he feels she ought to move he simply manhandles her into place with his arms. He hears no pauses in the music being somehow in a hurry to get somewhere. I have deliberately made this sound ugly, but the reality is that, for a somewhat insecure and inexperienced follower, this may be a wonderful trip. Such men, as long as they have a good sense of rhythm and strong balance, can be very attractive to dance with, until the follower becomes sufficiently skilled herself that she is able to listen to the music and make her own moves when offered the space. As soon as the follower raises her tango to that plane, the bully-boy leader becomes a potential combatant and not a partner.

I have stuck my neck out about this being a male attitude, and I think it is generally the truth. A group of us, sitting over dinner after a long tango workshop, fell to talking about – among other things – tango. We dwelt on the different nature of men and women and the roles played by the different genders as leaders and followers. The Argentine member of the group held that, while it was perfectly acceptable for same-sex couples and for women to be leaders, the 'real thing' was possible only when the man led a woman. For him this was simply the direct link back to the origins of tango, and was about sensuality, not sexuality. He himself frequently enjoyed dancing with men and would not go out for an evening's dancing, find himself without a female partner and just go home. However...there was a difference. Same-sex dancing was play, a bit of fun – like kicking a football about or mock wrestling. Dancing with a woman, when the mood was right and the music spoke to the soul and the chemistry between the man and the woman was almost palpable – that was the real thing.

The women agreed. They had all felt the satisfaction of mutual respect and playfulness when dancing as leaders and followers with other women. They enjoyed it and felt that, as followers or leaders, they were given more opportunity to express themselves by women partners. They too recognised that to find that in the arms of a man was less likely, but that, when you did, it was the best. All were agreed that the feeling was one of sensuality and not sexuality.

The bottom line would seem to be this. Two people, in love with the genre of tango but not necessarily each other, agree by mutual consent to spend time with each other in an intimate embrace. They agree that one of them will be responsible at all times for health and safety. Few will realise that the nature of the music and the dance means that they are not merely a couple; they are a threesome: the man, the woman and the music. All three elements in this mixture must have their full share of oxygen to create the 'real thing'. The bonds that tie the man and the woman to each other can be no stronger that the bond between the man and the music and the woman and the music. Where there is a serious imbalance, when only one is with the music, for example, there will be a dance; but it will not be as it can be. It will not be the fully satisfying thing; the 'real thing' called tango.

CHAPTER 17

Navigation and endings

Navigation

I'm sure it must have occurred to any who begin to dance to wonder why it is that the convention for dancers progressing round the dance floor is always to move anticlockwise. In giving the title of 'navigation' to this section I raised in my own mind images of the sea, where, for safety's sake, the convention is that ships pass each other port to port; that is, left side to left side. If we were dancing in a long and narrow room, as we travelled anticlockwise we would in fact, as leaders, be passing left side to left side those leaders coming in the opposite direction. Oddly, for many parts of the world – including, stubbornly, the United Kingdom – the rules of the road are the opposite.

Leroy and Sonia   *Photo DM*

Actually, the reason we dance this way is for safety, taking into consideration the field of vision of the leader. If we stand alone, our arc of useful vision extends very widely to our sides. Of course, we cannot read a newspaper held beside our right ear, but we do know it is there. If we are moving and allow our heads to turn a little from side to side, our field of view – for prevention of collision, at least – is almost 180 degrees. The big problem is that we *dance* with another person blocking our field of view, and this is where the trouble begins. Most couples you see dancing in a social mêlée dance a little offset; the man holds the woman a little to his right side and turns his head a little to his left. While this offers a wider arc of vision in general it produces a very significant 'blind side'. I should just point out that, when dancing with tiny partners, this may be quite different, but what I have discovered is that I tend to dance in the same posture in any case; although I could look to my right more, I still have the habit of turning my head slightly towards my left. I discussed this with two very small leaders, a man and a woman. They find their visual fields are extremely closed down but deal with it by frequently turning, as they dance, to gain more information. Their dance is punctuated by half giros and 'cortes' or cut steps that permit a greater awareness of the couples around them

So, how does this all impact on the way we dance? It's very simple. In the dance hall we encounter two kinds of hazard, in general. The fixed hazards are the walls and tables and chairs around the periphery. They are no problem. They are entirely predictable and reliable. It's the people who use them we need to look out for. Of course, those people, when not dancing, can still, occasionally, move a chair or a handbag onto the dance floor; and, if they can do it, be sure: they will do it. When up and dancing, they are a menace to shipping.

This is why we travel anticlockwise along the edge of the dance floor and keep our best field of vision for the main hazards, the other dancers. With my partner slightly to my right, she can walk next to the wall. I shield her from the back and I can see the space behind her and to her right, well enough to be able to take evasive action. If we were to dance around the floor in a clockwise direction in the same hold I would be blind on the dangerous side, but would have a lovely view of the walls and would be able to smile at those sitting at the tables and chairs!

I now have to make a confession. One lady I dance with on a regular basis always closes her eyes when she dances. In a moment of devilment one evening I took her a complete clockwise circuit on a packed dance floor. I am proud to say that we had no collisions and, what's more, she was totally oblivious that we had done it. I admit that she is tiny and so my field of vision was not restricted. It was great fun but I promise I will never do it again.

I love to watch a packed dance floor ebb and flow to the music, like a tide. It is almost spooky to watch, particularly when the floor is full of mature dancers who have danced as a group for years. The music starts and they wait for a few bars, then, as if by a prearranged signal, off they go. If the music stomps along, so do they. When the music becomes lyrical and the beat less insistent, the flow slows and the movements of the dancers become more sinuous, not just as individual couples but 'en masse'. Each couple is moved by the music but also senses the general mood of the crowd.

The safest place to put my lady, therefore, is in the outside lane with the moving hazards to one side only. When we move to the next lane in, we have moving hazards on both sides. To my blind side now are the unknown kickers and the outstretched, coupled fists at my lady's ear level. In the centre of the floor, the matter is worse. Chaos reigns here because there is no sense of direction. At least in the outer perimeter we are all travelling in the same direction. In the middle, nothing is predictable. But surely, if most are circling, there is a lovely space to dance in? Well, there was when I saw it and began to pilot towards it. The problem is that three other guys saw it at the same time and we all arrive together.

I think we need, as leaders, to focus strongly on what the point of tango is. We have a woman in our arms whose company we wish to enjoy and we want her to enjoy the experience of dancing with us. More than any other thing, I want women who dance with me to have had such a good time they want to repeat the experience every time we meet. I am old-fashioned enough to believe that, when a man walks along a pavement with a woman, he should place her to the side of him that is away from traffic. The same courtesy in the dance floor means that I must protect her from injury and embarrassment. To that end, if I see a hazard looming I should have the technical skill to impose my frame between her and the trouble. At the same time, I need to realise that, in certain places on the dance floor, hazards come from several quarters – sometimes all at once. Because of this I get no credit for swiftly moving my partner away from one couple's impact and into another.

Hours and hours of milonga experience allow us to derive a sense of the 'envelope' in which we travel. It is a little like when we drive a car; we need to leave enough stopping space between us and the car in front. There is not much we can do about the car behind, but at least we can be aware of it. It is tempting, on the dance floor, to sit behind a reliable couple and put the cruise control on, but it rarely works for long and lulls you into a false sense of security. I am told that in some dance venues there is a version of road rage, when couples behave antisocially, hogging the floor. When one couple is not listening to the music and holding up traffic, voices have been raised and nudges not unheard-of. I also heard stories a few nights ago about the way flashy couples, who occupy twice the space they should, have their style cramped by the regulars blocking their moves. It all sounded like the Argentine version of what happens to me when I drive to the Norfolk coast. However I want to drive, it seems that a regular series of men in beaten-up cars force me to travel at 45 mph. I once began to believe that they were all members of a single organisation, because the hats they all wore looked as if they were in uniform!

Endings

I have to start this section with a frank confession. I am rotten at endings most of the time. If I worry about the ending and concentrate on that during the last few bars of the song, sure as fate I stop connecting to my partner. If, on the other hand, I am in a dream world with her, the ending arrives and catches me unawares unless the song is a real old chestnut.

When you first start to dance tango the songs are unfamiliar and the level of concentration so intense that couples often find they are caught out by the music. They have started a manoeuvre, not realising that the band is about to wind it up to a halt. All over the dance floor, people are laughing because they have been caught out. They either felt obliged to take another step after the music had stopped, or froze in a bizarre position, halfway through a 'sentence'. Well, that's not a bad thing, and I have had many a laugh on the dance floor when the band tricked me. They used to do it deliberately in the old days in any case, so I would like to visualise those 'old guard' bandleaders watching us from 'tango heaven' and having a good chuckle at the way the trick still works. So, it really does not matter a whole lot in the context of social dancing if you don't finish the dance with a flourish, but it is just one other refinement worth learning to be able to end well. Basically, endings look good to me when definite, positive lines are shown by both dancers maintaining their 'oneness' to the very last. Irrespective of the look of the ending, there is no doubt that most people I dance with express a sense of glee if we end deliberately and together. Unfortunately, some tracks I dance to regularly catch me out with false endings. I'm sure there are parallels in other, not wildly unrelated areas of life that I could draw on, but I'm not about to go there at this point.

It is in the nature of tango that many of the tunes we love to dance to are such old favourites that most of us know only too well how and when they end and can plan accordingly. Even if you are unfamiliar with a particular tango, you will remember that all tangos are multiples of eight bars in their basic construction and need to end on a resolution. By this, I mean that the tune needs to feel that it has been completed, just as a hymn tune does. When you learn tango using the basic eight system, the last three steps of the eight are actually referred to as 'la resolución'. However much these tunes wander off the beaten track to entertain us, they always have to 'come home' at the end. Sometimes the band will signal the end by slowing up in the last few bars, and more often than not the whole tune will end with the flourish of a solid chord or – most frequently, in tango – two chords. Why does the band do this? Well, we may think it is to help the

Hilmar and Mary   *Photo DM*

dancer, but in reality the musicians need these stock endings for themselves so that they come to a satisfactory ending as an ensemble, and also so that they signal to the audience that this is the time to get ready to applaud.

However, if you study some of the earlier recordings, the endings appear to be much more obvious and predictable, and at the same time the tempo is much stricter. This is because the dance powered the music at that time and the band was obliged to keep the dancers happy. Later on, as the bands became more powerful and the cult of personality surrounded the band leaders and the singing stars, more liberties were taken with the tempo and the endings were – and still are today – sometimes less easy to read.

It's not too hard when the band is giving off a big signal of slowing up and coming to the end of a musical phrase for the leader to engineer a simple but quite satisfactory ending. It may be useful to stop leading complicated and rapid movements and thus be able, even within a couple of beats, to lead a simple, relaxed closure of the feet at the end. While this may sound boring, it actually feels quite satisfying to do. It just demands that the leader is actually listening to the music and thinking forward a few beats. If the band puts in an unexpected final beat, it is quite easy to simply lead a slight and connected upper body rotation without causing another step, to acknowledge the fact that the music had not in fact stopped when you led the halt. Similarly, you may see couples stopping, as it were, one beat too soon but marking that beat with a pose, perhaps involving an upper body tilt to the leader's right, the closed side of the embrace, with a balancing sway of the pelvis the other way.

The chords used by orchestras to signify the end of the piece tend to vary from pretty crisp 'stingers', like the closing of a door, to rather more vague affairs that peter out. Sometimes the chords are single and sometimes in pairs. Occasionally a loud, sharp chord is followed by a sort of orchestral sigh. It is nice to be able to select an appropriate ending to suit all these variations and take a little time to think about their musical and dance significance.

I find it convenient to consider all the possible endings in category headings using a nomenclature that works for me and may help you. 'Woofs and blings' are the brainchildren of Mike Rose and Stephanie Gögelein. Their class on endings helped me think about the whole issue in a constructive way. I soon realised that they had overlooked one particular type of ending that has caused me a problem, and so I coined the term 'Bleaarrgghh' to fit the bill. It sounds silly but it works. I know that, whenever he hears about woofs and blings, dear Rodolfo reacts as if he has heard a fart at a funeral. I hate to think what he would think of a Bleaarrgghh!

Woofs

These are the single, positive, full-ensemble chords that I likened earlier to the closing of a door, but they also remind me of a short, sharp dog bark; hence their nickname seems so appropriate to me. Singly they are rather rare. They are more likely to be found travelling in pairs and become 'woof-woofs'. The movement that fits them best is what Mike Rose refers to in his class as a 'larger body movement'. Being a fairly large body myself, I have little trouble in managing the easiest woof, which is a brisk, slightly larger than life sidestep to my left, leaving my right leg elegantly extended with the toe pointed. If at the same time as I step left I raise our joined hands, I signal a well-known, not to say clichéd, ending. I cannot say that I expect my follower to run her left thigh up to my right armpit at this moment but I have never been known to complain if she did.

As the years progress, I worry a lot less about such endings and I'm blowed if I want to cloud my mind for long planning one while enjoying the moment with my partner. Why not then just continue the movement you had already begun but, realising the end was upon you in a couple of beats, converting the last motion to one with a little more fire? You were about to take a step forward? Well do so with a spark of attitude and hold it. Then relax!

Blings

These are the rather more gentle chords and sometimes come in thoughtful pairs at the end of some wistful song, but frequently enough they follow a woof, thus producing a 'woof-bling'. A movement to accompany a bling would be something positive but of a lesser power than the woof movement. What fits the moment well here is something as understated as an intention move. In contrast to the woof, where body mass transfer is needed, in the bling the axis stays where it is but there is a limb movement.

Blearrgghhs!

An all too frequent ending in later music recordings and quite hard to do any really satisfying ending to. The bleaarrgghh is the sort of long, formless chord that suggests that the conductor of the music was in doubt as whether to stop or not.

I suggest that you familiarise yourself with the sort of music likely to be chosen by most DJs at a milonga. You know the sort of thing; the D'Arienzo or Di Sarli, straightforward-to-dance-to, early stuff through to the later Pugliese from the 1950s, and even some of the classic recordings of Piazzolla. Each DJ has his own favourite set.

Using a piece of software called Goldwave I managed to sample the very last half minute of a large number of classic tangos and made a CD compilation of dozens of them to use as a learning and teaching tool. I am happy to report that it always produces a hilarious class and works extremely well as a way of concocting and executing a wide variety of useful satisfying endings for daily use. I entitled the CD 'Something for the Weak End Señor?' which dreadful pun continues to amuse me anyway, if nobody else.

Without worrying too much about whether you perform some sort of stagy ending, with the lady exposing her stocking top or the man risking a double hernia carrying her on his hip, I suggest you consider some simple ways you can come to a neat finish in two beats. Most simply, you can step to one side and close feet together in a purposive sort of way. If the band has fooled you and puts in another chord, all you need to do is a modest, static chest rotation to cover that extra beat with something.

Good endings can be so simple and yet so satisfying. A woof is well enough managed by leading a powerful, single forward step, or a sidestep leaving a trailing leg. Woof-woofs can look good if you combine the crisp sidestep with a brisk body rotation, and woof-blings lend themselves to a softer rotation after a sharp step. A bling can be covered by a movement of intention alone. None of this is complicated, but it all works better with a touch of thought in advance.

I'm sure I have said enough to get you thinking for yourself – which is what tango is about, anyway. All I do is listen to the standard repertoire and think about the dynamics of the last bar of music. I ask myself: "Where are the important accents that convey feelings as the tune comes to a halt, and how do I feel it should be matched by my movements and those of the woman in my arms?" So, it's the same thing, right up to the last note, as the rest of tango. I think it is quite acceptable to interpret the music as we see fit, in the full context of the connection we have with our partner of the moment.

Just one further thought about the ending of a tango and the ending of a few moments of deep concentration on whoever is in our arms, leader or follower. It is a common experience for me that, when you have truly been 'in the zone', you find yourself holding your breath as the music dies. There is a precious moment of stillness when the spell has yet to be broken. Sometimes it feels as if we don't want the moment to end. Well, let it last, I say. Frequently, laughter breaks the tension at the end of a dance of that level of connection. I love that about tango. Let's not fall away from each other as if it had never been real and we feel silly though. Let us allow the moment to melt. And, Gentlemen, please, I beg of you, if this was the last tune of the tanda, escort the lady back to her seat. Don't just abandon her in the middle of the floor and clear off. Just because the mechanics of that dance is complete, it doesn't mean that the point of it all has gone. We must always remember that the ending is the last memory before the next beginning.

CHAPTER 18

Adornments and variations

I have to confess that, when I come to writing a chapter about adornments and other variations, I run into some difficulty. The reason is twofold. Part of me thinks that each tango dancer must develop his or her own style and that extra movements outside the simple things I have described (and which are universally taught) should be driven by the music. By this, I mean that when we dance freely we may feel motivated by the music to put in little flourishes of our own invention. Why not? What it is to have fun! However...there is a danger in learning a set flourish. Firstly, when an advanced dancer improvises an extra adornment to the dance it is set against

Tony   *Photo DM*

the background of their good balance and elegant technique. The added movement enhances the dance and is appropriate to the moment because it was driven by feelings inside the dancer at that specific time. When a poor dancer copies such a move, it looks absolutely ridiculous. I have seen it, and I am ashamed to say I have done it myself.

Am I suggesting that beginners should not adorn their dance, then? Not at all. I am just trying to put into context what an adornment is all about. An adornment is a well-placed, well-executed extra movement that enhances the look and the feel of the dance, without detracting from the pleasure of the partner. A clever adornment, even perfectly executed by an otherwise clumsy dancer, does not enhance that dancer's performance. Worse still, if a poor dancer makes it uncomfortable for the partner by performing adornments, by doing so he or she negates the true meaning and essence of tango.

So, the idea that adornments should not be taught at all has some merit. Most of the adornments I use, however, I have copied from others I watched. They are not exactly spontaneous, though I only use them when the music makes me want to. I mean, I did not invent them. I suppose that, if I had been taught them, I might be better able to do them than I am.

To begin with, we need to remember that any extra movement will take up time, and we have to decide where that time will come from. The easiest time to make an extra movement might be at the end of an eight-bar phrase, when we commonly bring a movement to a resolution. It's where the music returns to base, as it were. As long as we are not attempting any very quick manoeuvre, as we step we are quite able to add a little something on the way. Occasionally, you will hear these added movements referred to as 'firuletes', this being the Spanish word for 'frills'.

The most basic adornment of a simple walking movement would be a brief deviation of the foot's passage en route, so to speak, by allowing the free foot to play about the weight-bearing leg. For a moment the free foot can hook behind the fixed ankle before returning to its original path without breaking the rhythm. The ankle joint of this free foot must be relaxed for this to work well. Similarly, the free foot can hesitate in front of the weight-bearing ankle before continuing. I find this more difficult. It may be possible to include both these movements, one after the other, in the time available. This is the hardest for me, and I am indebted to my friend the supermarket trolley for his support in this matter over the years. Incidentally, when wheeling a trolley, the occasional simple firulete probably goes unnoticed. When I become more exotic, I am aware that I may have become an innocent source of amusement. I shall start to worry when I hear the sound of flapping white coats coming to take me away.

'Golpes' are little toe taps, either against the fixed foot or on the ground. They are not supposed to be loud because that smacks of vulgarity, though you do sometimes hear a dancer making a pronounced bang with his foot. I think that, within the context of the music and driven by the feeling of the moment, this is colourful and acceptable. I am less enamoured of the repetitive stamping I sometimes hear.

The 'lapiz', or pencil, is a circular gesture of the pointed toe that may be single or multiple – or complex, as when the circle begins small and widens.

I think we do well to remember that, when tango began, adornments were the province of male dancers, who used them to show off, both to prospective women partners and to the men about them with whom they were in fierce competition. Perhaps it is an indication of the seriousness of the problem of successful mating in Buenos Aires at the end of the 19th century that we see the behaviour of men resembling that of animals and birds, which display instinctively to attract the female. For a woman to adorn in those early days was considered very vulgar. Tango has evolved, as has the relative power of the sexes. In the same way that it is quite acceptable for women to ask men to dance, in Europe at least, it has become more common for women to dance as they wish and to feel more powerful in the relationship. Sometimes I dance with a woman who is an accomplished leader as well as being a great follower. She enhances our joint pleasure by adornments, hesitations and tensions, but – more than that – she occasionally 'back-leads'. By this I mean that, without any change in our embrace, or her role as a follower in most respects, she senses where I am and makes a move that dictates the way *I* dance. She has learned to read where my balance is, where I am vulnerable – perhaps even a little predictable – and changes her response so as to give me a little jolt out of my complacency. Dancing with Dr Sam is a true voyage of discovery and immense fun. She and I can have an intellectual, funny and rewarding tango 'conversation' just as we might sit and chat over a glass of wine. This sort of relationship may well have been possible even from the very beginnings of tango between some couples, but, when we hear that in present-day Buenos Aires women still have to wait to be asked to dance, I suspect that it was always rare. This is another reason why I feel that the evolution of tango and its modern, international influences are very much in its interest when we think of its survival.

I think it is useful to widen the brief when thinking of adornments to include other variations that are essential for the full enjoyment of the dance. Long before we get concerned about extra movements that might well cause a disturbance to the balance or interrupt connection we might think about simpler variations of the familiar themes.

When I first started to dance tango I found it was all I could cope with to walk on each beat, and, because there is such a positive beat with so much of the older music we hear, it becomes all too easy to simply plonk along, one step per beat. Teachers often find it best to use the old recordings to begin with because they are so steady. As I became more taken up by tango I discovered Carlos Gardel and Piazzolla. I loved their music but was a little confused to learn that many people felt it was impossible to dance to these two great musicians. I guess the problem was that they both deviate from the strict tempo. But life is not about rigid rules, and one problem of dancing to a strict beat is that it can sometimes numb your mind and make improvisation more difficult. If we are dancing as the music makes us feel, when the rhythm becomes obscured we really ought not to plod on regardless, ought we? I accept that our brains can carry a beat for a while even if the CD player dies, but if we just carry on we can't have been that involved with the music, can we?

I think that, if we listen intently to some of our favourite tracks, we can see how different feelings from the orchestra might make us want to take long steps, and make other parts shorter. Some of the phrases, either in the tune or the lyrics, are so complicated that it makes more sense to do less footwork and more minimalist movements. Many tunes begin with the main theme, which is often very positive, and have moments later that have quite a contrasting feel about them. Little intention movements and checks (small body rotations on the spot) suit some parts of a tune – say, in the middle section – before the orchestra returns to the main theme. Even when there seems to be minimal variation in colour, during one song I have discovered that I can introduce variety of step by taking two steps to a beat, or even one step every two beats. Some tunes positively cry out for these sorts of variations. I think particularly of 'Gallo Ciego'. This means, literally translated, the 'blind cockerel', but I suspect that the word 'gallo' is used here in its slang meaning of 'guy' or 'bloke', and may well have been one of many fairly cruel jokes at someone's expense originally. The tune has two very different sections, one staccato and the other more lyrical. It would make no sense to dance these in strict tempo as if they were identical. In 'Libertango', the insistent, fast first tune is overridden by a slower, more lyrical theme, and I find that it feels good to switch into this and dance as it moves me rather than simply following the almost machinery-like feeling of the background throughout the piece.

I am strongly of the belief that, when we come to consider adornments, we must keep to the spirit of tango if we invent our own as we are moved by the music, just as they did in the old days. To that end, therefore, we ought to consider adornments as spontaneous extras and not concentrate too hard on learning to adorn for adornment's sake. That, surely, is the path to tango pastiche and not true tango at all.

CHAPTER 19

Tango Zen

It has long seemed to me that there are two distinct wings of tango. I used to think of them as 'techys' and 'feelys' but over the years a more significant division has appeared. For the sake of discussion I want to characterise these as the introverts and the extroverts.

The introverts concentrate on the music and the person in their arms, tending to dance more slowly with more pauses and tension. They are content in their own little world and find pleasure by tiny variations of a very modest number of movements. Their eyes are glazed or focused who knows where and often the followers dance with eyes closed and

Chan Park and Eugenia   *Photo CP*

dreamy expressions on their faces. They are most likely to be seen dancing in close embrace.

The extroverts tend to dance further apart, faster and with more flashy moves per mile. What mainly characterises them is the fact that they tend to look about them to see who is watching them. You can be kicked or barged by either tendency, but you are more likely to be trampled underfoot by the extrovert couple who will finish the figure they have started whatever happens around them.

The next time you are taking a rest in a milonga, watching the world dance by, it might be amusing to try to guess which wing of the tendency the dancers fall into. Long established couples make the job of assessment easy because they share the tendency. Where the fun lies is watching the mismatched couples. My experience leads me to believe that leaders are more likely to be extroverts but in any case it is not hard to spot the introverts among them. Because leaders shape the dance they can, to some degree, impose their feelings on their partners but it works in reverse too. I suspect that most followers would be more comfortable on the introvert side. That's not to say they don't like the odd mad fling; they do. Many genteel followers can become temporary gangster's molls in the arms of some leaders. In addition, there lurks in the bosom of most introverted leaders the desire to look flashy from time to time. It rarely works out as planned. Flashy moves rarely succeed spontaneously. The show dances we so admire spend hours honing one or two exotic moves as a couple for a totally choreographed dance and even then things go wrong in the performance. How then can we mere amateurs bring off something flashy that we have spent a few minutes working at, often alone. It's all a bit like air guitar. Fun in the bedroom but no use in front of fifty thousand people in Wembley Stadium.

I long ago realised that I had a problem. Naturally, I am of the extrovert tendency. Well, what did you expect from someone prepared to write a book? The problem is that I am no good at it. To begin with I am too tall and heavy. My centre of gravity is too high for easy swift movements and changes of direction. Besides, most partners I meet are a foot shorter than I am. The worst thing however is that I did not discover tango until I had pass the age of fifty. This is not an excuse for not trying. It is merely my acknowledgement of the barriers that are insurmountable between where I am now and any ambition I might have to be a show dancer. The same handicaps would prevent me winning an Olympic Gold medal on the parallel bars. I have watched great show dancers my age doing amazing things. The difference is that *they* started in childhood and are now still trading on experience and muscle memory. I sometimes have difficulty tying my own shoelaces, now my back is so stiff. One of my near contemporaries has not grasped this . Maybe he never will. I think that the sight of this fat incompetent man performing flashy but inelegant complex figures with younger women is very unappealing. He would be horrified to realise how vulgar and ungainly it looks. I think he would be better occupied working with the grain of his body shape, not against it, but it is all a matter of taste. Perhaps if he saw a video of himself he would change his point of view but I suspect he might take the line of giving up tango and that would miss the point altogether.

What makes tango so different from other dances is the concept of deep connection throughout a fully improvised dance that needs no checklist of ingredients to satisfy it. To coin a metaphor, my ungainly colleague is piling cream on the jam on the butter of his bread because, in my view, his bread is in itself tasteless and lacking in meaning. Having watched so many tango masters dance great 'bread', I am delighted to attempt to suppress the extrovert in me and concentrate on making a really good loaf of bread because that is well within my ability. That is not to say it is easy; it is not. The point is that it is possible to dance simply, elegantly, and with deep strong connection but we need to choose that as a goal and work at it. The other thing is actually a mirage for most of us and the path to it is uncomfortable and may be doomed to produce unhappiness. Still, I have to admit that there will always be those who prefer to attempt to climb Everest to growing geraniums.

I had already come to this conclusion when I discovered the work of Chan Park. Chan is a writer with a background in engineering, martial arts and oriental philosophy but he is also a tanguero and bandoneonista. He tours the world teaching Tango Zen that combines the principles of

Zen Buddhist meditation with tango dancing. The purpose of meditation in Zen is to free the mind from intrusive thoughts that are likely to create tension. As Chan says in his excellent book on the subject, 'Zen practice, when reconciled with one's everyday life, creates balance, calmness, 'grounded-ness', centering and harmony in mind and body''. How wonderful to take the excitement and sentiment of tango, the closeness of a partner and with the help of Zen principles dance towards complete fulfilment.

Chan teaching   *Photo DCT*

I realise this sounds a little 'airy-fairy' at this moment, but bear with me as I explain the steps that Chan recommends for us to arrive at this point where we enter 'the zone' or achieve the Zen moment or 'Satori'.

To begin with, Chan encourages us to consider posture and breathing. These are surely the vital elements that will allow us to free ourselves to comfortable relaxed body contact with our partner. In my view, the biggest handicap to my dancing has always been my accustomed body posture and my tendency to hold my breath when concentrating on something difficult.

Chan's second principle, the one that has struck home most forcibly for me is the business of 'dancing in the here and now'. The most attractive tenet of Buddhism is the notion that we only have this present moment in which to live. The past is gone and dwelling on it clouds the mind for the tasks we have right now. Nor may we have the future, for it may never arrive. What we have and hold is *this* very moment. Instead of wasting whole chunks of useful mentality just re-examining the movement we got wrong or planning some complex figure to come, we should spend all our mental energy concentrating on the moment; the person in our arms, the music and, when we have to, the space immediately around us.

Naturally, most of us are not in total control of our thoughts when we dance. I am particularly thinking about some extremely smelly people I have danced with. Tango Zen teaches us to allow such intrusive thoughts to enter and immediately drift away. It is not helpful to dwell on anything that spoils the precious moment of the here and now. The thought arrives and passes without hindering. Actively pushing the thought to one side is just as intrusive. The mind is being highjacked for a secondary purpose. Chan refers to this as 'letting go'. A more difficult thing to let go of is the ego, particularly for the extrovert leader. I love this quote Chan Park offers us from Johanna Siegmann from Tango-L:

" *The magical leader's first concern is the couple, not the steps he wants to lead. For this to happen, the magical leader must surrender to his partner in the same way as the follower must surrender to his lead. He must surrender any image of what he wants/expects to do and open himself to the possibility of what might develop.*"

How different is that from the fantastic - but choreographed and essentially sterile - shows we see presenting themselves as Tango? There, ego is everything. Even the perception of connection is rehearsed and connived at in advance, not truly created and shared. I particularly detest the false frown of feigned passion on the leader's face. When we watch, we may be fooled into believing that there is true connection but for all we know the professionals have just had a flaming row backstage and are harbouring feelings of hatred and loathing for each other. They have learned to suppress true feelings to evoke a feeling in the onlooker that is entirely bogus. Why do so many of us not realise this and see though it as being pure fantasy, as synthetic as a cartoon. I suppose we live in a world where people want fame at any price and we idolise show business. We have people looking up to an actor because he played Moses in a movie or hounding some poor man who took the part of a villain in a soap opera. So many people are unable to distinguish the shadow from the substance because the shadow looks so like the real thing. I think we all see the problems those people in the media get into once our adulation has boosted their egos to dangerous levels. As someone once said of a young composer he admired, ' the worst thing that can happen to him is if he becomes successful'.

Chan believes, and so do I, that Tango is a medium we can all use to express our own nature. This means we are free to dance in our own style and should not think that the goal is to dance like this or that person. A young pianist I know was upset not to win a competition and moaned that he had 'played it just like Horowitz did!' 'Ah!' said one of the panel of judges when this was reported to him, 'But we didn't need *another* Horowitz; we needed a fresh young *him*'.

Buddhists believe that goals and desires are responsible for the suffering in life and I am reminded that there is no consolation in coming runner-up in a boxing match. Dance is an art form. The true artist does his thing, whether we like it or not. When he starts to pitch to what he thinks will sell, something just died.

For me the unique nature of tango is simply the one-ness we can achieve and I suspect that Chan would agree with me. We need to strive to overcome those elements in each of us that stand between us. They may be height differences, or age. They may be presence -or absence- of sexual attraction. We do best when we sink our differences and pool our resources toward a common feeling and total unity in the moment. Dancing with the feet won't do this. Dancing with the hearts together can.

In the same way that Buddhists use mantras to assist in the arrival at full concentration, in tango, we use music. By their very nature, the earlier recordings are rhythmical with a repetitive, unswerving beat and recurring themes. They allow us to tune into the demands of the music, without taking out attention from our partner. In comparison, Tango Nuevo and later recordings more designed for listening than dancing, can make finding the deepest levels of concentration harder, but can be refreshing for that reason. Since both of us are moved simultaneously by the music, in general it should be an aid to unity. I have danced with so many followers who did not listen to the music at all because they were so intent on concentrating on my lead. In retrospect I realise that I was abusing them. I was asking for so much stuff moment by moment, that I was depriving them of the joy of moving to the music as they would normally wish. My ego had taken over the entirety of the couple. How much better it would have been if I had left them enough mentality to enjoy the dance, not just survive it?

I have always been an opponent of the basic eight school of teaching tango because it seemed to me that it enslaved us and led us into dangerous areas of sterility and shopping lists. In Tango Zen it can be a positive advantage. In order to free the mind from needless anxiety about what to do next, the use of repetitive movements positively helps meditation and unity. After all, meditation during tango can only be achieved with practice and there is little point in re-inventing the wheel. In addition, familiarity breeds confidence and we need to feel confident if we are to take full charge of our dancing and release to each other as we dance, finding ourselves and each other as we go. Let us remember what Henry Ford once said, ' Whether you think you can or you can't, you're right'

Finally, Chan Park has something to say about those of us who are wrapped up in the philosophy of tango and I recognise myself in this category. He makes the most valid point of all. As he puts it - much better than I could -

'Like Zen, Tango can be beyond what words can express. It can open a door only to the one willing to experience pure and delicate joy in its pure form. In Tango, like all other practices, to taste essence, one must do; that is, one must dance. So drop your pen. Turn off your computer. Go out dancing Tango'

I will, Chan, and I have.

CHAPTER 20

A Taste of Buenos Aires

(Or some things I wish someone had told me before I arrived!)

Having just returned from a visit to Buenos Aires, I thought I would write a few words in the hope that it would assist tango lovers to plan their own trip. I wish to make it plain at the outset that this was a short visit, just before Christmas, and what I am about to say is one person's entirely subjective experience. Nonetheless, I wish I had known these things at the start of the trip.

Many tangueros and tangueras feel the need to make a pilgrimage to the place in which tango was born and they are tempted all the more when they see fantastic Argentine dancers who tour our countries teaching. I don't quite know

Buenos Aires architecture   *Photo DCT*

what I expected to see. I had delayed for a long time fearing that what I would discover was that the whole thing was a sham, a facade of tacky nonsense. I have to admit that I saw plenty of that but there was enough wholesome, solid dancing to be seen and done if you had good advice about where to look for it. One UK dancer with considerable experience of the tango scene in Buenos Aires, going back many years suggested to me that the 'real, authentic tango' had all but disappeared and made it plain that nostalgia was all that was left. I found this assessment most discouraging but I now believe it to be quite false. Tango continues to evolve wherever it is enjoyed.

The flight from the UK is long. To make it anything like economical you simply have to travel like cattle in economy class and that usually means hopping first to Frankfurt with Lufthansa, Rome with Alitalia or Paris with Air France. British Airways offers a direct flight from Heathrow but it is more expensive and only sensible if you live near to London. For us in the

Midlands it made more sense to start at Birmingham and fly to Frankfurt. However, as far as I can see, all the long haul flights stop to refuel at Sao Paulo. This means that after the quick flight to a European staging hub you suffer another 11 hours in the air, then an hour on the ground and then another 2-hour flight from Brazil before you arrive, shattered, in Bs As.

The best advice I was given, and took, was to avoid alcohol, wear flight socks and take a really good neck pillow, not one of the inflatable sort but something much more substantial. It worked for me.

Accommodation

Buenos Aires, as you might imagine, is full of hotels and several friends of ours have been quite comfortable, even in the most Spartan of these. We decided however that renting an apartment would work better for us and so it proved. We like to slob about without worrying about maids needing access. We like a decent bath and a sitting room separate from the bedroom in case one of us wants sleep and the other to watch TV. Hotels rarely provide this and besides, we wanted the ability to cook and wash and iron a few things so we could travel very light. When I talk about cooking, I want to make it plain that, particularly in a city with millions of great restaurants and amazingly cheap food 24 hours a day, what I mean is the nice thing of having a fridge stocked with breakfast goodies, bottled water and wine and fruit. It's nice too to have somewhere to hang out a pair of knickers to dry without offending the management.

To start with, we had arranged a small flat through an Internet acquaintance but, when we told our closest friends in Buenos Aires exactly where it was, they were appalled. It seems that there are certain areas of the city where crime is rife, usually because of drugs. Our friends suggested some safer alternatives and we were glad they did. In the end, using a company called ByTargentina we rented a superb apartment in Puerto Madera. This is the area that used to be the docklands and is in the process of being converted from warehousing into hotels and apartments. It is the swankiest part of town with the biggest Hilton Hotel I have ever seen and we felt very safe there. Part of the reason for that was that being under the dock authority, it has its own distinct police force. In case you think I have over stated the security issue, let me tell you that every bridge entrance to this 'island' of Puerto Madera has a police car with two armed officers standing on guard 24 hours a day as well as beat officers seemingly at most street corners. That has to tell you something.

We were able to rent for as many days as we wished. It was an easy process to arrange this online and everything we had been promised was correct. We liked the fact that we had a 24 hour concierge and were given several emergency numbers to use in case of problems. I think the company earned their commission and it was good to feel that you could walk to shops and restaurants in safety. Otherwise, they general advice given to us by our local friends was never walk the streets after dark but always call a taxi.

This all made us feel both anxious about general security but reassured that we had a safe bolthole and we would recommend ByTargentina from that point of view. However - just to underline the fragile state of the local economy – you might like to consider this fact. Unlike any arrangement you might make in the UK, we were obliged to pay in cash in US dollars up front on arrival and pay an additional returnable one week's rent, also in US dollars. I assume that this was to ensure we did not smash the place up and skip with the furniture. The company were excellent and honoured the agreement to the letter. On the day of departure, at the crack of dawn, along came the owner's representative to check us out, ensure we had left the place clean and tidy as we had found it. We were obliged to clean it well though not deal with linen or towels provided.

Had we not stayed in Puerto Madera, we would have liked to have stayed in a flat in an area called Palermo where one of our friends lives. This too is a peaceful area with wonderful restaurants, parks and, best of all, some amazing dress shops. Walking around this area with our friends felt quite safe. ByTargentina had several pleasant looking flats to let there too.

Communications

We found to our dismay that our UK mobile phones were useless and our house phone could only be used for local landline calls. The reason our phones did not work even with 10 pesos (£2) of sim card was that they did not have enough 'bands'. Check this out before you go. However, I wish someone had told me about the 'locutorio' system sooner. Locutorios are shops selling Internet access and private safe phone booths. They are much safer and nicer than trying to use a coin box in the street where there is so much traffic noise you could not expect to hear yourself think and, besides, your back is to the crowd. No, the locutorio is so much nicer and as cheap as anything, costing a mere few pence. In the town centre they were every few yards it seemed and once you knew what they were for they were easy to spot. However, the mobile phone is such a useful way to communicate with friends that when I next upgrade, I shall ensure that I can use it anywhere in the world just by buying a local sim card and I advise you to do the same. Charging your mobile's battery up in Buenos Aires is no problem because their electricity system is compatible. You make the connection simply by buying an adapter in Boots or at the airport.

Money

Credit cards work in some places but, for example, even in a reputable travel agent, to book a hotel up in Iguazu, even the Sheraton, meant that I was expected to pay in cash to avoid the agency having to wait for months to get their commission. Incidentally, please, PLEASE, do budget both 3 days and the money it costs to visit Iguazu Falls, up on the Brazilian border. It's where they filmed 'The Mission' and the combination of subtropical rainforest and the biggest waterfalls on earth is absolutely un-missable and a wonderful break from the city noise and stress. We also felt it was well worth the extra expense of staying at the Sheraton, the only hotel actually inside the National Park, where we enjoyed an astounding view of the falls from our bedroom window. Other, cheaper hotels are a few miles away in the small town of Puerto Iguazu, just on the Brazilian border. They looked nice enough but the advantage for us, apart from the view, was to have full access to the National Park from 7.30 am to 6.30 pm. Those people billeted outside the park were obliged to pay a daily entrance fee and were only allowed in between 10 am and 4.30 pm along with busloads of schoolchildren.

We found we needed daily modest amounts of cash for food, milonga entrance fees and taxis and these were easily obtained through ATMs (Cajeros Automaticos) which have the facility to deal in English. They are inside banks, not on the walls outside as in the UK, and you gain access by swiping your credit or debit card through a slot. This enables you security and privacy and the ability to leave after you have safely stashed the loot. Unlike those we use in the UK, these machines greet you by name when your card goes in and the money appears before the card comes out. Then you are asked if you want any other service, you say no and out comes the card. I found there was no notion of any limit I could withdraw per day, which surprised me and at the same time allowed me more freedom to pay for big items. Using a debit card will incur a few percent for exchange handling but the convenience makes that well worth while. On the other hand, if you use your credit card in an ATM, beware, When you get home you will discover an additional obscene amount charged for that privilege.

The economy in Argentina has gone through a really sticky time and not many months ago, some towns even printed their own currency for local use. Forged banknotes are common and you can even get them from an ATM so in the higher denominations it is worthwhile checking the authenticity by looking at the metal strip which should look as if words are written though not legible. Also check that the watermark has the same geezer's face as the picture and that the number changes in colour between blue and turquoise when you tilt it in the light. What fun! And you thought it was just like home?

One thing to know is that it is important to save up your receipts (and sometimes therefore insist that you get one!) so that when you leave the country, just before immigration control you report at a special desk to reclaim any tax you may have paid. Not all items you buy will qualify but since the tax will have been 20% it's worth getting back. I suppose the most likely items of purchase to fall into this category will be those that have had tax imposed on them by being imported into Argentina.

Another thing worth realising is that when you leave Argentina, you have to buy your way out by paying an airport tax which while only being 18 pesos a head could leave you feeling foolish if you did not know about it.

Taxis

One of the fantastic features of this city is that taxis are incredibly numerous and ridiculously cheap 24 hours a day. They are yellow and black and called radio cabs. To begin with you think they are all the same. Then as you hail a few you discover that there are reputable companies and less so. Some are illegal. Some rip you off but it is still peanuts to us. To give you some idea, the most expensive trip, taking us many miles out of town cost a mere 12 pesos (£2.40 then) The less reputable have homicidal maniacs or crumbling geriatrics as drivers, no seat belts (but notices advising you that you must wear one!) and noisily worn back axles. Some of our drivers appeared to have a death wish with ridiculous speeds, sudden sharp turns, loads of horn use and generally risk- taking of the silliest type.

The ideal thing is to establish a relationship with one good company and ring them whenever you want a cab. I found el urbano were excellent. After the first call when they took my name and phone number, all I had to do was to tell them my name. Their computer system did the rest. We took some risks by hailing cabs and had some white-knuckle rides. On one trip, our driver's behaviour so offended a local cop, he was pulled over and his boot was searched and his papers checked while we sat in the sweltering heat wondering where it was all going to lead. He got off with a caution but I nearly decided to abandon him. He calmed down after a while

Before leaving the subject of taxis, it is useful to know how to manage the business of getting to and from the airport at Ezeiza. The simple advice on arrival is to ignore the first wave of taxi touts and to walk through a ring of kiosks offering taxis and 'Remises' to the main foyer before you leave the airport building. In the centre of that is an open kiosk run on behalf of the local Ezeiza town drivers. They will take you in safety and comfort for 50pesos (£10) though their knowledge of central Buenos Aires may be limited. If you like your driver and his car, keep his card to organise the return trip and save another 10 pesos by so doing. I wish we had done so. As it was, I left it too late and rang to book through another company and was promised a car by a woman with excellent English. It arrived on time but it turned out to be an illegal taxi; just a private Joe in a beaten up jalopy who insisted that I sat in the front so that the police would not realise he was working. The seatbelt had barnacles, it had so rarely been used. He drove like a clown, used his mobile frequently at high speeds and as we left him, shaken but not stirred, he was trying unsuccessfully, to start the old banger up again

We never found English speaking taxi drivers but all of them were happy to chat in Spanish about the 'futbol'. One truly memorable night Boca had just won the Southamerican cup, having won the league only days before. We went home by taxi after a milonga through a city heaving with celebrating fans. To say that they were a little 'over the top' is to put it mildly. I was glad of the skill of our driver and his knowledge of the streets, getting us home safely with lunatic fans causing havoc all around us. Next morning on the TV news we could see that the fans had trashed the city in celebration.

Shoes

Before we went, everyone told us that, what with the fantastic leather quality and quantity and the exchange rate we would be coming back with loads of dance shoes. Well, we only bought 5 pairs! There were lots of outlets but the one we liked the best was a shop in the 1900s on Sarmiento called Neotango. They weren't the cheapest but the choice was fantastic. I am referring to the sexiest and most comfortable of high-heeled women's shoes. I did not find one pair of men's that I thought were worth buying. They looked pretty but the quality was simply not the same as for ladies. Perhaps I did not look hard enough to find the good stuff. There are limits to the effort you want to put into such a trawl in my view and I really did not need more shoes. Prices were about 125 to180 pesos (£25 to £36) for truly beautifully made, wonderfully stylish leather lined shoes for women but you could find bargains at half that price. The other nice thing about Neotango was the staff who were charming and we were very glad of their recommendation of a superb Italian Restaurant, called Prosciutto, a block and a half away, where we had a truly wonderful lunch.

One outstanding feature of Buenos Aires is the way people feel comfortable when asked to recommend places to eat that they like. No one was ever shy to tell us where to go and their advice always worked for us. While on the subject of shopkeepers, I could easily get used to receiving a kiss from some of the most attractive women in the world (one cheek, Bs As style) after I have spent significant sums of money.

Several Milongas were held in venues with marble floors which was a new experience for me. I really liked dancing on marble although to begin with I found it incredibly slippery, probably due to the amount of resin my soles had picked up over the years, I think. Noticing my problem, a kind local milonguero with a similar tendency soon put me right. He poured a tiny amount water on the floor and we both went paddling. That was the instant solution of the problem that night at the Confiteria Ideal and for the remainder of our stay. If you hear that the Ideal has collapsed into a heap of rubble, thanks to rotten woodwork, you now know whom to blame.

Food

One of the absolute highlights of a visit to Buenos Aires must be the food. My guess is that those who buy an all-in package including board could miss out badly. Argentineans are like the French and the Italians.; they take food very seriously. I cannot recall one lousy meal but I still remember some fantastic ones. The local beer, Quilmes, is light and refreshing if not particularly flavoursome and is on offer as draught (known as 'Chopp' for some reason) Drink is normally served with some nibbles and before a meal you might well be served delicious 'empañadas' miniature meat pasties. Totally delicious. Food is attractively served by pleasant staff, who are quite happy to help you decide, explain dishes, make recommendations and appear to enjoy their work. Food here is not fast food. Indeed, eating is a very slow and relaxed process indeed, which patently irritates some tourists. We happen to enjoy the relaxed feel and hate being hassled. Most places we went to segregated smokers from non-smokers which is quite important considering what a high percentage of Argentineans smoke. On the moment of touchdown in Buenos Aires, three smokers sucked on unlit fags throughout disembarkation, customs and immigration before being able to strike a match. I had never seen that before

The renowned Café Tortoni   *Photo DCT*

The big thing in Buenos Aires is the beef (Bife) barbecued at a Parrilla. Just to remember those ribs of beef on racks in front of piles of glowing wood ash at the front windows of Parillas still makes me salivate. I ate some of the most succulent flavoursome beef I have ever experienced in my life. The problem is the portions. How anyone can comfortably finish almost half a kilo of beef, after bread and empañada, maybe a side salad and then go for a postre (desert) beats me. More importantly, how on earth are these people so slim? It must be the Atkins- like diet and the frequent milongas. I put so much weight on despite failing to finish meals. Lord help those who start with the notion that you have to clear your plate!

Argentineans have a sweet tooth and their wonderful ice cream reflects the Italian ancestry of so many of them. Their croissants (Media Lunas) are wonderful but covered in sticky syrup. And the petit fours! Well! At the healthier end, we enjoyed some fantastic smoothies and fruit salads and outside of Italy, this must be *the* place for handmade pizza.

Milongas

We went out most nights to one milonga or another and found them to be very interesting and extremely varied. Most opened at about 10.30 but really did not get going until midnight when hoards of people arrived. We were always greeted warmly, often with a kiss, usually asked if we had made a table reservation. We never had but were always seated somewhere pleasant. We mostly drank bottled water and so did most of the locals as far as I could see. One interesting thing to see was people coming in parties to celebrate somebody's birthday. The milongas we enjoyed most were at the Confiteria Ideal on Suipacha 384 first floor, near the junction of Suipacha and Corrientes. This is a lovely old venue with marble floor and a very comfortable feel. The night we were there was a band called 'Sans Souci' and a brief demonstration by one couple but the best thing about it was the floor etiquette. The floor was packed but there was that cohesion that you read and hear about which gave an illusion of more space and nobody was showboating. In comparison, I found myself kicked and elbowed to death at La Milonguita, which was utterly vile. El Beso on the other hand was a tiny venue full of delightful mature couples and it would have been hard not to feel at home there. At the younger end of the scale, La Viruta was also a good place to be with a group class on some aspects of sacadas in the milonguero style before the milonga, included in the 7-peso (£1.40) entrance fee.

We never got to experience a Matinee, that is a milonga in the afternoon, but there are plenty of those to choose from. The best magazine for finding out where they are seems to be a glossy one called Tangauta. The reason we did not try a Matinee was that you have to sleep sometime!

Other than tango

Of course we go to Buenos Aires to sample the tango and it is wise to have a local friend in the scene that can advise you when and where the good milongas are. Yes, there are lists in monthly newspapers but they are not reliable. The scene changes day to day and often no decision can be taken until late in the afternoon for a Milonga that will start at 10.30pm. If you go on a tango package, you can expect this to be sorted out by the organisers, but it will be very much their idea of what you want and not necessarily your idea. Arrogance is common here, though well intentioned.

One night we turned up at the 'Ideal' expecting from the magazine lists that it would be open and found it closed. Feeling a little peckish at midnight we crossed Corrientes to discover one of the nicest restaurants we ever encountered. That sort of serendipity seemed commonplace during our stay and it cannot just be put down to good luck. I think the reality is that Buenos Aires is full of good places to eat at any hour you need one.

Outside of the tango scene, you simply must find time to visit the Teatro Colón. Seats are amazingly cheap in comparison to, for instance, Covent Garden. You can sit in the stalls for an opera or ballet for £18. One nice feature is that you can visit the official website of the Teatro Colon, find out what is going to be on when you are in town and ring up and book seats from the UK, paying by credit card. I did this once I discovered that Turandot was to be staged. The day after I paid for the tickets, the staff went on strike and for a few weeks the rest of the entire season was cancelled. The money was reimbursed to my credit card without fuss. Luckily, by the time we arrived all industrial strife had been brought to a satisfactory conclusion but it was not possible to mount the opera at short notice. Instead, we saw a magnificent concert of several pieces of various operas which the organisers had put together at short notice. It had that extra buzz you often see when something out of the ordinary comes off. In the same week we attended an impromptu tango night given by a large

Dancing in the street in Mataderos   *Photo DCT*

'orquesta tipica' with five bandoneons and seven violinists, the singer Suzanna Rinaldi and the dancer Miguel Angel Zotto. We sat in the front row of the stalls. It was truly a night to remember.

On Sunday from 11am, I would recommend anyone who has a free weekend in Buenos Aires to take a taxi to Mataderos, a northern suburb where the slaughterhouses used to be to see the Feria. This is a slightly sleazy street market with some nice things for sale at better prices than in the centre of Buenos Aires but also some interesting, if often crude, arts and crafts. More importantly, there was to be had some very and excellent barbecued beef and sausage. In cooler seasons gaucho riding skills are demonstrated but, for me at least, best of all, was genuine folk-dancing in the street. One or two dancers in folk costume were there to spark it off but then it was apparent that anyone can join in the fun and they do with gusto. There is some tango of course but better than that, Chacarera and Chamame. These are delightful, folkloric dances which preceded tango. Although they bear no resemblance to tango, having music much more reminiscent of the Andes, there was one salient similarity which touched me. Chacarera is an energetic but flowing dance in ¾ time in which a man and a woman circle each other, their arms raised, fingers snapping, sometimes waving kerchiefs and take turns to show off their fancy footwork. In particular, the man shows off with a great deal of flamboyant tap-dancing. However, throughout the dance the couple maintains a flirtatious eye contact. Within the restrictions of the sequence of the dance, they only have eyes for each other. For me, this makes Chacarera very special and to some extent ties in with the entire notion of dance as a courtship ritual much more than a show.

In addition, since the Feria is populated by locals rather than tourists, we were able to sit in a bar for a beer, enjoy some excellent food and experience the 'craic' of an old chap singing folk songs and tangos to a guitar and everyone singing their heads off. Much of what is being sold on hundreds of stalls is tourist tat but plenty of locals were buying things like engraved mates speciality foods and leather items as well. It was sad to see the selling of worn shoes and clothes, underlining how poor many are in Argentina. In comparison, the Feria at San Telmo, also on a Sunday seemed to a dreadful, unappealing tourist trap and, to me, to be much tackier. To see the place for its architecture and history, it would be better to go during the week unless you are into the grotesque.

Crime

We had been rather sensitised to the potential for a nasty experience. As it happens, the only thing we saw was a man fighting another to reclaim his bicycle. That felt more like theatre than scary although the victim was quite upset, even after he had won the tug of war. We had been told that Argentineans dressed smartly and imagined we ought to do the same. Nothing could be further from the truth. Most of them are as scruffy as we are. The thing not to do is stand out in the crowd as being a rich tourist. We were advised not to wear ostentatious jewellery or carry a camera obviously. When consulting a street map, it seemed wise to go into a shop or bank or at least stand with your back to a doorway. Women in Buenos Aires carry their handbags looped over their shoulder but also tucked into their armpit and we saw several people wearing belly bags or cross shoulder sacks. Wearing shorts might well mark you out as a tourist. People walk fairly slowly in the heat but always purposefully as if they know where they are going and it seems wise to merge with the crowd in that way.

Buenos Aires is an amazing crowded and busy city that never sleeps. We saw some drunks but they seemed affable. There were lots of beggars but they always took a shake of the head as a 'No' and cause no trouble. I am always saddened by seeing children begging but here, you can see very poor looking children of as young as eight or nine busking with bandoneons In some places we saw people evidently sleeping off drink or drugs. Police were everywhere and we found them pleasant and helpful when we asked directions. We never tested their English but we never needed to. By day, we never felt any anxiety. People were universally polite, warm and helpful, possible because we approached them with deference and about-adequate Spanish skills. I think night-time is a different matter although walking around the tree-lined and elegant Palermo district at 11pm seemed very safe but it was still vibrant and bustling at that hour. Local friends were very insistent that we never walked anywhere after dark. They also would have looked askance at our habit of hailing taxis in the street but perhaps we were lucky. We were advised to protect our cash by stashing it in several pockets rather than wear a body belt. The theory is that a mugger would probably get you to empty one pocket, possibly two but rarely go further. I asked if it would be best to hide money inside my shoes. It seems however that some tourists have been stripped stark naked at gunpoint so I suppose it is all a matter of degree. We saw nothing like any of this but I would not to presume it was urban myth.

Our conclusion

We are very glad we went. It was the holiday of a lifetime and we learned a great deal and enjoyed absolutely everything, other than the flight home, always a nasty thing as far as I am concerned. We saw great tango and bad tango. We discovered that the eternal truth about tango is universal; there is nothing specifically Argentine about it. Even the style of dancing that we now think of as Argentine can be seen in Milongas all over Europe. We saw people dancing for dancing's sake, deeply engrossed in each other. We saw old couples, odd-shaped couples, all bringing their own distinct styles to the dance and it gave us more heart to think that we should continue to develop our own particular style that suits our ages and our body shapes. We also saw people concerned only for how they might look to others and whom they were seen with. We had no difficulty rejecting that view of tango since we never subscribed to it in the first place. We never believed there was some Holy Grail to be achieved somewhere by finding a 'secret'. This trip reinforced that view. Speaking for myself, before I went, I feared discovering that I would be inadequate in a crowd of dancing porteños. I was not. Would we go again? Probably not. Would we encourage other tango dancers to go? Absolutely.

EPILOGUE to the First Edition

The writing of this book occupied my mind for two years in total, though it was not a continuous process. The journey began with me coming home after a lesson and writing notes in a ledger so that I might teach myself again at a later date. After a while I had gathered quite a thick dossier, and I began to try and make some sense of it all. Certain basic truths seemed to be common to most teachers but it was clear that not all teachers really understood the things they were teaching. It was immediately apparent that, after a lesson with certain teachers, I could fill pages with information. On the other hand, some who taught me appeared to have said nothing memorable at all. Some teachers had offered me insights that helped me understand the whole of tango and not just the small area that they had been concentrating on that day.

Those first few weeks of collation and assembly went by in a flash. I wrote compulsively, almost as if the words were bursting out of me. I was excited and some days I had difficulty thinking of anything other than tango. I have compared that first phase of writing as being similar in almost all respects to a bout of diarrhoea! Words fell onto the page in a torrent. I couldn't help it. Eventually, I was able to steady up and reread what I had written. Initially, all seemed as I thought it had been, but over the months something interesting happened. I soon discovered that what had seemed so sensible at the beginning needed to be revised as my understanding of tango progressed. Better still, I showed the work to some very experienced dancers and teachers, and they were able to add to my understanding. They changed my dancing, too. When I come to read it now, I realise how far this journey through tango has taken me.

I know that this book, although it deals with the bread and butter of tango, hardly scratches the surface; I have so much more to learn. What I have covered here merely represents the place I have arrived at now. I am still travelling – and I love it. I believe that tango is so like life itself and is, therefore, such a vast, wide open subject that there will never be a time when any one person could know it all. I just hope that what I have grasped up to now is interesting and useful to others. I would have loved to be able to take a book like this out of the library when I first started to learn, but I looked in vain for some information that was both accessible and entertaining.

More importantly, I would like to imagine that someone who is having a problem with tango or who needs some encouragement to stick at it might be able to gain greater insight into how he or she might progress as a dancer. Sometimes the problem in any human endeavour is not so much the not knowing the answer to things; if we already knew the answers we would not need to attend classes. The big thing for me whenever I want to learn something is to discover the important questions to ask those who are teaching me. My hope is that this book will open your mind to the questions *you* ought to ask.

¡Viva el tango!